THE ELIZABETHAN
SONNET SEQUENCES

THE ELIZABETHAN SONNET SEQUENCES

STUDIES IN CONVENTIONAL CONCEITS

By LISLE CECIL JOHN

NEW YORK
RUSSELL & RUSSELL · INC
1964

COLUMBIA UNIVERSITY STUDIES
IN ENGLISH AND COMPARATIVE LITERATURE
NUMBER 133

COPYRIGHT 1938
COLUMBIA UNIVERSITY PRESS, NEW YORK

REISSUED, 1964, BY RUSSELL & RUSSELL, INC.
BY ARRANGEMENT WITH COLUMBIA UNIVERSITY PRESS
L. C. CATALOG CARD NO: 64—15038

MANUFACTURED IN THE UNITED STATES OF AMERICA

TO MY MOTHER
AND TO THE MEMORY OF
MY FATHER

ACKNOWLEDGMENTS

IN WRITING this study of the conventional imagery of the Elizabethan sonnet sequences and in preparing it for the press I have incurred various obligations which I acknowledge with pleasure. For the subject, the opinions expressed, and the several inadequacies, I alone am responsible. For the rest my debt to Professor Harry Morgan Ayres is as great as it could be, for without the sustaining resources of his distinguished scholarship and his long-continued encouragement this work would not have been possible. I owe much, too, to several other scholars of Columbia University. To Professor Jefferson Butler Fletcher as author, translator, teacher, and kindly critic, my debt is greater than I can express or than he can possibly imagine. Professors Oscar James Campbell, Samuel Lee Wolff, Roger Sherman Loomis, and John L. Gerig, and Dr. H. W. Wells have aided me immeasurably by reading the manuscript and giving me many helpful suggestions.

I am grateful, also, for the valuable assistance which several others have given me in preparing the manuscript or in reading the proof—Mr. and Mrs. J. Lee Harlan, Jr.; my colleague Miss Jean Stirling Lindsay, of Hunter College; Professor Mary F. Patchell; and my sisters, Mrs. A. E. Crissey and Mrs. P. J. Eklund. Lastly, I wish to thank Miss Ida M. Lynn, of the Columbia University Press, for the benefit of her patient and kindly editorial assistance.

LISLE CECIL JOHN

Hunter College of the
City of New York
July 12, 1938

CONTENTS

INTRODUCTION

SCOPE

IN THE *Defense of Poesy* Sir Philip Sidney comments upon his having been admitted into "the company of the paper-blurrers" before he aspired to be called a poet:

But, as I have never desired the title, so have I neglected the means to come by it; only, overmastered by some thoughts, I yielded an inky tribute unto them.

That inky tribute appears, however, to be no less a work than the sequence of sonnets which, appearing in a pirated edition in 1591 as *Astrophel and Stella,* changed the course of Elizabethan verse by inspiring every poet of note of the day except Jonson, Harington, and Donne to write a sequence of love sonnets.

The twelve or thirteen hundred sonnets thus induced include, among the poems of Sidney, Spenser, and Shakespeare, some of the most cherished lyrics of the language. A Petrarchan sequence in its entirety is, on the other hand, often dismissed today as a genre dead and "nayled in his cheste" along with Petrarch himself. This situation has arisen largely because of the difference between the point of view of the sixteenth century and that of the present day. The Elizabethans, we may believe, were primarily concerned with the poetic quality of the work before them. Later readers, however, have usually turned to the sequences for evidence in regard to one of two points—their autobiographical reality or their relation to foreign sources or analogues. The first has always yielded more conjecture than fact; the second has been admirably treated in Janet G. Scott's *Les Sonnets élisabéthains.*

There remains, however, an approach to the sequences, a point of view perhaps closer than any other to the Elizabethan manner of reading them, which has never been considered for the vogue as a whole [1]—their relation to the conventional Petrarchan pattern and the actual nature and scope of the *concetti* which an imitation of Petrarch's *Canzoniere* of necessity employed. For, whatever emotion the poet may or may not have brought to his writing, whatever the provenance of his themes, his problem as a craftsman was that of making his own pastiche of the conventional Petrarchan motifs. In the belief, therefore, that the English sequences in their entirety are best understood today if read in that light, it is the purpose of the ensuing study to examine in some detail the poets' "precious tablet of rare conceits." In the belief, too, that the style of the sequences can best be determined if comparison is made of the treatment given the different versions of conceits such as those of sleep, absence, and the "eternizing" of the beauty of the beloved, reasonably complete listings of them are given either in the text or in the footnotes, and each conceit is to be found in the index under its respective headings.

A brief discussion has been appended, also, of some of the problems of Sidney's sonnets. The sincerity of the love "Astrophel" professes to have for "Stella" has so often served as a test for the merits of the whole vogue that, despite the length to which the discussion has already been carried, the question is reopened and the suggestion made that as yet the larger autobiographical implications of the cycle have not been invalidated by any evidence brought against them.

It should be said, perhaps, that, in view of the excellence of Miss Scott's *Les Sonnets élisabéthains,* no attempt has been made in this work to trace foreign sources or analogues. Nor has any attempt been made to deal particularly or exhaustively with Shakespeare's sonnets, although they are noted whenever their themes are the conventional ones of the other sequences.

Any study of the conventional conceits of the English sequences must presuppose, however, a familiarity with the history of the sonnet. The reader may therefore be not ungrateful for a brief account which seeks to assemble facts available only in widely scattered sources. It will be understood, then, that the introductory chapter of this study makes no pretense to originality in recalling the course of the Petrarchan sonnet in England, the Italian origin of the sonnet form, and the growth and establishment of the form in France. The sonnet material is for convenience divided into conceits of Eros or Cupid as the conventional symbol for the power of love, conceits describing the poet's woes, and conceits setting forth the beauty and cruelty of the lady.[2]

THE EARLIEST ENGLISH SONNETS

THE HISTORY of the sonnet in English literature begins with the work of Sir Thomas Wyatt (1503?–42) and Henry Howard, Earl of Surrey (1517–47).[3] One who would ascertain the impulse which prompted these poets to translate and imitate Petrarch's sonnets can only say, with Wyatt, "In a nett I seke to hold the wynde"; presumably, however, it grew out out of the acquaintance with Petrarch's *Canzoniere* which Wyatt may have made during his stay in Italy in 1527. It is unlikely that Wyatt's interest in sonnets came indirectly through France, where he was in 1525–26, for, according to Pierre Villey, the earliest French sonnet extant was written in 1536, too late to have affected him.[4] Direct Italian influence is also implied in Wyatt's occasional departures from the usual Petrarchan form of octave and sestet in favor of a scheme of quatrains and couplet, since he appears to have found a model for that scheme in the verse of Italian sonneteers less known than Petrarch.[5] Whatever the genesis of Wyatt's knowledge of Petrarch, tradition has it that the immediate object of his inspiration was Anne Boleyn, and the association of at least a part of his verse with her receives fresh support from the investigations of E. K. Chambers.[6]

The thirty-two sonnets of Wyatt which are now known from manuscript sources and from Tottel's *Songes and Sonettes* of 1557 include a number of translations and adaptations: seventeen, in whole or in part, are from Petrarch; one is expanded from a *strambotto* of Filosseno; two are from Serafino d'Aquila; and one is from Sannazaro.[7] The translation from Sannazaro has called forth extended discussion because it was thought to involve the question of the priority of the French or the English sonnets. Wyatt's "Like to these unmesurable montayns" (Foxwell, No. 19; Tottel, No. 97) is so similar to Mellin de Saint-Gelais's "Voyant ces monts de veuë ainsi lointaine" that Koeppel, Lee, Padelford, and others assumed that the English sonnet was translated from the French.[8] Both sonnets, however, are now known to be translations from Sannazaro.[9] Berdan then advanced the opinion that the English version came first and that Saint-Gelais had based his translation upon it. Kastner, on the other hand, held it to be improbable that Saint-Gelais could have known Wyatt's poem, and believed that the poets had translated independently.[10] There the matter rests. Yet, whatever the facts of the relationship between Wyatt and Saint-Gelais, the probability that there were no French sonnets before 1536 [11] indicates that the English version of Sannazaro's sonnet comes earlier than does the French.

Wyatt's sonnets, historically important though they be, are significant for the glimpses they afford of a man remarkable in an age of remarkable men. Even his translations, especially "My hert I gave the not to do it payne" and "Who so list to hount," which may allude to Anne Boleyn, appear to bear in intaglio the imprint of his own unhappy experience. Personal experience seems, too, to have provided the themes of the eleven sonnets which are original.[12] One is on his unlucky month of May (No. 27); two are on his imprisonment at Windsor (Nos. 31–32). Those upon themes of love show a range of moods, including the disillusionment of "Mye love take skorne my servise to retaine" and the rebellious, anti-Petrarchistic sentiment of "Ffarewell Love and all thy lawes for ever." [13] Yet we cannot today ascertain the circumstances which evoked these sonnets or attribute with certainty the inspiration of all of them to Anne Boleyn.

The almost inevitable linking of the names of Wyatt and Surrey has no doubt been unfair to both poets, but especially to Wyatt. Wyatt's sonnets, it is true, are less musical than those of Surrey; yet the younger poet himself acknowledged his obligations to his master by saying that his was the hand "that taught what may be sayd in ryme," that "reft Chaucer the glory of his wit." Surrey appears to have written only fifteen sonnets, for one of those usually printed with his verse (No. 7, "Brittle beautie") is perhaps by Lord Vaux. Those certainly his include six for which he is indebted to Petrarch and one evidently adapted from Ariosto.[14] The remaining eight[15] are, like the original ones of Wyatt, important for the bits of autobiographical information they yield. Like Wyatt, he wrote while in prison (No. 30). Unlike him, however, he wrote no original sonnets on themes of love, although that called "From Tuscan cam my ladies worthi race," addressed to the nine-year-old Elizabeth Fitzgerald, was the source of a deal of romantic conjecture about Lady Geraldine after the publication of Nash's *Unfortunate Traveller*.[16] The sonnet, written in 1545 or 1546, when Surrey was in Boulogne, seems to refer to the hardships of his separation from his family.[17]

The other sonnets are occasional. Two appear to allude to Henry VIII. No. 38, in praise of Wyatt's *Penitential Psalmes,* contains the biting lines:

> In princes hartes Godes scourge yprinted deepe
> Mowght them awake out of their synfull sleepe.

No. 40, based on the life of Sardanapalus, would indicate that the scornful young Howard had in mind the private life of his sovereign. The remaining sonnets are elegiac. One (No. 47) is on his friend Thomas Clere; two (Nos. 44–45) give generous praise to Wyatt.

The verse forms of both Wyatt and Surrey are of sufficient importance to require a summary here. Wyatt's rhyme scheme is usually *abba abba cddc ee*.[18] The sestet always ends in a couplet.

But Wyatt did not depend solely upon the form of octave and sestet; he used, as well, the rhyme scheme consisting of three quatrains and a couplet which is sometimes attributed only to Surrey: Sonnet 30 rhymes *abab abab abab cc,* and the final double sonnet *abba cddc effe gg.* Wyatt probably found his model for this form in a contemporary Italian anthology.[19]

It was Surrey, however, not Wyatt, who established this metrical form of the quatrains and concluding couplet as a convention of English sonnet writing. Surrey regularly uses quatrains and a couplet, and his rhyme scheme is usually *abab cdcd efef gg.*[20] He may, of course, have studied at firsthand the Italian models which Wyatt appears to have followed in his three sonnets of this type, but, more probably, he imitated his master directly. Since this "English" or "Shakespearean" form is used in eight of the sonnets in Tottel other than those of Wyatt and Surrey (the three by Grimald and five of the nine by unidentified authors),[21] the influence of Surrey in establishing this characteristic English form seems to have begun very early. The scheme is the predominating one in the sonnets after 1557, and, despite Sidney's use of the Italian pattern, it was the prevailing Elizabethan form.[22] It seems doubtful that this form can have come from France or from French influence. Marot's sonnets never end with a new rhyme in the couplet. Three sonnets of Saint-Gelais end *cee,* and three others, *dee.* Similar forms are found in the Pléiade poets. No structural division, however, of these final tercets seems to be intended.

The sonnets in Tottel's *Miscellany* other than those of Wyatt and Surrey, the "lanterns of light" of the Tudor court, are interesting as showing the practice of sonneteering in Henry's court. The three by Grimald are occasional verse;[23] the nine by unidentified authors are on the typical Petrarchan themes of the constancy, joys, and sorrows of the lover.[24] Except for the sonnets preserved in Tottel, very few written in this period appear to have survived. Among them, however, are two by John Harington the Elder in the *Nugae antiquae,* one headed "Upon the Lord Admiral Seymour's Picture," the other, "To Sweete Isabella Markham." [25] Others are a curious didactic sonnet in the 1557 edition of Thomas Tusser's *A Hundreth Good Pointes of Husbandrie,* called "A Sonet, or brief rehersall of the propercks of the twelue monethes afore rehersed"; [26] and the dedicatory sonnet by Thomas Sackville for the 1561 edition of Hoby's translation of Castiglione's *The Courtier.*[27]

For more than three decades after the publication of Tottel's *Songes and Sonettes* the sonnet appears only as occasional verse in the work of Googe, Howell, and Gascoigne, and in the miscellanies, songbooks, and pastoral romances. The first experimental cycles are those of Thomas Watson in 1582 and John Soowthern in 1584. Even a brief glimpse of the period between 1557 and 1591 shows the debt of later English lyric verse to Sir Philip Sidney's *Astrophel and Stella.*

From Tottel to Astrophel and Stella

THE HISTORY of the sonnet from the time of Tottel to the year 1591 is an unaccountably brief chronicle [28] of scattered and inferior verse. Yet the sonnets of this period are neither better nor worse than the other verse of the period preceding the full flowering of the Elizabethan genius, and, whether they occur as dedication, funeral elegy, or love lament in miscellany, songbook, or pastoral romance, they often have lines of surprising grace and skill. The word "sonnet" itself, it must be remembered, is an untrustworthy clue to the nature of an Elizabethan poem, for the word was used loosely throughout that century [29]—as, indeed, it was in the eighteenth century by Collins and Goldsmith —to mean a short song. Outstanding examples in the sixteenth century of these so-called sonnets are the "Sonnets to Sundry Notes of Music" in the *Passionate Pilgrim,* and the "sonnet" al-

luded to by Thurio (Act III, scene 2, ll. 91–94) in *The Two Gentlemen of Verona,* which proves to be the lyric "Who Is Sylvia."

Irregular forms (along with lyrics of several types) are likewise present in some of the regular sonnet cycles, particularly
in those of Greville and Lodge. Several series of six-, eight-, and
ten-line stanzas were also termed "sonnets" by their authors.[30]
The true sonnet, on the other hand, is commonly called a *quatorzain.*[31]

Of the regular sonnets themselves, the majority are occasional
and express a single, often didactic, idea. Many an Elizabethan
volume, even the *Faerie Queene,* was fortified by several prefatory sonnets, while this commendatory "praising of bukes" was
the chief use King James noted for the sonnet in his treatise on
verse in 1584. Gascoigne, for example, wrote such dedications
both for himself and for others, while his friends wrote similar
eulogies for his *Posies.*[32] Gascoigne also used sonnets as the foreword and the final chorus of *Jocasta,*[33] as Shakespeare was later
to use them as an epilogue to *Henry V* and as the choruses of
Acts I and II of *Romeo and Juliet.*[34] (The first quarto of *Romeo
and Juliet,* however, shows a very different and incomplete version of the first of these sonnets.)

Perhaps none of the occasional sonnets of the century are more
interesting than those written as "epitaphes." The example of
Dante, Petrarch, Boccaccio, and other Italians had given ample
precedent for this use of the sonnet. Surrey's sonnets on the death
of Wyatt and of Thomas Clere are presumably the first elegiac
sonnets in England. This type of sonnet was not affected by the
passing of the Petrarchan vogue but has continued to be written
in every century. It is illustrated by Milton's sonnet on his wife
and Thomas Gray's sonnet on Richard West. Sixteenth-century
examples are Thomas Howell's "Ultimum vale" (in *Devises*)
on the Countess of Pembroke, Whetstone's sonnets upon Gascoigne and the Duke of Bedford,[35] King James's and Henry Constable's sonnets upon Sidney and others,[36] and Queen Elizabeth's

sonnet upon the death of the Princess of Espinoy.[37] The sonnet
of Queen Elizabeth, little known, may be quoted for its own
sake.[38] The final quatrain shows an unusual use of a conventional
conceit noticed later on, that of Cupid's dwelling place as the eyes
of the lady; and the "our" of line 8 is presumably the regal use of
the pronoun:

> When the warrier Phoebus, goth to make his round,
> With a painefull course, to too ther Hemisphêre:
> A darke shadowe, a great horror, and a feare,
> In I knoe not what clowdes inueron the ground.
> And elien so for Pinoy, that fayre vertues Lady,
> (Although Jupiter halie in this Orizôn
> Made a starre of her, by the Ariadnan crowne)
> Morns [*moans?*], dolour, and gréefe, accompany our body.
>   O Atropos, thou hast doone a worke per-lierst [*perversest?*]
>   And as a byrde that hath lost both young, and nest,
>   About the place where it was, makes many a tourne.
>   Even so dooth Cupid, that infaunt, God, of amore
>   Flie about the tombe, where she lyes all in dolore,
>   Weeping for her eies, wherein he made soiourne.

The only other English sonnets of the sixteenth century so far
attributed to a woman writer are also elegiac: four "epitaphes"
and the last quatrains of two other sonnets, which John Soowthern published in 1584 in *Pandora* as the work of the Countess of Oxford. The Countess, the unfortunate Anne Cecil
who was married at fifteen to Oxford, wrote the sonnets upon
the death (1583) of her infant son. Stiff classical allusions provide
the texture of the poems. In one Venus mourns for the "marble"
of the mortal child, thinking it is Cupid; the gods, nymphs, fates,
and all the muses except Beauty (who has lived and died with
him) mourn for the child. Yet these poems, especially that in
which the Countess says the gods and destinies might better
have taken her twenty-odd years than the two days of her son,[39]
have a poignancy unusual in any verse of that century.

The isolated sonnet had, to be sure, other uses than as "epitaphes." Following Italian and French examples, poets paid tribute to their patrons in sonnets. Tusser, for example, not only made "Chapter LV" in his *Five Hundred Points of Good Husbandry* (1573) a sonnet against a slanderous tongue but also made "Chapter LVI" a sonnet to Lord Paget. Howell wrote sonnets in acrostics to the daughters of his patron.[40] Again, the isolated sonnet, following Italian practice, was a poetic epistle or an address to a friend, as in Gascoigne.[41] Lastly, there are several moralizing or didactic sonnets [42] which are usually distressingly dull and never achieve the elevation Milton and Wordsworth were to give such themes. Among the better ones is Gascoigne's "If yelding feare, or cancred villanie," one of several sonnets he wrote on Latin mottoes furnished by friends at Gray's Inn.[43] Among didactic sonnets belong, too, Spenser's early work in the form: the translations which appeared in Van der Noot's *The Theatre*,[44] his translation of Du Bellay's *Antiquitez de Rome* (later published as a part of the *Ruines of Rome*),[45] his allegorical *Visions of the Worlds Vanitie* (which has the linking rhyme scheme later used in the *Amoretti*), and his sonnets which are a part of *The Ruines of Time.*

Sonnets on the joys and sorrows of the lover appeared in print only infrequently during this era. Those that have survived are in the volumes of Googe, Howell, and Gascoigne; in the pastoral romances; and in the unidentified work of the songbooks and miscellanies. Googe, whose *Eglogs, Epytaphes, and Sonettes* of 1563 contained two sonnets, one of them didactic, wrote, in his "Unhappye tonge, why dydste thou not consent," a surprisingly pleasing version of the conventional theme of the lover's unhappiness.[46] Howell's *Devises* of 1581 contains four Petrarchan sonnets—two showing the poet's faithful love, two showing the baleful effects of love upon him.[47]

The most considerable sonneteer in this transition era is George Gascoigne, the first in England, it will be recalled, to record a definition of the sonnet.[48] The possibility of divided

authorship of *The Hundreth Sundrie Flowers* precludes a cate-
gorical statement of the number of Gascoigne's sonnets, yet
enough certainty exists to give him first rank in the extent and
accuracy of his work. If, as Bowers suggests,[49] all the work of
The Hundreth Sundrie Flowers is Gascoigne's, he wrote in the
Petrarchan manner (either for himself or, as his statements in the
1575 edition indicate, for other men) a large number of sonnets
which must be mentioned here.

Eight of these are in the 1573 edition of "The Adventures of
Master F.J." [50] The others are occasional: one is to a "Skotish
Dame whom he chose for his Mistresse in the French Court"; a
second is "An other sonet written by [that is, 'about'] the same
Gentlewoman"—although it is doubtful to what "an other" can
refer, since no sonnet had preceded it.[51] A third is in praise of
"the brown beautie," an unknown "Mistresse E.P." In one mood
he praises constancy in love; in anti-Petrarchistic vein, he writes
an "uncurteous farewell" to an "inconstant Dame." A sonnet
written to a "gentlewoman because she challenged the Aucthour
for holding downe his head alwaies" employs the convention that
the lady's blazing eyes cause all his woes.

None of these love sonnets of Gascoigne is, unfortunately, sufficiently forceful or striking to linger in the reader's mind. The
same judgment must be made of the sonnets—six in all—preserved in the two chief miscellanies of this period, *The Paradise
of Dainty Devices* (1576) and *A Gorgeous Gallery of Gallant
Inventions* (1578). The first edition of the *Paradise* has a single
sonnet on a favorite Petrarchan theme, the sighs of the lover.[52]
The *Gorgeous Gallery* has four sonnets on Petrarchan themes [53] in
addition to a characteristic didactic one on "How to choose a fayth-
full Freende." One of the four Petrarchan sonnets is on a subject dear to the poets of that century—"Aske what love is? it is
a passion." [54] The second celebrates in correct fashion the beauty
of the lady as being superior to that of Helen, Polyxena, Venus,
and Cressida. The third and fourth (one of them irregular), are

part of a translated tale of Pyramus and Thisbe. One presents the amusing situation in which Pyramus, holding Thisbe's hand, recites a sonnet to her through the chink in the wall. Thisbe, on her side, hears it all with evident pleasure. After the sonnet vogue began in 1591 the miscellanies contained, of course, a large number of sonnets. Many are occasional. Some on themes of love are reprinted from the sonnet sequences; many appear in no other work.

All the sonnets so far discussed in this chapter were presumably intended to be read by the recipient or recited by the writer. It is quite another matter to consider the sonnets which were given musical accompaniment. The entire subject of the relation of sonnets to musical notation needs investigation by a musician —preferably E. H. Fellowes. Did the earliest Italian sonnets actually have musical settings? Did Petrarch compose his sonnets or only his lyrics by testing them to his lute? [55] Did any English musician of this period compose a sonnet expressly to set it to music, and, if so, to what extent was its form affected by the requirements of the musical form? None of these things is clear at the present. We know, however, that Nicholas Yonge's *Musica Transalpina,* of 1588, furnished English musicians with models of Italian sonnets treated as two-part songs which had separate music and new headings for the octave and sestet. This method of composition was followed by William Byrd and the later English madrigalists. The earliest English musical settings given to sonnets are apparently those in Byrd's *Psalms, Sonnets, and Songs of Sadness and Piety,* of 1588. The two sonnets of that volume,[56] beginning "Ambitious love" and "As I beheld," are treated as two-part songs—the octave sung as two quatrains (using the repeat sign), the sestet sung straight through. Both are for five voices. The same general procedure is used in Byrd's second book, *Songs of Sundrie Natures.*[57] These anonymous sonnets are interesting, not only for their musical settings, but also as indications of the quality of verse written and circulated presumably with no thought of publication. Most of them are conventional in theme and situation, and, of course, lose much when they are merely read and are not heard with the accompanying melody. Yet, even so, one encounters phrases and lines of filigreed beauty. Although the madrigalists and lute singers usually preferred poems shorter than sonnets,[58] it is pleasant to know that an age that set even stanzas from the *Faerie Queene* to music [59] provided the musicians with sonnets as graceful as the anonymous ones known from manuscripts or commonplace books.

Last to be noticed among the dispersed English sonnets of the transition era are a few appearing in the English pastoral romances. These, like their counterparts in the Italian and Spanish pastorals, are often sung by the characters in the story as being their own compositions. It is quite disconcerting, nonetheless, to find Bartholomew Yonge stating in his translation of Montemayor's *Diana* [60] that certain sonnets of that work were to be sung, not only to a rebeck and a "delicate harp," but also to a bagpipe! Greene has many so-called sonnets in his novels, but none of the early editions of *Menaphon* has any genuine ones, although Dyce and Collins printed from late seventeenth-century editions one which is attributed to him.[61] Lodge's *Rosalynde* has one true sonnet in an eclogue between Rosalynde and Rosader.[62]

Sidney's *Arcadia* contains a large number of sonnets which, as Miss Scott and others have observed, are frankly exercises in verse [63] and are interesting chiefly as showing the apprenticeship preceding the more mature sonnets of *Astrophel and Stella.* Among Sidney's experiments is a sonnet ("What lengthe of verse serve") in the manner of Berni, which ridicules Mopsa's opal-hued cheeks, sapphire lips, and silver hands. Sidney also tried intricate experiments, such as a sonnet with all the lines ending in "dark" or "light" and one with lines to be read either vertically or horizontally, "lately with some arte curyously written," beginning (and so numbered throughout) as follows:

1   2   3   1   2   3

Vertue Bewty and Speeche, did stryke, wounde, Charme.

The delightful "My true Love hathe my harte and I have his," often reprinted later without the last six lines, has been given several musical settings, one of the earliest being that by John Ward in 1613. Several Petrarchan themes of the sighs, sleepless-ness, and contrary passions of the lover are fitted into the context as devices for carrying on the narrative. A meditative sonnet (the last one of Bk. V, composed by Musidorus "before Love turnde his Muse to another subject"), however, best deserves to be remembered from the twenty-one sonnets of the *Arcadia:* [64]

> Since Natures worckes bee good and Deathe dothe serve,
> As Natures worckes, why shoulde wee feare to dye?
> Synce Feare ys vayne, but when yt may preserve,
> Why should wee feare that which wee can not flye?
>
> Feare ys more payne, then ys the Payne yt feares,
> Disarming humane myndes of Native mighte,
> While eache Conceipt, an ugly Figure beares
> Whiche were not evill well wayed in Reasons light.
>
> Oure Owly Eyes which dymmed with passions bee
> And scarce discerne the Dawne of Coming Day,
> Lett them bee Clearde, and nowe begin to See,
> Our Lyfe ys butt a Stepp in Dusty Way.
>   Then lett us holde the Bliss of peacefull Mynde,
>   Since this wee feele, great Loss we can not Fynde.

Comparison of the original draft of the *Arcadia* (first published in 1926 by Feuillerat) with Sidney's revision about half-way through Book III reveals that fourteen of the original twenty-one sonnets had been discarded. The revised Book I kept both the sonnets of the first draft but placed one ("Transformde in Shew") into a new context, where the singing of it enabled Musidorus to penetrate the Amazonian disguise of Pyrocles. The revised Book II retained three sonnets but dropped two wailing pastoral ones beginning "Feede on my sheepe" and "Leave of my sheepe."

The revised Book III discarded all the twelve sonnets of the first draft, including the lyric beginning "My true Love hathe my harte." Consequently, the 1590 *Arcadia* (that is, Books I, II, and 164 pages of III) contained a total of only five sonnets. The composite edition of 1593,[65] however, replaced the twelve discarded sonnets in Book III and published for the first time the two from the unrevised Books IV and V—one from IV and the one on death just quoted from V. (Later editions, however, inserted the sonnets in changed contexts.)

When we leave behind all these dispersed poems and come to the earliest series of sonnets in England, we approach one of the most important but least-read books of the century, Thomas Watson's *Hecatompathia,* of 1582, dedicated to the Earl of Oxford. This work, a series of adaptations and translations based upon a wide range of classical and foreign sources,[66] has a prose note to each poem explaining its purpose and stating its source. All are eighteen lines in length except Watson's Latin translations of Petrarch (Nos. VI, LXVI, XC, and the epilogue); a regular sonnet which precedes the cycle is called a *quatorzain.* Watson's work as a whole seems to have inspired no imitative cycles, yet individual sonnets were imitated, and he presents interesting versions of conceits that proved to be the favorites of later writers.[67] His function was chiefly that of transmitting classical material to English readers, but, even so, he deserves more credit than has been bestowed upon him.

After Watson comes John Soowthern, or Soothern, whose *Pandora* (1584) includes thirteen sonnets, some of them poor translations and adaptations from Ronsard. Soowthern, like Watson, dedicated his work to the Earl of Oxford and published the four elegiac sonnets already discussed in this chapter as having been attributed by him to the Countess of Oxford.[68] Soowthern's bad rhymes and curious neologisms cause his verse to seem almost the nadir of Elizabethan versifying. One of the more intelligible sonnets (No. 9) will suffice as an illustration:

It is after our deathes, a thing manifest,
We bothe goe to hell, and suffer hellische paines,
You, for your rigour, I, for my thoughts haultaines,
That attempt to lolie a Goddesse so Celest.
But as for mee I shall be lyttle afflicted,
Tis you (my warrier) that must halie the torment:
For I that but, in seeing you, am content:
You, with me, I'll blesse the place so much detested
And my soule that is ralied with your fayre eyes,
In the midst of hell, wyll establishe, a skeyes:
Making my bright day, in the eternall night.
And when all the damned else are in annoy:
I'll smyle in that glorie, seeing you my ioy:
And being once there, goe not out of our [your?] sight.[69]

The English Sequences

THE ACCOUNT just given of the sonnets before 1591 makes clear the indebtedness of English lyric poetry to the post-humous and surreptitious publication of *Astrophel and Stella* in that year. Sidney's cycle presents problems which will be considered in the appendix of this study; only a few facts need be noted here. The printer Newman published an edition of 108 sonnets in 1591, including within it twenty-eight sonnets by Samuel Daniel, several lyrics by different hands, and, as a separate group at the end, songs by Sidney which later appeared as a part of the sonnet cycle. This edition was suppressed because of complaints to the Stationers' Company,[70] but Newman soon published another. A third edition, published by Matthew Lownes, appeared the same year; and it was not until 1598 that one authorized by Sidney's sister appeared. In this edition the Countess of Pembroke inserted the songs within the sequence. The Countess also added a few other sonnets, among them one satirizing Lord Rich and the two now generally placed last in Sidney's cycle, "Thou blind man's mark" and "Leave me, O love, which reachest but to dust," which appear to round out the story ending in the earlier editions with despair and separation.

In 1592 Daniel published an authorized edition of his sonnets under the name *Delia*.[71] He omitted nine of the sonnets published in 1591 by Newman, but added thirty-one new ones. In 1594 he further revised his work. The dedication of *Delia* to the Countess of Pembroke, sister of Sidney and mother of Daniel's pupil William Herbert, as well as the obviously early date of the sonnets published by Newman, makes it seem quite probable that Daniel knew Sidney's sonnets in manuscript and that he wrote under their inspiration. His work, often pleasingly lyrical, is notable in that it contains extensive translations from continental authors and in that it may have served Shakespeare as a model when he employed the theme of the poet's verse "eternizing" the beauty of the loved one.

The year 1592 marked, also, the publication of the first edition of Henry Constable's *Diana*. Constable's work offers problems discussed to some extent in the notes with regard to the text now read as his.[72] A few facts should nevertheless be mentioned here. The first edition of *Diana* contained twenty-three sonnets. The second edition, containing seventy-six sonnets, was published in 1594 by a printer who "augmented" Constable's poems by "divers Quatorzains of honourable and learned personages." Eight are now known to be Sidney's; the exact number belonging to Constable is not known. Additional poems were published in 1812 in the "Harleian Miscellany" (Vol. IX) from a sixteenth-century manuscript.

Two points concerning Constable's verse have been cleared up by the important discovery by Ruth Hughey of the Harington Manuscript at Arundel Castle.[73] One is the identity of the person addressed as Diana: The Harington Manuscript contains twenty-two sonnets of the 1592 edition with the heading "Mr Henry Constables sonetes to the Lady Ritche. 1589." Miss Hughey states that the heading, the first two sonnets, and the first two lines of No. III are in the hand of Sir John Harington and that the other nineteen are in a hand that occurs nowhere else in the manuscript.[74] This date shows that Constable should take rank as one of the earliest sonneteers in England. There is no evidence to show that he knew *Astrophel and Stella* in manuscript,[75] and it is probable that his inspiration came from continental sources rather than from that work.

The year 1593 brought forth several volumes of sequences. Thomas Watson's *The Tears of Fancie* is unfortunately marred by the author's attempt to live up to the title. The pastoral conventions setting forth the misfortunes of love are present in the sequences of Lodge and William Smith, but nowhere are they so remote from reality, so much a sonnet world bounded on all sides by conventions, as in Watson's work. Watson's reputation suffers, too, from the extent of his indebtedness to other writers, especially to Gascoigne.[76] Yet it should be recalled that *The Tears of Fancie* was printed posthumously and that, as Watson had so carefully listed his indebtedness in the *Hecatompathia,* it is not impossible that he would have done the same for *The Tears of Fancie* had he chosen to publish it himself. Only one copy of the work is said to have survived.[77]

The second cycle of 1593 is that of Barnabe Barnes, second son of a bishop of Durham, whose *Parthenophil and Parthenophe* also survives in a single copy.[78] The work is inscribed to William Percy, a son of the Earl of Northumberland, and has word-play indicating that Parthenophe is a lady of the Percy family.[79] It is concluded by dedicatory sonnets to imposing personages—the Earls of Northumberland, Essex, and Southampton, the Countess of Pembroke, Lady Strange, and Lady Bridget Manners. Madrigals, sestinas, elegies, canzoni, and odes are included. Barnes has occasional good lines, even an occasional good sonnet. Best known is his "Ah sweet content, where is thy mild abode?" But the cycle as a whole is marred by hyperbole and by exaggerated, often incongruous, versions of the Petrarchan conceits. The cycle is of interest partly because Barnes's extensive legal phraseology may have influenced Shakespeare, while Barnes himself has attracted attention because Sir Sidney Lee believed him to be the "rival poet" of Shakespeare's sonnets.[80]

Two other cycles belong to the year 1593. Thomas Lodge "honoured" his Phillis with "pastorall sonnets, elegies, and amorous delights," forty sonnets studied today chiefly for their relation to their foreign sources.[81] Giles Fletcher's *Licia* consists of fifty-three sonnets which give versions of a number of classical themes from Marullus, Angerianus, and others.[82] Both cycles are dedicated to patrons, that of Fletcher having, also, a famous prose preface which successfully mystifies his modern readers, at least, as to the identity of Licia, and which disclaims in the conventional vein any personal sentiment in his imitations of the "best Latin poets" whom he follows.

The sonnet wave was at its crest in 1594 and 1595. In 1594 appeared the first of a series of sonnet editions and reprints by Michael Drayton—*Ideas Mirrour, Amours in Quatorzains*.[83] Drayton's sonnets are thought to have been written to Anne Goodere, but it seems impossible to substantiate that fact.[84] The collation of Drayton's 1594, 1599, 1605, and 1619 editions by Oliver Elton [85] shows how extensive were the revisions Drayton made in his work and how faithful was his devotion to the sonnet form in spite of his frequent protestations against it. Studies of Drayton's sonnets have been made, too, by Fleay and others to show the similarities between them and those of Shakespeare.[86] The work of Drayton, like that of Barnes, reveals the extent to which a poet's style could be affected by his search for new garbs to deck out old ideas. Yet, after all, Drayton was a genuine poet, and his "Since there's no help, come, let us kiss and part" appears in almost every poetic anthology.

Two minor collections of sonnets also appeared in 1594. One is by Barnes's friend William Percy (1573–1648), who professes that his *Coelia*, a cycle of twenty sonnets of which only two copies are said to have survived, was sent to the press without his knowledge. Percy, who later wrote some plays,[87] and who was probably about twenty at the time he tried his hand at sonneteering, has faults arising both from his immaturity and from imitation of the exaggerated conceits of Barnes. The second cycle of 1594, the anonymous *Zepheria,* is in one respect probably the most remarkable of all the sequences—obscurity of language arising from curious neologisms. *Zepheria* reflects, too, considerable imitation of the worst features of the imagery, phrasing, and sentence construction of Barnes, as well as legal phraseology used in so literal and prosaic a manner that it is later satirized in the "gulling" sonnets of John Davies. *Coelia* and *Zepheria* inevitably call to mind a description in the *Return from Parnassus* (Act IV, scene 2, ll. 187–88) of the character Amoretto, who was a "chief carpenter of sonnets, a privileged vicar for the lawless marriage of ink and paper."

The year 1595 is notable for the publication of Spenser's *Amoretti,* written, the publisher says, "not long since"—Renwick suggests between 1592 and 1594.[88] The first sonnet of the sequence was copied by the poet in his own hand in a 1590 copy of the *Faerie Queene* and may have been an introduction to that work rather than to the *Amoretti.*[89] The sonnets, chiefly in Spenser's interlocking rhyme scheme of *ababbcbccdcdee,* are, as a whole, in a twilight mood of sustained gravity and are addressed to a lady named Elizabeth (No. LXXIV), usually said to be the Elizabeth Boyle who became the poet's wife. This opinion gains plausibility from the suggestion of Garrod that the frequent references throughout the poems to the word "peace" are word plays upon "Peace" or "Pease" and that Elizabeth Boyle was the widow of a Tristram Pease or Peace when Spenser met her.[90] Renwick points out, however, that documentary evidence of this marriage is lacking.

The theory that the Elizabeth of the sonnets is Elizabeth Boyle has been disputed, yet the alternate suggestion that the Elizabeth referred to in Sonnet LXXIV is Lady Elizabeth Carey [91] has not gained wide acceptance. If Spenser did write the *Amoretti* to Elizabeth Boyle (whether or not she was the widow of Tristram Pease or Peace), the separation indicated at the end of the cycle must have been a temporary one. In short, the extent of the autobiography in the *Amoretti* is so uncertain that any assurance regarding it must be deferred until new facts are brought to light.

Spenser's sonnets stand secure in English verse, however, because of their genuine poetic quality even when they suffer in comparison with the best of Shakespeare and with the wittier and more vivacious sonnets of Sidney. Renwick's estimate of the cycle is excellent:

Spenser never wrote one outstanding sonnet to rank with Drayton's masterpiece or Sidney's best. He has not Shakespeare's compression, nor what comes from it, the magical phrase that strikes the throb of immediate response and lingers for ever in the memory. He never achieved the solidity of some of the *Sonnets pour Helène*, or the subtlety of some of the sonnets to Madonna Laura. But he kept a better level than most, and if he never wrote a great sonnet he never wrote a bad one. His sonnets neither march nor snap, but glide with an easy flow like all his poems, "tuning their voices to the water's fall." For that his rhyme-scheme, his only innovation, is responsible.[92]

The *Amoretti* was the only important cycle of 1595. Lesser works of that year were *Emaricdulfe,* by "E. C."; an irregular sequence called *Alcilia: Philaparthen's Loving Folly,* by "I. C."; and *Cynthia with Certain Sonnets,* by Richard Barnfield. By 1596 the sonnet wave was receding. The three cycles of that year are by writers about whom almost nothing is known. William Smith published pastoral sonnets, called *Chloris,* which he dedicated to Spenser; Richard Linche published *Diella;* [93] and Bartholomew Griffin, *Fidessa,* a work echoing Daniel and Sidney. (Lee says that only three copies of *Fidessa* are known and that *Diella* is very rare.) By 1597 the reaction against sonneteering had begun,

so that only one sonnet cycle appeared, Robert Tofte's *Laura,*
dedicated to Lady Lucy Percy, sister of the ninth Earl of Northumberland. This cycle, which includes verse by unknown hands,[94]
departs so far from the conventional pattern of a Petrarchan cycle
as a record of a poet's unrequited love that it has the dubious distinction of being the only English cycle to have a happy ending.
Tofte's use of the Petrarchan themes is almost uniformly characterized by excessive hyperbole and almost complete lack of
taste.

Several Scottish poets—notably William Drummond of Hawthornden and the Earl of Stirling—also wrote sonnets.[95] The English sonnet development includes, also, cycles of religious sonnets
such as those of Barnes, Constable, and Donne, the philosophical
sonnets of Chapman, and a series of nine satirical sonnets of Sir
John Davies. These non-Petrarchan groups, however, are disre-
garded in this study.[96]

Last to be mentioned of the sonnets written during the age of
Elizabeth are two sequences published only in the following century. Fulke Greville's *Caelica,* not published until 1633, five years
after Greville's death, was written, the title page says, in his
"youth and familiar exercise with Sir Philip Sidney." *Caelica*
shows so many resemblances to Sidney's work that it seems obvious that the poets sometimes wrote competitive versions of the
same themes.[97] The last sequence to be mentioned is the most
illustrious in the language—the unauthorized edition in 1609 of
Shakespeare which "T. T." dedicated to "Mr. W. H.," the "only
begetter of these ensuing sonnets." Probably no two initials have
ever evoked so much conjecture; certainly no other sonnet cycle
has been subjected to so much speculation. The latest and most
comprehensive account of the facts known concerning this cycle
is that in the Preface to Professor Tucker Brooke's *Shakespeare's
Sonnets.*[98] Since, however, it is not the purpose of the present
study to refer to Shakespeare except incidentally when the sonnet

themes coincide with those of the other sequences, no mention will be made here of the problems with respect to his work.

Such, then, is the sonnet's brief chronicle from the time of its naturalization in Tudor England to the publication of Shakespeare's sonnets, in 1609. The phases of the English sonnet which have received the most extended examination [99] are the metrics of the form [100] and the relation of the English sonnets to their continental analogues. For the last, Miss Scott's *Les Sonnets élisabéthains* (1929) takes precedence over other and earlier works because of its completeness.[101] Miss Scott's book, altogether the best one available on the English cycles, also clarifies the sixteenth-century point of view (so little considered by Sidney Lee) with regard to foreign sources. This conception, dating from the Middle Ages, of originality as personal application or new expression of the old rather than as new material itself, of substance as common property, with originality shown in the form, is further illuminated in Harold O. White's admirable *Plagiarism and Imitation during the English Renaissance*.[102]

After the early seventeenth century the Petrarchan sonnet sequence gradually disappeared from the English language. The growth of the anti-Petrarchistic feeling has been indicated by Sir Sidney Lee.[103] Habington's *Castara* (1640) is probably the last example of a sequence which pretends to follow the Petrarchan pattern. The fate of the genre in England after *Astrophel and Stella* was published reminds one not a little of the allegory of Tennyson's "The Flower"—most could grow the flower then, for all had got the seed:

> And some were pretty enough,
> And some are poor indeed.

Yet taste soon changed—

> And now again the people
> Call it but a weed.

Tudor England, as all the world knows had, however, brought this strange plant from Italy. Only an occasional reader, on the other hand, is really aware of the details of that origin or realizes the extent of the conventional material present in Petrarch's *Canzoniere*. Yet he who wishes to account for the nature of the English sequences, to take cognizance of the *concetti* which comprise them, must recognize the long duration of this usage and the continuity of the sonnet tradition. We must turn back, therefore, from the flowering of the form in Elizabethan England to consider as briefly as possible the sonnet origin in Sicily and the establishment of the genre in Italy and France.

THE ITALIAN ORIGIN OF THE SONNET

THE POEMS in Petrarch's *Canzoniere,* or *Rime,* consist of sonnets, ballades, sestines, madrigals, and odes written during the lifetime and after the death of Laura. The *Canzoniere* includes thirty-odd "friendship" sonnets addressed to persons other than Laura.[104] There are two manuscripts of the *Canzoniere,* Vatican Manuscript No. 3195, used for the Aldine edition of 1501 and most later editions,[105] and No. 3196, an earlier draft from which the latter was made.[106] Both are said to have been owned by Cardinal Bembo. Each manuscript is in two parts, for, although the 366 poems are given a consecutive numbering, there are seven blank pages between those to Laura in life and those to her in death.[107] Tatham says that the final manuscript might well be called a random collection of fugitive pieces which had been circulated in Provence and Italy and handed on to an ever-increasing company of admirers.[108] In later life Petrarch, he suggests, set to work to make an "authorized collection, containing his latest improvements and disposed in an order which he wished to be considered final."[109] Miss Phelps, in her comparison of the earlier and later forms of the poems, stresses the annotations which reveal Petrarch's continued revisions.[110]

The earliest edition of Petrarch was published in Venice in 1470. Ferrazzi states that 34 editions were published in Italy in the fifteenth century, 167 in the sixteenth, 17 in the seventeenth, 46 in the eighteenth, and (up to 1877) 128 in the nineteenth.[111] More than 200 of these were published in Venice alone. Several editions appeared in France in the sixteenth century; none, apparently, were printed in England until much later.[112] Of translations in England there were until the middle of the nineteenth century only isolated sonnets such as those in Tottel, Watson, and others, or groups of selections from the whole, such as those published in the eighteenth century.[113]

Since the poems of the *Canzoniere* must be referred to in each of the later chapters of this study, it will suffice to say only a word about them here. The work, best understood if read in the light of Petrarch's *Secretum* and his *Letter to Posterity,* expresses every phase of his joy and sorrow with so much care and artistry that it is not surprising that he became the archetype of all later sonneteers. It is of interest, however, to observe that the sonnets in the *Vita nuova* anticipate in some respects the scope of later sequences.[114] These sonnets are essentially a record of unrequited love, and that theme is the subject of later sequences. Then, too, Dante's verse is written, he says, at the command of the god of love. Later poets also profess to write at Love's command but nowhere does the convention have the intensity or the allegorical significance that it has in Dante. Dante's sonnets, again, are subjective; he speaks his innermost thoughts. Yet he is confidential, social; the book is written for his friend Cavalcanti. Dante anticipates Petrarch, moreover, in writing of the death of the beloved. No parallel is to be found here, however, in the English cycles under discussion. Those of Sidney and Spenser end with separation attributed merely to absence rather than to death; lesser sonneteers, as Lodge, Constable, and Fletcher, merely bring their cycles to a close as pleas for pity from the lady.[115]

The *Vita nuova* not only anticipates the scope of later sequences; it also incorporates sonnets of most of the types later used as unrelated or occasional verse rather than as part of a narrative.[116] It contains, for instance, sonnets written at the request of others and to persons other than Beatrice. The first sonnet is a request to friends for interpretations of his dream vision. He says he received many answers; those of Cavalcanti, Cino da Pistoia, and Dante da Maiano are to be found in Rossetti's translation.[117] This epistolary type of sonnet is sometimes used by continental sonneteers, but in England, although three of Sidney's are undoubtedly addressed to personal friends and although one of Spenser's is addressed to Lodowick Bryskett, such sonnets are usually separate or dedicatory verse.[118] Finally, Dante made use here of the sonnet as elegy for persons other than Beatrice. Two sonnets lament the death of a "damsel young and of gentle presence, who had been very lovely in the city I speak of," merely because Dante had seen her in the company of Beatrice. Two others lament the death of the father of Beatrice. In England no sequence contains this elegiac type of poem,[119] although the isolated sonnet was, and still is, employed for this purpose. In the *Vita nuova,* however, even such occasional sonnets do not seem irrelevant or inappropriate but contribute to Dante's idealization of Beatrice.

Whether or not the sonnets of the *Vita nuova* furnished Petrarch with a specific model for his *Canzoniere,* they were in themselves an expression of material and ideas already conventional before Dante made use of them. The similarities between Dante's work and that of his predecessors in Italy and Provence have been pointed out by L. F. Mott in his *The System of Courtly Love Studied as a Background for the Vita nuova.* Mott shows, as well, the points at which Dante elevates this conventional material, particularly in his portrayal of love as a powerful and ennobling divinity instead of the sensual deity of the Provençals. The Italian poets of the *dolce stil nuovo* had, however, brought some degree of elevation to this verse before Dante's time. It was for this that Dante acknowledged Guido Guinicelli as his master and called him

> That father of me and of my betters, who
> Used ever sweet and gracious rhymes of love.[120]

Also attributable to the Italian poets instead of to those of Provence is another quality adding to the ennoblement of love—an idealization of the ladies to whom they addressed their verse. Moseley's study of a set of images used by both Provençal and early Italian poets shows that this idealization was not found in the earlier verse but was added by the Italians.[121] Dante's sonnets provide the finest illustrations of this kind of elevation. Petrarch's *Canzoniere* contains, as R. V. Merrill points out, some elements of Platonism, yet, in several respects, is contrary to the spirit of Platonic doctrines.[122] The practical effect upon the writing of sonnets was the establishment of a genre which men of lesser gifts could utilize in recording an idealized love.

Dante and Petrarch, however, were no more the inventors of the technical form of the sonnet than they were the first to treat the themes they used. The sonnet form is nevertheless of Italian origin. The earliest sonnets known to exist were written in the court of Frederick II of Sicily.[123] Thirty-five survive, and it is probable that all but four were written between 1220 and 1250. Twenty-five are the work of King Frederick's imperial notary, Giacomo da Lentino, who accompanied Frederick on his journeys through Sicily and the south of Italy in 1233. Three by the Abbot of Tivoli, together with two of Giacomo's, compose a five-sonnet *tenzone,* or poetical debate, on the question as to whether love has a separate being or is only a state or condition. Giacomo also contributes to a three-sonnet *tenzone* in conjunction with Piero delle Vigne, Frederick's imperial chancellor, and Jacopo

Mostacci, imperial falconer in 1240 and King Manfred's ambassador to the King of Aragon in 1262. A sonnet by Monaldo d'Aquino is an independent composition. The four sonnets which are thought to be of a date slightly later than 1250 are, respectively, by Guglielmo Beroardi, Mazzeo di Ricco, King Enzo, son of Frederick, and Rinaldo d'Aquino, probably the older brother of Saint Thomas Aquinas, whom he had kidnapped in an attempt to prevent him from becoming a Dominican.

It is probable that Giacomo the Notary was the inventor of the sonnet. The earliest sonnet, Wilkins believes, may be any of the group of thirty-one except those in the second or a later position in a *tenzone:* [124]

The chances are that it is rather one of the sonnets of Giacomo than one of those by the other authors . . . No. XI, then, *Molti amadori la lor malatia,* is more completely primitive in character than any of the other sonnets; and has therefore a slightly more plausible claim than any other to be regarded as the earliest extant sonnet.

Wilkins analyzes the form of the Sicilian sonnets. They contain fourteen hendecasyllabic lines, with the octave rhyming *abababab.* The scheme for the sestet in twenty of the earliest thirty-one sonnets is *cdecde;* for ten it is *cdcdcd;* and for one *aabaab.* The octave was divided into four distichs, and there was a tendency to divide its meaning into two quatrains. The sestet was separated, not into distichs, but into tercets. The octave is derived from a popular Sicilian peasant song, the *strambotto,* and is not, as has sometimes been said, derived from a Provençal form. [125] Neither is it a single stanza of a *canzone* or a form derived from the north of France or from Germany. The sestet is of uncertain origin, but Wilkins suggests that an Arabian love song called the *zağal* could, if known to the sonnet inventor, have suggested the sestet rhyme scheme because of its similarity to the eight-line *strambotto.*

One sonnet of Giacomo may be quoted to illustrate his rhyme

scheme. In accordance with Provençal conventions he compares the lady to various gems and, in the words of Langley, finds "that she surpasses them all in beauty and should rather be compared to a star in brightness. Fairer is she than the rose or other flowers; may Christ bless her with life, joy, and honor!": [126]

> Diamante, nè smiraldo, nè zafino,
>   nè vernul' altra gema preziosa,
> topazo, nè giaquinto, nè rubino,
>   nè l'aritropia, ch'è sì vertudiosa,
> nè l'amatisto, nè 'l carbonchio fino,
>   lo qual è molto risprendente cosa,
> non ano tanta beleze in domino,
>   quant'à in sè la mia donna amorosa.
> E di vertute tutte l'autre avanza,
>   e somigliante [a stella è] di sprendore,
> cola sua conta e gaia inamoranza;
>   e più bell' è che rosa e che frore.
> Cristo le doni vita ed alegranza,
>   e sì la cresca in gran pregio ed onore.

Wilkins therefore summarizes the origin of the sonnet in the following words:

The sonnet, then, is Sicilian: certainly in the source of its octave; presumably in the person of its inventor; possibly in the source of the sestet. If the inventor was Giacomo, or any other member of the Frederican court, the actual invention may of course have occurred upon the mainland.[127]

Italian in its origin, the attitude toward love which the sonnet embodies is nevertheless largely that of the Provençal troubadours. Langley states that Giacomo carried on in both *canzoni* and sonnets the conventions of the Provençals in their worship of a lady; all his *canzoni* are on themes of love, and of the twenty-five sonnets only one (on friendship) is on a theme other than love. Eighteen are ostensibly based on personal experience or emotion, while the other six are impersonal discussions of the nature and power of love.[128]

The general similarities between Sicilian and Provençal verse pointed out by Gaspary in *Die sicilianische Dichterschule des dreizehnten Jahrhunderts* (1878) and by Jeanroy in *Les Origines de la poésie lyrique en France* (pp. 233–73) and *Le Poésie lyrique des troubadours* need not be noticed here. The probable Arabic influence which may have affected the court of Frederick II and even the Provençals is noticed by several writers, notably Gibb and Nykl.[129] Guillaume IX, the earliest troubadour, was perhaps influenced by Moslem culture through his experiences in the Crusades and through contact with Andalusian Arabic culture. Nykl believes that even the Ovidian and Platonic influences present (though misinterpreted) in later troubadour verse came through Arabic sources. Eleanor of Aquitaine was also probably influenced by Oriental culture.[130] Of less immediate importance, however, for the student of the sonnet than are the origins of Provençal verse are the nature of that verse and the fact that by the time of Petrarch the Provençal conception of love had been elevated by Dante and his followers.

With these observations upon the sonnet as shaped by the Sicilians and early Italians and upon the conventions from which Petrarch himself drew, we may return to him with the statement that after him a sonnet sequence without his influence would have been *Hamlet* without Hamlet. Imitators flourished in Italy, particularly toward the end of the fifteenth century and at the beginning of the sixteenth under the influence of Cardinal Bembo (1470–1547).[131] Three of the late fifteenth-century writers especially influenced the scope and style of the sonnets—the Spanish-born Gareth, usually called Chariteo (1450–1514),[132] Tebaldeo (1463?–1537),[133] and Serafino d'Aquila (1466–1500). Chariteo added themes from classical sources; Tebaldeo, who made the sonnet almost an epigram, had a definite effect upon the construction of French sonnets.[134] All three, but especially Serafino because of his great contemporary fame, affected later sonneteers

by making their sonnets more realistic and sensual than those of
Petrarch. All pointed the style and exaggerated the Italian *concetti* until preciosity almost obscured the beauty and sincerity of
Petrarch. Bembo's desire for a purer style and tone helped coun-
teract these qualities and recalled the Italian lyric, as Professor
Fletcher expresses it, "from this conceitful travesty of Petrarch
back to the real Petrarch, though more to the elegant stylist than
to the deeply moving poet that Petrarch is at his best." [135] All
this emphasis upon style left its mark, however, upon the French
and English sonnets.

THE EARLY FRENCH SONNETS

SUCH was the Italian heritage which, in the main, shaped the
destiny of later sonnet cycles. After the middle of the sixteenth century, however, another force was at work which also
affected the English writers—the writing of sonnets in France.
Since French, not Italian, verse was sometimes the immediate inspiration of the English poets (particularly of Lodge and of
Daniel) and since it gave one new theme to the English sequence, some account of the French sonnets is essential here.

Imitations of Petrarch did not appear in France until the second quarter of the sixteenth century. Clément Marot (1495–1544)
is, as it has been said, credited by Pierre Villey with having written in 1536, the earliest sonnet in France.[136] Marot's twelve
sonnets [137] include six translations from Petrarch, three of them
called "epigrams." [138] Mellin de Saint-Gelais (1490?–1558) wrote
almost twice as many sonnets as Marot, among them the translation from Sannazaro mentioned at the beginning of this Introduction in connection with Wyatt.[139] Marot and Saint-Gelais, like
Surrey and Wyatt, wrote some occasional verse. Saint-Gelais addressed one sonnet to Marot, wrote one each to preface works by

Ronsard and Herberay des Essarts, and still another as an epitaph on the wife of Herberay. His sixteen *Sonnets* also include occasional ones as well as those on themes of love.

No notice of the French sonnets, however brief, can overlook the influence of the writers of Lyons, especially of Maurice Scève. Scève, although he wrote only two regular sonnets, produced in the 499 *dizains* of *Délie* (published in 1544) a series of poems which were forerunners of the cycles of the Pléiade poets and which influenced them greatly. He took over, as Vianey expresses it, the whole arsenal of the images of Serafino and shows more of him than of Petrarch; but he elevated and restrained them in his use of the themes.[140] Less influential than the *dizains* of Scève, but perhaps of greater interest for their own merits, are the sonnets of another member of the Lyons group, Louise Labé.[141] Her twenty-four sonnets employ many of the Petrarchan themes—the eye as the abode of love, pleas for pity, songs to the lyre, sleeplessness, the loneliness of absence. Yet her sestets often depart from the usual conventional Petrarchan tone and treatment and gain in her hands an unusual degree of poignancy and autobiographical reality.

The work of the Pléiade group of poets, especially of Ronsard and of Du Bellay, is of particular interest to the readers of English sonnets; but the scope of their more than two thousand sonnets [142] makes it impossible here to do more than to note the fact that they added one new theme to the Petrarchan sonnet conception—the Alexandrian Greek personification of Cupid, derived from the newly recovered *Greek Anthology* and *Anacreontea*, which had, as we shall see, a marked influence upon the English sonneteers. Desportes, too, who wrote more than four hundred sonnets, exerted a great influence upon English sonneteers. Although the English poets sometimes directly translated him and the Pléiade writers, at other times they reveal only the similarity of analogues—the inevitable repetition of the definite set of ideas that make up a Petrarchan imitation. For Petrarch remained the head of all the sonneteers, and, as Sidney Lee observes, probably no sonnet of his and few of the popular ones of his Italian followers "were not more or less exactly and more or less independently reproduced a dozen times or more in the French verse during the last years of the sixteenth century." [143] The scope and the theme of a sonnet cycle had, except for the addition of certain classical subjects, been largely determined by Petrarch. And now we may consider the themes of the English cycles—first, the conventional methods used in portraying the theme of love.

CLASSICAL HERITAGE

A PETRARCHAN sonnet sequence, it has already been said, is a record of the poet's unrequited love. Yet, paradoxically, other sonnet themes reveal more convincing indications of autobiographical reality than do those purporting to set forth the theme of love itself. Indeed, the sonnets cast so little light upon the very subject about which they are professedly written that the modern reader sometimes dismisses them as trivial and insincere. The fact often overlooked, however, is that, until a period later even than the sixteenth century, love was still customarily and conventionally described in the classical manner as the exploits of Cupid.

Since it is apparently impossible to read a sequence today as a literal transcript of personal feeling, to translate accounts of Cupid's arrows and fires and sieges into the present-day terms of "reality" or "sincerity," some other basis of approach must be found for such sonnets. Considered from the point of view of their origins and the traditions reflected in them, they afford much light on the sonnet conventions; considered from the point of view of style, they afford an excellent basis of comparison for the treatment given by the different poets. It is therefore the object of this chapter to seek to assemble and to clarify somewhat the hundreds of sonnet allusions to Cupid as the conventional symbol for portraying the power of love, and to indicate the scope of the treatment given them by the English writers.

The historical approach employed here necessitates, however, a preliminary definition of the terms used. The first division is therefore given over to brief explanations of the Latin, or "Ovidian," and the Alexandrian Greek, or "Anacreontic," manners of representing love as Cupid. The two, to be sure, are not always mutually exclusive, and they often appear side by side within the same sonnet. Yet the fundamental difference between them affords a basis for dividing the personifications into two main groups. Since the first, or Ovidian, dominated the other forms of

Elizabethan literature as well as the sonnet, that phase of the historical background has also been given brief comment in order that the fact may be recognized that Cupid was the god of the Elizabethan idolatry. The last two sections of this division are then given, respectively, to the Ovidian and to the Alexandrian representations of love as they appear in the sonnet sequences themselves.

The Two Chief Guises for Representing the Theme

MOST of the conceptions and personifications of love known in later ages came from Greek literature. The Romans had no god of love of their own—"einen Kult derselben," says Furtwängler, "gab es nie bei ihnen." [1] Among the Greeks, however, the cult of Eros was very old. Furtwängler says: [2]

Die homerische Poesie kennt Eros als Gott nicht; nur einmal findet sich eine für einen augenblicklichen Zweck gemachte Art von dichterischer Personifikation . . . Bei Hesiod . . . jedoch ist Eros volle göttliche Person, doch mit einem ihr anhaftenden begrifflichen Charakter . . .

The conceptions of Eros in Greek literature as traced by Furtwängler and Floyd A. Spencer show that, although love was sometimes considered as a cosmogonic force, he was more commonly a blind, cruel deity whom not even the other gods could resist. Since he was a god, he was portrayed even in the earliest Greek art as winged. Euripides is said to be the first poet to describe him as having a bow; [3] later writers gave him other attributes such as a fascia and fiery arrows. "The appearance of Eros," says Professor Spencer, "is variously portrayed, according as he is thought of as a cosmogonic deity or as specifically the god of love." He adds: "The cosmogonic Eros is a veritable Ancient of Days; the god of love is at first a young man or a boy, then later (particularly in the Alexandrian period) a mischievous child (sometimes without wings—a mere *putto*) . . ." [4]

This Alexandrian, or "Anacreontic," conception of the mischievous child was largely lost sight of in later European literature until the Renaissance recovery and publication of Theocritus and the *Greek Anthology*. More particularly, it was known and disseminated through French verse after Henri Estienne had published the *Anacreontea* in 1554 and Remy Belleau had translated that work into French in 1556.[5] Its influence in England is therefore later than that of the Latin conception, and comment regarding it will be deferred until the latter part of this section.

The Latin writers, for their part, evolved certain modifications from the Alexandrian conception. By the time of Ovid the representation of love in the *Amores, Ars amatoria,* and *Remedia amoris* is that of a malicious, vindictive tyrant who had none of the playful, insouciant qualities of the Alexandrian Greek representations.[6] This Ovidian conception of the appearance, power, and nature of love in time dominated the literature of the Middle Ages, especially the romances of Chrétien de Troyes.[7] The conception of love held by the Provençals [8] was thus modified, for, in the Provençal language,[9] *amor* was a feminine noun and poets such as Bernart de Ventadorn had portrayed love as a goddess. Chrétien himself followed this feminine personification in his early works, but, after knowing the writings of Ovid,[10] he took over the "picture of love as a god who wounds his victims with his arrows . . . and this deity soon came to be generally recognized." [11] The Provençals sometimes blended the masculine and feminine conceptions, as in a poem of Guiraut de Calanso in which the goddess of love is given all the attributes of Cupid— "wings, nakedness, blindness, and the bow and arrows." [12]

The Provençals gradually evolved, moreover, from the Ovidian personification the composite figure of French poetry of the Middle Ages which portrayed love as a tall young man who is placed in the setting of a feudal court and who possessed at once all the

tyrannical powers of a feudal overlord and of the classical god.[13]
The epitome of this composite figure is the blind young god of
the *Romance of the Rose,* who looked like an angel and possessed such glory and beauty that the poet scarcely dared write
of him. On his garments were represented all the flowers and
beasts:

> Love's friends had woven from his bowers,
> In scorn of silk, a robe of flowers,
> All worked about with amorettes,
> And tied with dainty bandelets,
> Bedecked with lozenges and scutcheons,
> Leopards, strange outland beasts, and lions;
> While blossoms of all colours were
> Besprinkled o'er it, here and there.
> 'Twere no light task some flower to name
> That was not found thereon, each came
> To lend its beauty . . . and he
> One of God's angels looked to be.[14]

This composite figure acquired, too, additional attributes drawn
from the religious observances of the period, giving rise to the
so-called ecclesiastical conception of Cupid [15] and adding great
seriousness to the portrayal of the figure of love.

Thus the characteristics of the god of love were fixed conventions when Giacomo and the other Sicilians wrote the earliest
sonnets. The Sicilians appropriated from the Provençals both
their chivalric attitudes toward love and the Ovidian modifications made in them.[16] Giacomo wrote all but one of his sonnets
on the various aspects of the power and nature of love, even
though his *canzoni* sometimes protest against what Langley calls
the "simpering insincerities" of the Provençal code.[17] By the time
of the *Vita nuova,* the original Ovidian conception of the nature
of love had been so elevated in tone by the troubadours and the
singers of the *dolce stil nuovo* that it had lost much of its original
sensuality. Dante, through the seriousness with which he treated
it in the lyrics of the *Vita nuova,* the *Convivio,* and the *Com-*

media, further elevated it; as Rand expresses it, he raised it "to heights of which Ovid never dreamed." [18] Of this quality of the *Vita nuova,* Mott says: [19]

. . . the picture of a joyous youth surrounded by a gay court has given place to that of a veritable god. *Ecce deus fortior me, qui veniens dominabitur mihi,* says the Spirit of Life. Thenceforth Love ruled Dante so that he compelled him to do all his pleasure, yet never without the faithful counsel of reason.

Petrarch never portrays love as a tall young god, although he does address him at times as *signor,* a feudal lord. Nor does he employ any of the dream-vision allegory of the *Vita nuova;* Amor is rather the *saevus puer* of the *Amores.*[20] He is described once as "garzon con l'ali, non pinto, ma vivo" (Pt. I, No. C).[21] Yet the *Canzoniere* and the *Vita nuova* agree in personifying love as an irresistible god at whose command the poet writes and who causes the poet's woes. Few poems of the *Canzoniere* fail to record some aspect or attribute of Amor, while the seventh *canzone* of Part II is notable as summing up the ennobling effects and the grievous suffering love causes. Petrarch's pagan allegory is given, also, an infusion of Christian love when he turns after the death of Laura from earthly to heavenly love.

The representations of love found in English verse before the appearance of Tottel's *Miscellany* are largely those of the medieval period rather than of the straight Ovidian interpretation. Chaucer makes use, as Dodd shows, of the feudal, classical, and ecclesiastical guises of love, and he has, as well, some instances which are indeterminate. In the *Book of the Duchess,* for example, love is a feudal lord. The knight says:

> . . . I have ever yit
> Be tributarye and yiven rente
> To Love, hooly with good entente,
> And throgh plesaunce become his thral
> With good wille, body, hert, and al.
> (ll. 764–68)

Then the personification changes immediately to the ecclesiastical, for the lover prays devoutly to the god.[22] These examples illustrate how the conceptions veer back and forth in Chaucer's other poems. In *Troilus and Criseyde* the feudal and ecclesiastical portrayals far outnumber the classical ones.[23] The *Romance of the Rose,* of course, carries on the conception of the *Roman de la Rose* and represents the god of love as a tall, beautiful youth who wore a robe "all in floures and in flourettes, /Y-paynted al with amorettes." The Prologue to *The Legend of Good Women,* however, likewise represents him as a tall god but as wearing a robe of silk embroidered "ful of grene greves / In-with a fret of rede roseleves."[24] The *Parliament of Fowls* (ll. 211–17) describes Cupid and Pleasure tempering arrows[25] and the *Knight's Tale* (ll. 1963–66) mentions the blind, winged Cupid attending Venus.

Other poems of the period make use of a mixture of conceptions. Gower's *Confessio amantis* follows no one method consistently, veering from the feudal method to the ecclesiastical and back again without any reason. Although Gower uses the classical personification, names Ovid, and takes from the *Metamorphoses* the theme of the arrows of gold and of lead (*Met.* i. ll. 466–74), yet Venus is for him more important than Cupid, who "does nothing of any consequence except to pierce the lover, near the beginning of the poem, and to pull out the dart, just before the close."[26] A feudal poem about Venus, too, instead of about Cupid, for all its discourse about "Lufe," is James I's *Kings Quair.* Cupid is represented here, nevertheless, as sitting in a "chiere of estate" in the palace of Venus and as having arrows of gold, silver, and steel. He has "wingis bright, all plumyt bot his face," and wears a chaplet of green leaves upon his "longe yalow lokkis" (ll. 651–65).

The Cupid of Lydgate's *Assembly of the Gods* differs somewhat in appearance from the regular classical portrayal, but the "ouches and ryngs" with which he was so "beset" that the palace shone as if it were day appear to be a bright reflection of the passage in the *Amores* describing the way in which the god would be adorned in his triumphal progress.[27] Yet Lydgate's Cupid, curiously enough, wears a "kerchyef of pleasaunce" which "stood over hys helme ay." More nearly in the classical tradition is the "lytle Cupyde" of Hawes's *Pastime of Pleasure* who is sent to La Belle Pucell at the request of Grande Amour. The anonymous *Court of Love,* published in Stowe's 1561 edition of Chaucer, presents Cupid as a feudal lord, but in effigy.[28] One of the few echoes of this conception in the Elizabethan sonnets is Drayton's poem beginning:

> Cupid, dumbe-Idoll, peeuish saint of love
> No more shalt thou nor Saint nor Idoll be.

The Scottish Chaucerians gave surprising and original attributes to the god of love. Henryson's *Testament of Cresseid* must have been a well-known poem if we are to judge by the number of contemporary references to Cressida as a leper. Unfortunately, however, no later poet imitated Henryson's truly remarkable description of King Cupid calling up the planets by "ring-and ane silver bell" which men might "heir fra hevin unto Hell" (ll. 144–45). An occasional imitation, too, of the description of Cupid in Gavin Douglas's *A Palice of Honour* (l. 1501) would have lent variety to less colorful versions in the sonnets and elsewhere in the late Elizabethan era, for Douglas describes the god as wearing "cleithing" which was "als grene as ane huntair." There is at least one echo of this kind of tradition, however, in the *Faerie Queene* (Bk. VII, canto 7, stanza 34) in the line: "And Cupid selfe about her fluttred all in greene."

The English sonneteers, strangely enough, use the feudal conception of love chiefly in phrases such as Sidney's "my lord Love," Greville's "Cupid's knights and I," Smith's description of himself as a vassal of the glorious love-god, and Percy's reference to love as his liege and as "dread liege." [29] Constable and Fletcher both speak of themselves as thralls to love. Spenser reflects this feudal conception more than any other sonneteer: Sonnet X protests against the unrighteous lord of love; Sonnet LXX has lines in which the poet bids the lady wait upon love amongst his lovely crew in the springtime; and Sonnet XIX alludes to the song of the cuckoo as a warning to all lovers to wait upon their king, who comes forth crowned with a garland.

The Ovidian Conception of Love in England before the Sonnet Sequences

ALTHOUGH the Ovidian personification of love as a vindictive little tyrant had appeared rather infrequently in English verse before the work of Wyatt, Surrey, and their contemporaries, it soon became so well established that it was almost the only means by which the sixteenth-century poets recorded the theme of love in any type of work. Even after a few poets acquired at first hand or through French intermediaries a knowledge of the lighter, gayer Alexandrian personification of Eros as a merry, insouciant infant, the average Elizabethan poet continued to bewail his woes as resulting from the warfare or tyranny of the implacable god described in the *Amores* and the other works of Ovid.[30] So numerous, indeed, are these Ovidian descriptions of the tribulations caused by Cupid that the present-day reader longs, with greater fervor than Donne can have had, to talk with some old lover's ghost who died before the god of love was born. Yet to the Elizabethans—the gentlemen of the Inns of Court, for example, to whom some cycles were dedicated —these themes probably had little, if any, of the brittle artificiality that they connote today, and the sonnet vogue may no doubt be explained in part by the appeal they made to sixteenth-century poets. The Ovidian conception in the sonnets themselves is best understood, therefore, if we consider briefly the sixteenth-century attitude toward the subject of greatest moment to any poet seeking to produce a Petrarchan sonnet sequence.

Tottel's *Miscellany* is dominated by the Ovidian conception of love. Wyatt's translations of Petrarch range from the sonnet which represents love as steering his ship with cruelty to those showing love as dwelling in the poet's heart and in the lady's eyes.[31] His rondeau "Behold Loue, thy power how she despiseth" is from a Petrarchan madrigal;[32] his "Complaint vpon Loue, to Reason," a translation of Petrarch's *Canzone* VII, sets forth both the good and the bad effects of love. One short poem (No. 110) is called "Why loue is blinde." Wyatt's allusions to love in all the types of his verse succeed at times in conveying the emotion of love rather than merely describing the appearance or power of the god, yet certain passages of his work make sense only when the uncapitalized word "love" is read as meaning *Cupid*.

Although Surrey never writes of Cupid or of any aspect of love in his original sonnets, he translates several Petrarchan sonnets of this nature. One (also translated by Wyatt) begins:

> Love, that liueth, and reigneth in my thought,
> That built his seat within my captiue brest,
> Clad in the armes, wherin with me he fought,
> Oft in my face he doth his banner rest.
> (Tottel, No. 6)

The classical conception of the all-powerful divinity provides Surrey, as well as Wyatt, with themes for a number of long poems. No. 26, for example, shows how the poet observes the effects of love:

> Wrapt in my carelesse cloke, as I walke to and fro:
> I se, how love cā shew, what force there reigneth in his bow.

The poem called "Description of the Fickle Affections Panges and Sleightes of Loue," with its mention of the gold and lead arrows of Cupid and its general indebtedness to Petrarch's third

Trionfo, is another instance of the same kind of derivation. Ovidian in tone is a protest against Cupid in a poem (No. 5) warning other lovers of the futility of striving against love as he had done:

> . . . I curssed love, and him defied: I thought to turne the streame.
>   But whan I well behelde he had me vnder awe,
> I asked mercie for my fault, that so transgrest his law.
>   Thou blinded god (quod I) forgeue me this offense,
> Vnwillingly I went about to malice thy pretense.

Ovidian, too, are the sufferings endured when "blind Cupide did whippe and guide" him (No. 24) and those recorded in a "Description of the Restlesse State of a Loher" (No. 3):

> But all to late loue learneth me,
> To painte all kinde of colours new,
> To blinde their eyes that els shoulde see,
> My specled chekes with Cupides hewe.
>   And nowe the couert brest I claime,
> That worshipt Cupide secretely:
> And norished his sacred flame,
> From whence no blasing sparkes doe flye.

The "uncertain" authors in Tottel also express protests against the cruel god and his warfare against the poet. Only a few illustrations need be named. Lord Vaux's "Thassault of Cupide upon the Fort Where the Louers Hart Lay Wounded and How He Was Taken" (No. 211) treats a theme which recurs in the sonnet cycles. One poem represents a lover, wounded by Cupid, as wishing he had been stricken by death instead of by love (No. 292). Another shows a lover caught in the snares of Cupid (No. 175). Professor Rollins notes that the "uncertain" authors show comparatively little knowledge of the Italian poets who had dominated Wyatt and Surrey, and that classical and humanistic influences predominate over them and account for their "frequent references to classic mythology as well as for their translations or paraphrases from Ovid, Lucretius, Seneca, and Horace." [33]

Ovid's influence is strikingly apparent throughout the last half of the sixteenth century, not only in countless descriptions of love as a vindictive, malicious little tyrant, but also in the many protests uttered against the nature of love.[34] Poets who go to Ovid directly usually reflect his sensual conception; those who follow the more attenuated codes of the Middle Ages, where love is elevated by an infusion of Platonism and of chivalric idealism, show less of it. An interesting sidelight upon the Ovidian attitude toward love is revealed in Barnabe Googe's *Cupido Conquered*.[35] The young Protestant poet is obviously fascinated by the classical background of his story, yet in the end has the "gresye hoaste" of Gluttony overcome by Sir Abstinence, while Cupid's leaders—Idleness, Excess (who rides a camel because no horse can support him), and others—fall before the soldiers of Labour. A similar allegorical tale, yet much more censorious, is "Of Cupid His Campe," in "The Poor Knight, His Pallace of Private Pleasures."[36] The armies of Cupid and Venus rout the forces of Diana, but only because Mars aids Venus.

Protests on moral grounds against the god of love are far outnumbered in that age, however, by the tributes at every hand, especially in the miscellanies, to the figure described in *Love's Labour's Lost* as

> This wimpled, whining, purblind, wayward boy,
> This senior-junior, giant-dwarf, Dan Cupid;
> Regent of love-rimes, lord of folded arms,
> The anointed sovereign of sighs and groans.
> (Act III, scene 1, ll. 181–84)

An incredible number of poems, or parts of poems, are farewells to, or renunciations of, love; only a few, such as Wyatt's and Sidney's, appear to have any evidence of sincerity. Other poems pretend that love is dead or dying, as Sidney's "Ring out your bells" and Drayton's "Since there's no help, come, let us kiss and part." Again, the poets tell of their hardships by means of advice as to ways to escape love or the means to endure it. The largest number of these poems, however, are variations of a theme employed by Giacomo da Lentino, Cavalcanti, Petrarch, Beniviene, Serafino, and others—an attempt to define love.[37] Petrarch's version (*S'amor non è*), translated by Chaucer in *Troilus and Criseyde*, begins

> If no love is, O god, what fele I so?
> And if love is, what thing and whiche is he?
> If love be good, from whennes cometh my woo?
> (Bk. I, ll. 400–403)

The English poets obviously liked this phase of the subject, for a long list might be made of the poems they wrote upon it.[38]

A pleasant illustration of contemporary interest in poems on the power of love is a work called *The Debate betweene Follie and Love*,[39] which Robert Greene published "as translated out of French"—really a poem by Louise Labé of Lyons, with "Follie" akin to the Folly of the *Encomium moriae* of Erasmus, and Cupid the conventional Ovidian tyrant who, "how little so ever I be, am the most redouted of all the gods." [40] Individual poets, too, drew much of the content of their volumes from the Ovidian conception of the power and the effect of love. Turbervile, for example, owes to this tradition nearly all the poems, except "Of Lady Venus," in his *Epitaphes, Epigrams, Songs and Sonnets* (1567).[41]

Perhaps the most striking indications of the importance of the Ovidian tradition to the Elizabethan poets are Spenser's great interest in it and his obligations to it. (His use of the Greek, or Alexandrian, conception will be noted on pages 67–69.) We know from the comments of "E.K." in the *Shepheardes Calender* that before 1579 Spenser had written a poem called the *Court of Cupid* and had translated Politian's Latin version of the first Idyll of Moschus. The *Shepheardes Calender*, the *Teares of the Muses, Muiopotmos*, the *Faerie Queene, Colin Clouts Come Home Againe*, the *Amoretti* with the four epigrams following it, and the *Fowre Hymnes* among them make use of all the portrayals of love heretofore mentioned except that of love as the tall young god.[42] "The Cupid of Spenser," says Fowler, "is a sort of composite of the classical, the feudal, and the ecclesiastical conceptions." [43] *Colin Clout* and the *Hymne in Honour of Love* employ the conception from the early Greek cosmogonies of Eros as "one of the fundamental principles of nature, the power by which discordant elements were united and harmony brought out of chaos." [44] Throughout Spenser's works the customary classical elements are present in brief allusions such as those to Cupid's conquests over gods and men, to his arrows, snares, and yoke.[45] The feudal conception appears both in brief mention of Cupid as liege lord over the vassal lover, to Scudamour as "Cupid's man" and shield-bearer, and the like,[46] and, as Fowler points out, in the more extensive and significant passages in the *Faerie Queene* of the court of Cupid (Bk. VI, canto 7, stanza 32 ff.).[47] Cupid is here represented as holding court on Saint Valentine's day. Upon finding many of his vassals missing, he had his eyes "unblindfold both" that he might see his men and muster them by oath. A jury determines that the men have been betrayed and murdered by Mirabella and pronounces a sentence against her.

The Masque of Cupid in the *Faerie Queene* (Bk. III, canto 11, stanza 12) in particular combines the medieval conception with the classical, for Cupid's wars and victories are pictured upon the arras in the House of Busirane, and Cupid himself is represented as an image upon an altar.[48] The procession in the Masque proper comes from Petrarch's *Trionfi,* and in it, as in Petrarch, love is conquered by Chastity. Cupid rides a lion and unbinds his eyes that he may gloat over his victims:

> With that the darts which his right hand did straine
> Full dreadfully he shooke, that all did quake,
> And clapt on hye his coulourd winges twaine,
> That all his many it affraide did make:
> Tho, blinding him again, his way he forth did take.
> (Bk. III, canto 12, stanza 23)

Colin Clout criticizes the moral tone of the English court of the day as a place where even Cupid was ashamed of the "vaine votaries of laesie Love," where no one holds himself in esteem unless he swims in love "up to his eares"; yet the poem is chiefly an explanation of love's origins and perfections and of the way in which the god should be worshiped—a blending of feudal, classical, and ecclesiastical conceptions.[49]

The Englishman of the sixteenth century not only read—or wrote —such accounts as these just mentioned of Cupid; he was accustomed to seeing the little figure represented in pageants [50] and on the stage. Even in Scotland, Cupid figured in at least one pageant—that which welcomed James VI to Edinburgh in 1579. The king passed under a curious globe that "opnit artificiallie as the King came by, wharin was a young boy [Cupid] that discendit craftelie, presenting the keyis of the town to his Majestie . . ." [51]

A masque which Churchyard records as performed before Elizabeth in Norfolk in 1578 [52] turned the interest in Cupid into flattery of the queen. The narrative begins with an account of Venus and Cupid, thrust out of heaven, as homeless wanderers on earth. They meet a philosopher from whose taunts Cupid runs away. Cupid goes to court to complain of his fate to the queen, but she will have none of so disreputable a person. After further wanderings, Cupid finally encounters Chastity and her four handmaidens and is completely vanquished:

. . . encountring Cupid in a goodly coatche, and without any honest gard wayting on him, [they] sette upon him, threwe him out of his golden seate, trode upon hys pompe, spoyled him of his counterfeyte godhead and cloke, and tooke away his bowe and his quiver of arrowes (the one headed with leade, the other with golde), and so sent him like a fugitive away, and mounted up into the coatche hirselfe and hir maydes, and so came to the Queene . . . and because (said Chastitie) that the Queene had chosen the best life, she gave the Queene Cupid's bow to learn to shoot at whome she pleased. . . .

Cupid departs, falls in with Wantonness and Riot, and thus endures many hardships. In the end Modestie triumphs, and Queen Elizabeth no doubt considered both the performance and the compliment to her as quite satisfactory.

The god of love, presumably an attractive figure to the Elizabethan playgoer, frequently appears upon the stage. Some child from among the children of Paul's or from the Chapel Royal acted the part of Cupid, for instance, in four plays of Lyly—*Sapho and Phao, Gallathea, Love's Metamorphosis,* and *The Woman in the Moon.* Peele's plays also have Cupid on the stage, as in his *Arraignment of Paris* (1584), in which Helen enters "in her braverie" with four Cupids, "each having his fan in his hand to fan fresh ayre in her face." (This detail may be compared with *Antony and Cleopatra,* Act I, scene 2, ll. 197–200, the description by Enobarbus of Cleopatra's barge: on each side of the queen stood pretty dimpled boys, like smiling Cupids, who fanned her with divers-colored fans.) The nature of Peele's *The Hunting of Cupid,* now lost, is conjectural; but the fragment from it preserved in *England's Parnassus* (1600) describes arrows of love, hate, hope, and jealousy made for Cupid by Mars at the entreaty of Venus. Shakespeare's plays, especially *Love's Labour's Lost* and *Romeo and Juliet,* often mention Cupid,[53] but in none of them does he appear as a character. Later Elizabethan and Jacobean plays show his continued appeal on the seventeenth-century stage: Ben Jonson presents him in several masques—*Love Freed from Folly, Love Restored, The Vision of Delight, The Hue and Cry after Cupid, The Masque of Lethe,* and *The Masque of Christmas.* (In *The Masque of Christmas,* Cupid appears in a flat cap and an apprentice's coat, but with wings on his shoulders!) Cupid appears, too, as a character in Heywood's *Love's Mistress* (the Cupid and Psyche story) and Beaumont and Fletcher's *Cupid's Revenge,* while Beaumont and Fletcher's *Triumph of Love* ends with a procession in which Cupid appears in a chariot drawn by two other cupids.[54]

Such is the background of literary taste against which the sonnet cycles were projected, and such are a few of the works illustrating the fact that the conventional symbol for the power of love was the god Cupid. We may now turn to the sonnet sequences themselves to consider the representations there of the theme of love.

THE OVIDIAN CONCEPTION IN THE ENGLISH SEQUENCES

SINCE the Roman, or Ovidian, conception of love was the basis of Petrarch's *Canzoniere,* it naturally has a larger part in the English cycles than does the Alexandrian Greek conception gained through the Pléiade poets. In the Middle Ages the various aspects of the Roman conception had become widely known, partly through the romances of Chrétien de Troyes and, later, through Italian poetry. Yet, since the literature of Greece and Rome were also available, Ogle states that it is usually futile to seek specific sources for the fifteenth- and sixteenth-century versions of these personifications,[55] while Hutton suggests that, despite the fact that the conceits of Renaissance verse are often derived ultimately from remote classical sources, the poets who wrote them probably had in mind some much nearer source such as Petrarch.[56]

The sonnets which set forth the theme of love by means of the aspects of the Ovidian concept fall into three chief groups. Some attribute the presence of love to the fact that Amor establishes himself, willy-nilly, in the heart of the poet or in the eyes or breast of the lady, and employs her beauty as the means of torturing the poet. Other sonnets attribute the poet's woe to the cruel warfare of love; still others describe the fires caused by his arrows. Love's tyranny is also described as a maze, a labyrinth, or a yoke.

Such themes are usually inserted at any point in the cycles, with no regard for the continuity of the story, yet, in *Astrophel and Stella,* not a little of the autobiography apparent in the sequence comes from the fact that Sidney arranges them in chronological order: his sonnets on Cupid tell a story beginning with his realization that he loved Stella too late and ending with his despair and final renunciation of earthly love. Perfectly clear when removed from their context, they are more significant if read in their numerical order. Spenser, on the other hand, has little narrative in his sequence except for the one fact of the parting at the end; his sonnets on love might come equally well at any point in the sequence. They have a bookish, studied air of being motifs carefully chosen for their classical interest.

Before we consider the sonnets on the theme of love in the regular cycles, it is due to Thomas Watson to say that no sequence proper affords such a learned or comprehensive presentation of classical themes as does his *Hecatompathia* of 1582.[57] Yet Watson's service in introducing much of this material into England has usually been dismissed with casual statements to the effect that his work had little effect upon later writers and that the listing of the sources of his poems indicates only that the work shows no personal feeling.

Since classical literature everywhere expresses the concept that the eyes are chiefly responsible for love, that idea may be expected to figure prominently in all later discourses upon the subject. Ogle's study of the origins of literary conceits shows that the belief is present in one form or another from Hesiod through the *Greek Anthology* and down to the later rhetorical writers.[58] The Roman poets, however, were usually "content with the simple statement that the eyes are leaders in love." [59] The notion that the eyes emit flames of fire is likewise a commonplace of classical literature, especially of the later Greek epigrams: the fire came from the eyes of the lady and passed through those of the lover into his heart. Ogle says:

This idea that love flows through the eyes into the heart and the theory of the *eidolon* go back to Plato. . . Both occur frequently in the writings of later philosophers and rhetoricians. . . According to Philostratus, Ep. 12, it is through the eyes only that beauty enters the heart, "for the eyes," he goes on, "are not fortified by ramparts of wood and brick as are the citadels of kings, but by the eyelids only, and Love slips quietly and by degrees into the heart, quickly since he is winged, easily since he is naked, without a battle since he is a bowman; and the eyes, since they are the first things to perceive beauty, are all the more readily set on fire.[60]

Love, thus induced by the eyes, is represented in both Greek and Roman literature as having various dwellings—the heart of the lover, the eyes, the face, or the breast of the lady.[61] The idea that love dwelt within the poet is first expressed in a poem in the *Greek Anthology* attributed to Julianus: [62] "Once, weaving a garland, I found Love among the roses, and catching him by the wings dipped him in wine. I took and drank him, and now within me he tickles with his wings." [63] The popularization of this theme in the Middle Ages came, however, not from the Greeks, but indirectly from Ovid and the romances of Chrétien de Troyes, and entered the sonnet tradition through Italian verse.[64] Petrarch protests in almost every sonnet against the anguish caused by the presence of Amor in his heart, yet appears to take that presence for granted, with brief statements of facts similar to those found, for instance, in the first book of Ovid's *Amores—in vacuo pectore regnat Amor;* or *possessa ferus pectora versat Amor.* One of Petrarch's sonnets of this nature was translated both by Wyatt and by Surrey.

The English sonneteers, however, appear to have preferred the livelier and more expanded narratives of the Anacreontic stories, but Spenser once refers to the winged god who has ruled within him for a year; Constable says that love is not in his heart, for his heart is love; and Linche tells his grief at having admitted love to his heart.[65] He had been promised rest, pleasure, and endless joy, but received, instead, so much grief that he believes he has admitted the Trojan horse instead of love.

The notion, however, that love arises from the lady's gazing at the poet—in other words, that love's dwelling is the lady's eye—occurs everywhere in Elizabethan literature and ranges from phrases such as Sidney's "Cupid, because thou shin'st in Stella's eyes" (No. XII) to the lines of the Shakespearean "Who Is Sylvia":

> Love doth to her eyes repair
> To help him of his blindness,
> And being helped inhabits there.

It embraces, as well, occasional echoes of the other classical themes —the eyes as the windows of the soul and the image reflected in the pupils of the eye—*pupula duplex*—which the Elizabethans described as "looking babies" in the eyes of the lady.[66]

The Elizabethan gentlewoman—Sidney's Stella, for instance— no doubt felt quite complacent at the compliments implied in the sonnets describing love's dwelling as in her eyes. Sidney, with a proper Elizabethan flourish, accounts for the blackness of Stella's eyes by saying that nature, knowing that love will always dwell there, made them black as mourning for all who are destined to die for her sake (No. VII). Again, with less originality, but still with a flourish, he warns love that, even though he lives in Stella's beauty and shines in her eyes, he has not yet won the citadel of her heart (No. XII). (Sonnet No. VIII, in which Sidney alludes to Cupid's taking refuge in Stella's face, will be mentioned more fully on page 71). Another sonnet (No. LXII), showing the economy of detail characteristic of Sidney, compresses this motif into a single line: "She in whose eyes love, though unfelt, doth shine."

Fletcher also turns out compliments that should have softened the tiger-like heart of Licia—if, indeed, she was a person and not, as he hints in his preface, Learning's image, or some heavenly wonder, or even a college. Whatever her identity, she causes the poet's woe because love dwells in her eyes (No. XXXIX):

> My grief began, fair Saint, when first I saw
> Love, in those eyes, sit ruling with disdain.

The power of Licia's eyes is such that Cupid, taking refuge in her eyes from the anger of Jove, is able to defy even the greatest of the gods (No. XIII). Tofte also makes use of this idea by having his Laura conquer all who gaze upon her, because Cupid lies in her eyes (Pt. III, No. 23).

Daniel rarely uses classical personifications of love but does express this conceit in a brief allusion which employs the word "cabinet" in its sense of cabin or little room (No. LV): "I send those eyes, the Cabinets of Love." Constable's trick of giving negative versions to conceits is observable in his use of this one (Dec. VI, No. 5): Reason has bidden him see if love lives in Diana's heart and keeps there his royal bower; but the god is not there, for there is no god of love save her eye. Another negative version (Dec. VII, No. 3) is:

> What viewed I, dear, when I, thine eyes beheld?
> Love in his glory? No, him Thyrsis saw. . . .

Perhaps the most pleasing version is in Lodge (No. XIII):

> Love in thine eyes doth build his bower,
> And sleeps within their pretty shine;
> And if I look the boy will lower
> And from their orbs shoot shafts divine.[67]

This motif figures in a line in a sonnet by Drayton (No. II in the 1599 edition) describing the poet's heart as slain by the lady:

> But O see! See, we need inquire no further!
> Upon your lips, the scarlet drops are found,
> And in your eye, the Boy that did the murder,
> Your cheeks yet pale since first he gave the wound.

A second sonnet (No. IX) of this edition has the same conceit in the following version:

> Love once would dance within my mistress's eye,
> And wanting music fitting for the place,
> Swore that I should the instrument supply. . . .
>> Thus like a lute or violl did I lie,
>> While the proud slave danc'd galliards in her eye.

The conceit that love's dwelling is the lady's heart rather than her eye was, on the other hand, infrequently employed, perhaps because it was more difficult to execute. The best illustrations belong, moreover, among the Anacreontic sonnets to be discussed later—accounts of a perverse infant god preferring captivity in the lady's breast to freedom [68] and of an impudent, impertinent tiny god driven away by an enraged lady.[69] The influence of Catullus, however, is seen in the sonnet of Sidney which states that both love and Stella's sparrow sleep in Stella's breast (No. LXXXIII). Griffin, following Sidney literally, says that love must make his bed in Fidessa's heart if he wishes to sleep well (No. XXIII). Another sonnet of Sidney—a mediocre one at that—casts its shadow over two other poets: Sidney (No. XLIII) states that when love wishes a retreat from the world, he makes Stella's heart his room, for no one dares approach him there. Watson's *The Tears of Fancie* (No. XXII) carries this idea a step farther by saying that love, although imperious, dares not touch the lady's heart; Constable goes even farther in reproaching "uncivil sickness" for entering the breast which love himself dares not approach (Dec. III, No. 1).

Shakespeare wrote three sonnets on the conceit that love's dwelling is the face or breast of the beloved. No. XCIII says:

> But heaven in thy creation did decree
> That in thy face sweet love should ever dwell.

Sonnet CIX states that his "home of love" is the home of the beloved. Sonnet XXXI treats the theme at greater length:

> Thy bosom is endeared with all hearts
> Which I by lacking have supposed dead;
> And there reigns love and all love's loving parts. . . .
> Thou art the grave where buried love doth live.

The concept that love is caused by the eyes occurs no more frequently in classical lore than does that of cupid as wantonly shooting his arrows from the ambush of the lady's eyes and as otherwise carrying on his cruel warfare. Although Ovid's *Amores* and other works had brought about almost universal acceptance of these ideas in the Middle Ages by the usual route of the romances of Chrétien de Troyes and the poetry of Provence and Italy, the ultimate source for them is said by Ogle to be two early Greek poems. One is an epigram of Meleager, in which the town crier, proclaiming the loss of the infant god, finds him hidden in the eyes of a lady:

. . . and by all he is hated; but look to it in case he is setting now new springes for hearts. But wait! there he is near his nest! Ah, little archer, so you thought to hide from me there in Zenophila's eyes! [70]

The other is a fragment from the *Anacreontea:* [71]

> Thebes doth your verse employ,
> Another's, frays of Troy;
>   My tale shall be
>   The Sack of Me.
>
> No ships were my undoing,
> Nor horse nor foot my ruin,
>   But barbarous foes
>   With eyes for bows.

Echoes of these themes are, of course, well-nigh ubiquitous in Elizabethan literature. Most of them are today rather dreary accounts in the Ovidian manner of the warfare and tyranny of love, although a few are lightened by an infusion of Anacreontic narrative or description. [72] A faint-hearted modern might indeed quail before the task of setting forth his love by means of allegories and accounts of the combats and conquests of Cupid; the Elizabethan, however, took the method and manner for granted and exerted energy enough in tricking out the conventional conceits to have produced verse which would be "original" in the modern sense. "May not a man go a-wooing or a-mourning," Professor Fletcher asks, "as well in a borrowed song as in a borrowed suit?" [73] If today the sonneteers' coats sometimes seem to be shreds and patches of conceits, it is only fair to recall that, in all likelihood, the Elizabethan reader and writer liked the sonnet sequences because the conceits were familiar and had the sanction and challenge of usage.

Spenser's *Amoretti* leans heavily upon these themes of classical warfare, but often makes the siege that of the lady, not Cupid, against the poet. The "unrighteous lord of love" makes "huge massacres" through the lady's eyes; the poet's heart is "through-lanced everywhere" with a thousand arrows; he is falsely taken in a wicked ambush; and so forth.[74] Spenser achieves real originality, however, in a famous negative version in Sonnet VIII: [75]

> Through your bright beams doth not the blinded guest
> Shoot out his darts to base affections wound,
> But Angels come to lead frail minds to rest
> In chaste desires, on heavenly beauty bound.

Barnes (No. LX) has a version beginning "Whilst some the Trojan wars in verse recount" which should be compared with the Anacreontic just quoted. The idea of warfare is put into a sixteenth-century context: the poet is undone, not by the wars of Arthur or of Troy or even of Germany or of Spain, but by a blind captain whose men, in golden arms, wound him with darts of gold. Another of Barnes's sonnets explains that Cupid's darts are unseen and unheard until it is too late to escape them—and "thus a peasant Caesar's glory dares," although Cupid's soldier suffers greater torture.[76] Percy repeats the standard theme of the unwary beholder as being shot from the lady's eye, but wears his rue with a slight difference, for he calls Coelia's eye a chariot and asserts that he is being schooled for gazing at divinity.[77] Constable and the other minor writers reveal, on the other hand, little variety in the choice of phrase or of conventional classic images.[78]

Perhaps the most realistic imagery describing love's malicious nature and enmity toward the poet is that expended upon the conceit of his siege of the poet's heart as a citadel. This allegory was used in England at least as early as Tottel's *Miscellany* in Lord Vaux's "When Cupid Scaled First the Fort." Sidney (No. XII) warns Cupid that Stella's heart is a citadel so fortified with wit, so stored with disdain, that he must not think it too easily won. Another version, No. XXXVI, for which Miss Scott suggests numerous analogues, especially Tebaldeo,[79] begins:

> Stella! whence doth this new assault arise?
> A conquered, yielded, ransacked heart to win!
> Whereto, long since, through my long battered eyes,
> Whole armies of thy beauties entered in.
> And there, long since, Love thy Lieutenant lies:
> My forces razed, thy banners raised within.

The allegories in these sonnets are often very elaborate and no doubt appealed to an age that produced the House of Alma in the *Faerie Queene*. Barnes, in his tenth madrigal, writes of ivory walls which cannot endure Cupid's dart and of a turret of whitest porphyry, "inset with roses," which should warn Parthenophe that Cupid will overcome her as she has overcome Parthenophil. Percy (No. X) is extravagantly militaristic in his account of laying rams, mines, and plots to win his Coelia: Two redcoats (her lips) guard the "Larum bell"; Scorn, Fear, and Modesty toss their pikes, but "Pudicity" keeps him from the wall. Spenser wrote a sonnet of a siege but carried out the theme without mention of the god of love. He pleads, however, with his defeated forces to renew their siege against the cruel lady (No. XIV).

Some versions represent the heart as betrayed by the five senses. Barnes (No. III), Drayton (No. XXIX), and Linche (No. VII) are examples: Linche's version, filled with war terms, ends with an account of how the traitors Sweet Smiles, Fair Face, and Piercing Eye set fire to his heart and then flee. Smith's *Chloris* is notable for the abjectness of the surrender of the poet (No. XXVII). All these variations of the theme may be compared with Petrarch's sonnet in which he compares himself to a besieged city betrayed by his own heart.[80]

From the mass of brief allusions to the warfare of Cupid only two others need be singled out—the ingenuity with which Sidney professes himself the slave of Cupid without really sounding abject and the flattery the poets could muster to show love as yielding to the superior power of the lady. For the first, Sidney has a sonnet (No. XXIX), rather bad as verse but presumably effective as flattery, which compares Stella with a weak lord who sacrifices everything else to keep his coasts clear from the mighty kings who are his neighbors: she gives up Astrophel as a slave because his prospect lies upon that coast. Earlier (No. II), he had compared himself to a slave-born Muscovite glorying in his captivity. Again, when he is fighting in a tournament in the livery of Mars, he is detected by Cupid. The god makes his slave gaze upon Stella, and that, of course, makes him forget to fight (No. LIII).[81] Lastly, the poet says he will yield to Cupid's yoke and become his slave if he will observe the laws of arms and grant honorable terms for his surrender.[82]

The second of these conceits, that of love yielding to the lady, is usually a brief allusion, such as Sidney's statement that, although Stella's eyes made love conquer, they conquer love (No. XLII), and Barnes's description of Cupid as resigning his bow and arrows to Parthenophe (No. LIV). Several times, however, Fletcher expands this conceit,[83] while Griffin writes that Fidessa disdains love and lovers, that she makes love seem merely a foolish boy whom she snares with her love.[84] Spenser (No. X) asks love why he allows the lady to scorn him. Drayton's most famous sonnet (No. LXI), "Since there's no help, come, let us kiss and part," thus uses the conceit to show the power of the lady over love:

> Now at the last gasp of Love's latest breath,
> When, his pulse failing, Passion speechless lies,
> When Faith is kneeling by his bed of death,
> And Innocence is closing up his eyes,
>   Now, if thou wouldst, when all have given him over,
>   From death to life thou might'st him yet recover!

The ravages of Cupid's sieges against the poet's heart appear, however, to have been less devastating than the conflagrations caused by Cupid's arrows. These classical echoes are ubiquitous, and, in the hands of poets such as Barnes, who tends toward hyperbole in any instance, and Constable, who affects the exaggerated humility of the medieval lover, they constitute a sore trial for the modern reader's patience. Often limited to a phrase or a line in sonnets on other themes, they lose their point if taken from their context.[85]

Spenser, following his customary plan of limiting the images in his sonnets to one or at most to a few ideas, develops these themes at considerable length. He professes to fry in flames;[86] but, even so, is unable to melt the lady's heart (No. XXXII). He builds an altar to the lady and sacrifices his heart "burning in flames of pure and chaste desire" (No. XXII) and, in Sonnet XXX, says:

> Or how comes it that my exceeding heat
> Is not delayed by her heart-frozen cold;
> But that I burn much more in boiling sweat,
> And feel my flames augmented manifold.

Sidney's allusions, although numerous, are usually consistent and brief—a thread here and there instead of the design of the sonnet.[87]

Fletcher's comparisons, are, on the other hand, extensive, and they reflect his classical reading. As Miss Scott shows, they are based chiefly upon the neoclassic verse of Angerianus.[88] Only a few need be mentioned. He once says that, although he is burned to a cinder, the flint-hearted Licia feels no heat at all. A painter paints a portrait of Licia with her eyes closed so that the work will not catch fire from their flames. She touches the water of a stream and it burns with love; love and Licia, in a boat, fling balls of fire into the seas to burn them, he with his bow, she with her eyes. Lodge also has a large number of these allusions, including comparisons of himself to Etna, to a phoenix, to ice, and to fire. His love serves for fire, his heart is a furnace; his thoughts freeze and burn, and so forth.[89] The other minor writers set forth the pain of their professedly unhappy loves and of the tyranny of love in comparisons that range from the trite and the commonplace to the unconscious humor of inconsistent figures and hyperbole.[90] Tofte's versions are especially incongruous to modern taste. In a dozen or so of his sonnets on the usual aspects of the subject are accounts such as those in which the "outward ashes" of his face are caused by the fire burning in his veins and in which his heart catches fire from gazing upon a portrait of Laura.[91]

A few scattered classical reflections, chiefly Ovidian, remain to be noted as available to the poet for revealing the tortures inflicted by the "almighty dreadful" little Cupid. Latin and Greek poets had written of love as a hunter who ensnares lovers in his net,[92] and Petrarch many times used the figure. Ovid and others also write of love as a yoke.[93] The English sonneteers describe love as a labyrinth and as a maze [94]—but with what degree of originality it seems difficult to say. All the figures in this group are infrequently used, perhaps because the figures are so obvious and do not easily lend themselves to variety of treatment. Yet they have a charm of their own because they are consistent and recognizable.

The two Shakespearean sonnets which protest against the tyranny of love are totally unlike any other Elizabethan sonnets, for Shakespeare's sequence is in no way more notable than in its almost complete emancipation from the allegory of Cupid. In the two instances in which Shakespeare does make use of the classical vehicle, the allegory is deeper and more philosophical than it is in the work of any other sonneteer. In the closely knit Sonnet CXLVIII love keeps the poet blinded with tears lest he discover the foul faults of the god: he places his eyes within the poet's head, but either they have no correspondence with true sight or the poet's judgment has left him, for he censures what he looks upon. For, if what he dotes on was fair, why does the world say it is not? Love's eyes, he believes, are so vexed with watching and tears that they cannot be true, and it is, therefore, not to be wondered at that the poet mistakes what he sees.

The other instance of these themes, No. CXLIX, is the chief example in Shakespeare of the classical conception of love as a tyrant, and it may therefore appropriately conclude the discussion of this phase of the sonnet material:

> Canst thou, O cruel! say I love thee not,
> When I against myself with thee partake?
> Do I not think on thee, when I forgot
> Am of myself, all tyrant, for thy sake?
> Who hateth thee that I do call my friend?
> On whom frown'st thou that I do fawn upon?
> Nay, if thou lour'st on me, do I not spend
> Revenge upon myself with present moan?
> What merit do I in myself respect,
> That is so proud thy service to despise,
> When all my best doth worship thy defect,
> Commanded by the motion of thine eyes?
>> But, love, hate on, for now I know thy mind;
>> Those that can see thou lovest, and I am blind.

THE ALEXANDRIAN CONCEPTION IN THE
SONNET SEQUENCES

THE "borrowed coat" of the Elizabethan poet often seems to be worn with more grace when it is rather well ornamented, the "borrowed song" to be more pleasing when heightened by narration and description. The Anacreontic conceits are therefore often more readable than the Ovidian, yet they appear rather infrequently in Elizabethan verse; for, although the Ovidian Cupid must have been familiar to every Elizabethan reader, the Anacreontic conception was, on the other hand, little known before the publication of *Astrophel and Stella* in 1591.

This Alexandrian or Anacreontic conception of Cupid became, as was said at the beginning of this section, a part of the sonnet cycle chiefly after the publication of the *Greek Anthology* in 1494 and the *Anacreontea* in 1554. Tebaldeo and Chariteo added some classical subjects to their sonnets.[95] It was, however, from the imitation of the *Anacreontea* by the Pléiade group that that conception became more widespread. The whole of the Alexandrian characterization is thus stated in Laumonier's *Ronsard:*

L'Erôs alexandrin est ailé, armé d'arc et de flèches, parfois d'un tison enflammé; il a des frères en grand nombre, roses, joufflus et potelés comme lui, qui lancent avec lui une grêle de traits sur la même personne. C'est un enfant espiègle, étourdi, capricieux, un lutin effronté, un incorrigible touche-à-tout. Bref il est tel dans la poésie qu'on le voit dans la sculpture, la peinture et les bas-reliefs gréco-romains, par exemple dans les fresques de Pompéi; et c'est cet Erôs-là, léger et mondain, qui, après avoir été adopté par la Renaissance italienne et néo-latine, a envahi nos arts poétiques et plastiques depuis Marot jusqu'à nos jours, surtout au temps de Louis XV.[96]

Spenser was the earliest English writer to use one Anacreontic conception and the most distinguished Elizabethan poet to make extended use of others. The March eclogue of his *Shepheardes Calender* gives what is perhaps the first English version of the

Moschus idyl of love and the fowler.[97] Spenser adds details such
as wings spotted with purple and blue like the tail of a peacock.[98]
Love flies lightly from bough to bough and at length shoots the
lad who has thrown stones at him in the belief that he is a bird.[99]
Barnes has echoes of this theme in two madrigals in his sequence.
The first (No. III) shows Cupid softly creeping about the myrtle
bushes to drive away the small birds that might waken the sleep-
ing Parthenophe, calling them and hushing them from branch
to branch. The other (No. XXV) describes the little god as sitting in a cherry tree, smiling and lightly waving his motley wings
as he gathers a branch of cherries and places it against the lips of
Parthenophe. Greville (No. II) refers to himself as one whom the
light-winged god had long pursued; and Watson mentions love's
"parti-colored wings" (No. VI).[100]

A second detail of the Alexandrian conception, that of love accompanied by many little loves—*putti* [101]—adds lightness and
grace to some of Spenser's lines. Love and his young brother
Sport are mentioned in the *Muiopotmos* (ll. 288–89), and the
little loves that attend upon Venus are described in the *Faerie
Queene* (Bk. IV, canto 10, stanza 42):

> And all about her necke and shoulders flew
> A flocke of litle loves, and sports, and joyes,
> With nimble wings of gold and purple hew;
> Whose shapes seem'd not like to terrestriall boyes,
> But like to angels playing heavenly toyes;
> The whilest their eldest brother was away,
> Cupid, their eldest brother: he enjoyes
> The wide kingdome of Love with lordly sway
> And to his law compels all creatures to obay.

One sonnet of the *Amoretti* (No. XVI) likewise presents these
little loves—legions of them flying with little wings, darting
deadly arrows at every rash beholder passing by; the *Epithalamion* (l. 357) also speaks of a "hundred little winged loves / Like
divers fethered doves." The two other sonneteers who echoed

this notion of the many little loves are Barnes (No. XXIV), who says that, since all the loves have burned their wings at the torch of his heart as if they were gnats, they are compelled to remain there afterward; and Lodge (No. XXV), who professes that a swarm of loves confound him when he gazes upon Phillis.

Spenser's interest in the Alexandrian Cupid is shown still further in the four short Anacreontic poems published between the *Amoretti* and the *Epithalamion*. The second and third poems are taken from Marot; the fourth is the incident of the bee-stung Cupid which comes ultimately from the *Anacreontea* (No. XL) or Theocritus (No. XIX). Spenser probably knew the story through Ronsard,[102] although it had appeared in England in 1577 in Timothy Kendall [103] and in 1582 in Watson's *Hecatompathia* (No. LIII). The Anacreontic story which appears to have attracted Spenser most, however, is that of the runaway Cupid. The first idyl of Moschus represents Venus as proclaiming the loss of her son in the manner used in advertising runaway slaves. Spenser narrates the story in the *Faerie Queene* (Bk. III, canto 6, stanzas 11–26). Venus is aided in the search for the child by Diana and her nymphs, but in the end they find Chrysogone and her babes instead of the god of love. This story, introduced into England by Turbervile, had long been a favorite on the continent; Hutton and Fucilla trace it from Moschus to Meleager through the neoclassic poets Marot, Jamyn, and Desportes, down to Spenser.[104] Barnes includes a translation of this story in his sonnet cycle as "The First Eidillon of Moschus." [105] The narrative became very popular in England, one of the most important later versions being Ben Jonson's masque *The Hue and Cry after Cupid,* presented at Court in 1608.

Several sonnets are traceable to this story of Cupid's flight. It explains, incidentally, the allusion from Moschus in Barnes (No. LXXV) of love's going "red-coloured in his skin." Most of the sonneteers give reasons for the flight of Cupid. Greville recounts the fact that Cupid, bound as apprentice to his mother, took an oath to escape from her fetters (No. XXXII) and, again, that he fled because Venus mistreated him:

> Cupid, my little boy, come home again!
> I do not blame thee for thy running hence,
> Where thou found'st nothing but desire's pain,
> Jealousy, with self-unworthiness, offence.

The conclusion of Greville's sonnet is quite characteristic of the original and allegorical turn which this poet usually gave his themes: Cupid could not return to the poet's heart, for, after having taken refuge in Myra's eyes, his "right wing of passion" dies and he is so scourged by modesty and truth that he finally loses all hope of escape. He then takes malicious pleasure in enticing his "school-fellows" to a similar fate so that they may be plagued as he is and cannot make sport of him when he cries for mercy (No. XXXV).

A third sonnet of Greville springs from the same concept of Cupid's flight. No. XIII relates how Cupid, angry because Venus alternately forbids him to shoot his arrows and scolds him because he does not shoot them at Mars, weeps himself blind over the vagaries of womankind. The little god wanders far and wide in his blindness; but finally his foe Absence captures him, destroys all his weapons, and keeps him prisoner until he changes his sportive nature. Then Absence releases him, cures him of everything except blindness, and forbids him nothing except constancy. The sonnet concludes with a couplet which suggests that Greville read the poem aloud to his friends:

> Ladies, this blind boy that ran from his mother
> Will ever play the wag with one or other.

A fourth sonnet of Greville (No. XI) represents Cupid as being banished below the tropics by Juno.

Linche (No. XVIII) likewise gives a reason for the fact that love comes begging for admission to his heart: his flight was attributed to his rage at his mother's punishment for "some heinous act or other" that caused her to "whip him very sore." Sidney, for his part, gives an entirely original turn (No. VIII) to the story. He does not mention Cupid's misdeeds or his anger at his mother, but explains how the little god came to be in England:

> Love born in Greece, of late fled from his native place;
> Forced by a tedious proof, that Turkish hardened heart
> Is no fit mark to pierce with his fine pointed dart:
> And pleased with our soft peace, stayed here his flying race.[106]

When love finds that he is freezing in the cold climate of England, he seeks warmth by flying to Stella's sunny face. She drives him away, and he then seeks and gains admission to the poet's heart. There, laying firebrands to warm himself, he burns his wings and cannot fly away.[107] This story shows Sidney's great skill in adapting derivative material and making it his own. The opening quatrain is original, the underlying idea of love dwelling in the poet's heart is a conventional Petrarchan (that is, Ovidian) conceit. The conceit of love remaining in the poet's heart because he has lost his wings and cannot fly away comes ultimately from a poem by Paulus Silentiarius in the *Greek Anthology,* while the conceit of the fire built in the poet's heart is from Serafino.[108] For all its composite nature, however, Miss Scott states that this sonnet is one of the three Anacreontic poems of Sidney for which she was able to find "definite" foreign sources! [109]

Another Greek narrative, that from the *Anacreontea* of the fugitive Cupid begging admission to the poet's heart, so often gives the point to the Elizabethan sonnets that the Loeb translation is quoted here for the sake of comparison:

> 'Twas at the mid of night,
>   Whenas the Wain doth wheel
>   Close on Arcturus' heel,
> And every mortal wight
>
> Is sunk in slumber; then
>   One stood my gate beside

And knocked. "Who's there?" I cried,
"Who rends my dreams in twain?"

Says Love, ('twas he) "Pray let
   "Me in, nor send his ways
   "A babe forlorn that strays
"This night so dark and wet."

Eftsoons I fetched a light,
   And opening did descry
   A babe, but winged to fly
With bow and arrows dight.

By th' ingle then and there
   I set him, chafed amain
   His hands, and wrung the rain
From out his dripping hair.

And when he found him warm,
   "Go to, let's try together"
   Says he, "if this foul weather
"Hath done my bowstring harm."

This said, he drew the string,
   And straight with madding arrow
   Had pierced my very marrow;
Then laughing loud took wing,

And cried as off he flew
   "Rejoice, my friend, with me;
   "My bow is sound, I see,
"And pain's in store for you." [110]

This narrative, appearing in sonnets by Sidney, Greville, Barnes, Constable, and Drayton, came into the English sonnets with *Astrophel and Stella*. Greene, however, had already used it in 1588 in *Alcida,* and, in 1589 or 1590, in *Orpharion,* it appeared as "Cupid Abroade Was Lated in the Night." Lyly had also suggested it in his *Endimion*.[111] Sidney's witty and urbane version of the story [112] explains that he was the only man of his too modern world who would give aid to the runaway god (No. LXV):

Love! by sure proof I may call thee unkind,
That giv'st no better ear to my just cries!
Thou, whom to me, such my good turns should bind,
As I may well recount, but none can prize.
For when, naked boy, thou couldst no harbour find
In this old world, grown now so too too wise,
I lodged thee in my heart: and being blind
By nature born, I gave to thee mine eyes.
Mine eyes, my light, my heart, my life! Alas,
If so great services may scorned be!
Yet let this thought thy tigerish courage pass,
That I, perhaps, am somewhat kin to thee,
Since in thine arms, if learned Fame truth hath spread,
Thou bar'st the arrow; I, the arrow head.

Greville's version (No. XII) is:

Cupid, thou naughty boy, when thou were loathed,
Naked and blind, for vagabonding noted,
Thy nakedness I in my reason clothed,
My eyes I gave thee, so was I devoted.

Greville, usually allegorical where Sidney is merely narrative, here represents the mischievous god as first afflicting the poet with a "seeing blindness," and then, for the greater torment of the poet, as flying to Myra's heart.

Barnes, stressing the wily nature of Cupid portrayed in the Moschus idyl already mentioned, rejoices that he has detected the identity of the beggar at his gate (No. XCIII):

Begs Love! which whilom was a deity?
I list no such proud beggars at my gate!

Constable represents love as begging in vain for food from Diana, who ought to have been charitable to poor orphans; and as starving at the gate of Beauty because Pity denies him the two cherries—her lips, of course—that would have saved his life.[113] Drayton, in his 1599 edition (No. XXIII), gives the old theme a sixteenth-century context: love, banished from heaven, is held in scorn on earth, and, although the son of a goddess, has to beg

alms until the devout and charitable poet admits him to his heart,
clothes him, and feeds him on his tears and sighs. But the ungrateful little beggar sets fire to his lodgings, and the poet then philo-
sophically remarks:

> Well, well, my friends! when beggars grow thus bold,
> No marvel then, though Charity grow cold.

In 1619 (No. XLVIII), however, Drayton gives the story a much
livelier tone by assuming the rebellious attitude of the Cavaliers
rather than the professed humility of the Petrarchists:

> Cupid, I hate thee! Which I'll have thee know!
> A naked starveling ever mayst thou be!
> Poor rogue! go pawn thy fascia and thy bow
> For some poor rags, wherewith to cover thee!
> Or if thou'lt not, thy archery forbear!
> To some base rustic do thyself prefer!
> And when the corn's sown, or grown into the ear,
> Practice thy quiver and turn crowkeeper!
> Or being blind, as fittest for the trade,
> Go hire thyself some bungling harper's boy!

Not all the Anacreontic allusions to Cupid, however, are as specific as are those describing Cupid in flight and the vagabond as
setting fire to the lodging given him in the poet's heart. The
roguish, childish nature of the tiny Eros was often sketched in
merely by epithets such as "wanton," "wag," or "little lad Cupid." [114] Sidney once sets forth the childish irresponsibility of the
god by comparing him to a child who examines the gilded leaves
or colored vellum of a book but does not try to read the text (No.
XI), and Greville several times writes in the same vein.[115] Sidney compares love, also, to a school boy who misses his lessons
and must smart for it (No. XLVI). He twice compares Love to
a page—once as "sworn page to chastity" (No. XXXV), and,
again, as faithful page to Stella in her illness, going "up and
down" to help assuage her pain (No. CI). Griffin appropriates
these lines outright (No. XVII):

> But Love twixt us will prove a faithful page,
> And she will love my sorrows to assuage.

Drayton (No. XXII) writes in sportive vein of love as a baby who plays with "gauds and toys" and "like a wanton sports with every feather":

> He still as young as when he first was born
> No wiser I, than when as young as he.

Still another Anacreontic theme represents Cupid weeping like a disappointed child. Sidney's seventeenth sonnet presents Venus angrily driving Cupid from her lap because his arrows are no longer sufficiently powerful to affect Mars. Miss Scott says of this sonnet: [116]

Sidney a donné une variation de ce thème plus intéressante que la pièce quelque peu monotone de Pontano. Dans le sonnet anglais, Vénus joue bien le rôle d'une mère courroucée et Cupidon d'un enfant insouciant et irresponsable.

Fletcher, who uses Anacreontic material more than any sonneteer except Sidney and Greville, writes of love weeping when outwitted by Licia (No. IX), but neither he nor Sidney achieves the lively realism of the first quatrain of Greville's twenty-fifth sonnet:

> Cupid, my pretty boy, leave off thy crying,
> Thou shalt have bells or apples; be not peevish;
> Kiss me, sweet lad, beshrew her for denying.

Indeed, no aspect of Greville's verse is more remarkable than the intricacy of imagery he expends upon allegory of love. In one instance (No. LXXI) Cupid is represented as an apprentice to beauty who has gone forth clad in "seizin and livery of beauty's sky" and "enamelled fair with hope." Wounded, however, by a rival and lean with despair, he returns and asks to be apprenticed, not to womankind, but to knowledge, honor, fame, or honesty. Greville's reference (No. LII) to Cupid as a meadow-god, which seems to be the only one of its kind in the cycles, is thought by Bullen to have been suggested by the *Pervigilium veneris*.[117]

Even Greville's farewell to love (No. LXXXV) has a mocking, Anacreontic tone rather than the serious, almost religious one of Sidney and Spenser:

> Farewell, sweet boy, complain not of my truth,
> Thy mother loved thee not with more devotion;
> For to thy boy's play I gave all my youth;
> Young master, I did hope for your promotion . . .
>   But Cupid, now farewell, I will go play me
>   With thoughts that please me less, and less betray me.

Shakespeare's sonnets contain two brief allusions to the childish aspects of love. Sonnet CXV says:

> Love is a babe; then might I not say so,
> To give full growth to that which still doth grow?

Likewise, Sonnet CLI says: "Love is too young to know what conscience is." Two other Shakespearean sonnets, the final ones, describe the fires of Cupid and are derived ultimately from the work of Marianus in the *Greek Anthology*.[118] They bear little, if any, relation to the narrative of the sequence, yet, considered merely as an illustration of Elizabethan interest in the exploits of the Alexandrian god, they form a not-inappropriate conclusion to the sonnet material given over to that aspect of the personification of love.

In brief, the sonneteers whose poems are explainable in the light of this classical tradition of the Alexandrian, or Anacreontic, conception are Sidney, Greville, and Fletcher. Sidney popularizes it.[119] Although Watson's *Hecatompathia* had sonnets of this type,[120] that sequence had little influence. Since the conception is the chief motif of *Caelica,* it is impossible to read that work understandingly or to recognize the originality shown in it without reconsidering its background. Greville's verse, however, was unpublished until 1633, and so he can have exerted at best only a limited influence. Watson's *The Tears of Fancie* opens with seven sonnets in the Anacreontic vein; Barnes probably takes some of his material directly from Greek sources.[121] Spenser, on the other hand, for all the interest shown elsewhere in the Greek conception, here follows his master Petrarch rather closely and in the *Amoretti* presents Ovidian patterns almost exclusively. Drayton had none of these themes in his 1594 edition but adds them to his later editions. Constable and the minor writers make occasional pleasing allusions.[122] Of Fletcher, Miss Scott's statement may be aptly quoted: [123]

Des poèmes anacréontiques, il est vrai, se rencontrent partout dans la poésie anglaise de la Renaissance, mais où les contemporains se contentent d'un ou deux sonnets sur l'*Amour annuité,* Fletcher en fait une vingtaine, introduisant des exploits de Cupidon inconnus aux autres sonnettistes élisabéthains.

Yet, as it was said early in this chapter, this Greek conception was never popular in the sixteenth century in the sense that the Latin, or Ovidian, conception was. It must surely have been the Ovidian Cupid as the conventional symbol for the power of love that caused Donne, "rebel and atheist, too" against love, to render English lyric verse so signal a service by helping to free it from the classical vehicles for setting it forth.

ANATOMY OF MELANCHOLY

"In piercing phrases, late,
The anatomy of all my woes I wrote."
SIDNEY, SONNET NO. LVIII

A SONNETEER'S chief concern was presumably that of portraying the theme of love, his next task was that of analyzing the baleful effect of love upon his mental and physical state,
and his tablet of rare conceits offered him an even greater variety
of ways for setting forth that theme than it did for the other. In
neither instance can the reader of today determine with certainty
what is fact and what is rhetoric, for any actual feeling would almost of necessity have been cloaked in some conventional figure.
Even so, however, these sonnets often appear to reveal greater evidences of emotion than do the sonnets on the theme of love. Shakespeare alone sometimes expressed himself without the intervention
of conceits, and, when he did use them, he transmuted them. Yet
this theme of the sonneteer's melancholy produced the best of
Sidney, Spenser, and Shakespeare—the finest love sonnets, in
short, in the English language. Such sonnets are best understood
if considered in the light of the literary conventions they embody.
These conventions bring us again to Ovid, this time to his method
of analyzing the effects of his love. From that vantage point, we
may observe the sonnet themes themselves.

THE OVIDIAN MANIFESTATIONS OF LOVE

THE OVIDIAN symptoms and analyses of love, drawn
chiefly from the *Ars amatoria,* the *Remedia amoris,* and the
Amores, were the sources of the conventions by means of which
Petrarch portrayed the effects of his love. These concepts were
widely known to the Middle Ages, partly through the twelfth-
century romances of Chrétien de Troyes,[1] and furnished both
the standards in France and Italy for amatory conduct and the

materials for such codifications in France as the *De arte honesti amandi* of Andreas Capellanus.[2] The troubadours, for their part, made no formal codifications, but the rules were fully exemplified, and lovers' symptoms, especially sleeplessness, were frequently mentioned.[3]

These Ovidian concepts were disseminated after the thirteenth century chiefly through the *Romance of the Rose,* where the commandments laid down by the god of love had no formal numberings, yet were clearly regarded as statutes to be observed by all true lovers.[4] Neilson enumerates some of these symptoms of love:

. . . solitariness, alternations of heat and cold, absent-mindedness, restlessness in absence, insatiable desire to look on the lady, bashfulness, secret haunting of her neighborhood, dumbness in her presence, sleeplessness, dreaming of her and waking to disappointment, humility, rising before dawn and going to her house in all weathers, and leanness.[5]

Giacomo da Lentino and the earliest sonneteers acquired these ideals of the correct conduct of the lover through Provençal verse, for here, as elsewhere, they took over the formalized attitudes and symptoms of love found there. Giacomo writes often of the symptoms of his love, of his sighs and despair. Using imagery which he had drawn from Provençal conventions, he compares himself to a butterfly entering a flame, to the phoenix, peacock, swan, basilisk, and so forth.[6] Succeeding Italian poets wrote in a similar vein. Dante describes in the *Vita nuova* his pains and sighs, his bitter weeping and grievous sickness. He is often so abstracted that he fails to note his surroundings; his feelings are in a whirl of contradictions. He dreams of Beatrice and trembles when in her presence.[7]

It was Petrarch, however, who transmitted these conventional motifs, modified as they then were by chivalry and Platonism alike, to all later sonnet sequences. For one thing, they gain great beauty and apparent subjectivity at his hands, since they appear to be more than mere conventions and to express direct personal experience; for another, Petrarch's sonnets were easier to imitate than those of the *Vita nuova,* since they lacked both the prose commentary and the greater mysticism of Dante. Briefly summarized, Petrarch's description of the effects of his love include the following: he is pale, meek, sleepless; he refers often to his sighs and tears, to the sorrows of absence. He compares himself to many things, among them a ship tossed upon perilous seas, a moth, a gnat, a bird caught in a trap, a pilgrim, a blind man. He envies the happiness of Pygmalion and the attention bestowed by Laura upon her mirror. His love makes him able to perform many seemingly impossible things; his love will last, for example, until the snow turns black. He writes to gain relief from his woes, to praise Laura's beauty, or to fulfill the command of the god of love.

The modern reader who feels only embarrassment at the delineation of emotion in the English sonnet cycles, who finds himself unmoved by the distressing symptoms brought forth as proof of the poet's unswerving devotion, must occasionally remind himself that such analyzing and attitudinizing were familiar enough to the average Elizabethan. Sighing, melancholy, analytical lovers were not only the heroes of their romances and pastoral fiction but trod the boards realistically enough upon the Elizabethan stage. Indeed, too little recognition is usually given to the extent to which the Ovidian symptoms and the medieval love conventions affect the conduct of many Shakespearean characterizations. Troilus,[8] Orsino, Orlando, Shallow, Valentine, Romeo—even Benedict, who, in the end, was reduced to writing a "halting sonnet of his own pure brain" to Beatrice—these and others often seem to be either the very prototypes of the sonnet lovers, or, in some instances, to satirize the conventional attitudes toward love. Only two need be noticed here—Valentine as representing the comedies and Romeo as representing the tragedies.

The *Two Gentlemen of Verona* affords numerous parallels between the conduct of the sonneteers and the romantic heroes of the drama. Speed satirically points out the symptoms by which he has recognized the fact that Valentine is in love:

VALENTINE: "Why, how know you that I am in love?"

SPEED: "Marry, by these special marks. First, you have learned, like Sir Proteus, to wreathe your arms, like a malcontent; to relish a love-song, like a robin redbreast; to walk alone, like one that had the pestilence; to sigh, like a school-boy that had lost his A B C; to weep, like a young wench that hath buried her grandam; to fast, like one that takes diet; to watch, like one that fears robbing; to speak puling, like a beggar at Hallowmass." (Act II, scene 1, ll. 16–25)

More in the same vein follows, both from Speed and Valentine himself, as in his speeches to Proteus in Act II, scene 4. Proteus, too, recounts some of the correct symptoms for lovers in his advice to Thurio in describing the "wailful" sonnet which is to "entangle Silvia's desires." Its rhymes should be "full-fraught with serviceable vows":

> Say that upon the altar of her beauty
> You sacrifice your tears, your sighs, your heart.
> Write till your ink be dry, and with your tears
> Moist it again, and frame some feeling line
> That may discover such integrity . . .
> After your dire-lamenting elegies,
> Visit by night your lady's chamber-window
> With some sweet concert: to their instruments
> Tune a deploring dump; the night's dead silence
> Will well become such sweet-complaining grievance.
> This, or else nothing, will inherit her.
> (Act III, scene 2, ll. 72–76; 83–88)

The fact that Thurio's "deploring dump" proves to be no sonnet at all but the lyric "Who Is Sylvia" in no way invalidates the analogy between the conduct of these characters and of sonneteers.

Romeo and Juliet, however, contains the best example of a Shakespearean character explainable only in terms of the Ovidian tradition. The Italian sources of the story no doubt account for some of the situations in Arthur Brooke's *Romeus and Juliet,* yet a comparison of Brooke's poem with Shakespeare's play shows that Shakespeare greatly expanded the delineation of Romeo's character. Brooke, for example, describes in only a few lines (92–101) the conduct of Romeus when in love with Rosaline, while Shakespeare gives almost an entire scene (Act I, scene 1, ll. 125–245) to the same part of the story. Romeo's mental state is revealed through the eyes of his parents and friends as well as through his conversation with Benvolio. His sighs and tears are described by his father in a long passage beginning:

> Many a morning hath he there been seen
> With tears augmenting the fresh morning's dew,
> Adding to clouds more clouds with his deep sighs.

Romeo is abstracted, all but out of his wits from despair at his unrequited love for the pale, hard-hearted Rosaline. He converses with Benvolio upon the contrariety of moods caused by love; he describes love as the warfare of Cupid and says that Rosaline lives unharmed by "love's weak childish bow" (Act I, scene 1, ll. 217). He speaks, with apparent seriousness, of the god of love as the cause of his woe. When Mercutio mockingly says that Romeo should borrow Cupid's wings and "soar with them above a common bound," he replies:

> I am too sore enpierced with his shaft
> To soar with his light feathers; and so bound
> I cannot bound a pitch above dull woe:
> Under love's heavy burden do I sink.
> (Act I, scene 4, ll. 19–22)

Rosaline is worshipped in the conventional manner as a divinity (Act I, scene 2, ll. 93–94):

> When the devout religion of mine eye
> Maintains such falsehood, then turn tears to fires!

Shakespeare adds to this play not only the two sonnets which are the prologues of Acts I and II but also inserted the sonnet form of the dialogue between Romeo and Juliet at the time of their first meeting (Act I, scene 5, ll. 95–110). After Rosaline disappears from the story, Romeo, it need not be said, discards his conventional posturing.

In spite of instances such as these, however, of conventionally correct romantic heroes in Shakespeare's plays, it is clear enough that Shakespeare recognized the discrepancy existing between these literary ideals and the actual conduct of the average Elizabethan gentleman. Speed, Don Pedro, Feste, Mercutio, and others appear to serve as touchstones of common sense for the romantic lovers. Feste, for example, when leaving the presence of Duke Orsino, says:

Now, the melancholy god protect thee, and the tailor make thy doublet of changeable taffeta, for thy mind is a very opal! I would have men of such constancy put to sea, that their business might be every thing and their intent everywhere; for that's it that always makes a good voyage of nothing. (Act II, scene 4, ll. 74–81)

Hamlet's reference to the crocodile in a speech to Laertes (Act. V, scene 1, ll. 297–300) implies his scorn of the convention he is nevertheless ready to follow:

'Swounds! show me what thou'lt do:
Woo't weep? Woo't fight? Woo't fast? Woo't tear thyself?
Woo't drink up eisel? eat a crocodile?
I'll do't.

Yet such characters do not appear to be intended as vehicles for social satire as are certain characters of the plays of Ben Jonson and Marston. Nor, on the other hand, do they appear to be the true malcontents or genuine hypochondriacs among whom Jacques, as Professor Campbell shows, belongs.[9]

These illustrations from Shakespeare suffice to show that the Elizabethan reader took for granted a definite code of action as a manifestation of the symptoms and effects of love. The symptoms and effects of love were revealed in a variety of ways. We may consider first the treatment given to the theme of the effect of love upon the poet's sleep.

CARE-CHARMER SLEEP

ONE OF THE conventional manifestations of love which was stressed in every medieval code was the sleeplessness of the lover. The twenty-third statute in Andreas is: *Minus dormit et edit, quem amoris cogitatio vexat.* Petrarch addresses sonnets to night and to his bed, and dreams that the image of Laura appears to him in his sleep. The successors of Petrarch often made use of the theme of the sleeplessness of the poet. It was written in Italy, for instance, by Chariteo, Sannazaro, della Casa, and Serafino and in France by Ronsard, De Baïf, and Desportes.[10] Many epithets are applied, but probably few of them are original: Sir Sidney Lee points out that both Homer and Hesiod had called sleep the "brother of death" and that the favorite Elizabethan adjective "care-charmer" comes from Daniel's translation of Desportes' *chasse-soin*.[11] In England the themes sleep and night called forth some of the most distinguished verse of the Elizabethan age.

The sonnet apostrophes to sleep written by Sidney, Drayton, Daniel, Griffin, and Drummond of Hawthornden usually devote the first quatrain, sometimes the entire octave, to the attributes of sleep. Sidney's sonnet (No. XXXIX) begins:

> Come, Sleep! O Sleep, the certain knot of peace,
> The baiting place of wit, the balm of woe,
> The poor man's wealth, the prisoner's release,
> Th' indifferent judge between the high and low.

The sestet of such sonnets sometimes states the reward offered to Morpheus, but, more frequently, it makes some request of him or laments his fickleness. Sidney, blending the conceit with a second one, that of the portrait or image of the lady engraved in the poet's heart, offered to Morpheus smooth pillows, sweetest bed,

> A chamber deaf to noise and blind to light,
> A rosy garland and a weary head:
> And if these things, as being thine by right,
> Move not thy heavy Grace, thou shalt in me
> Livelier than elsewhere, Stella's image see.[12]

Daniel's sonnet on this subject (No. XLIX) is generally conceded to be one of the most beautiful lyrics of the Elizabethan age. Although the poem has several analogues, among them Desportes, the originality of Daniel is proved by the fact that the critics cannot agree as to the closest source or nearest analogue.[13] The tone, in contrast with the more playful one of Sidney, is serious throughout, and the poem ends with the wish that the poet may not wake from his dream of happiness. Daniel's English construction may be compared with the Italian form used by Sidney:

> Care-charmer Sleep, son of the sable night,
> Brother to death, in silent darkness born;
> Relieve my anguish and restore the light!
> With dark forgetting of my cares, return!
> And let the day be time enough to mourn
> The shipwreck of my ill adventured youth;
> Let waking eyes suffice to wail their scorn,
> Without the torment of the night's untruth.
> Cease, dreams, th' imag'ry of our day desires,
> To model forth the passions of the morrow;
> Never let rising sun approve you liars,
> To add more grief to aggravate my sorrow.
> Still let me sleep, embracing clouds in vain,
> And never wake to feel the day's disdain.

Griffin's version (No. XV) owes more, line by line, to Sidney than to Daniel in spite of his appropriating Daniel's phrases "care-charmer" and "brother of quiet death." Altogether, Griffin's poem is an illuminating illustration of how a young poet could make a pastiche from his favorite poems without being able to sustain his powers to the end:

> Care-charmer sleep, sweet ease is restless misery,
> The captive's liberty, and his freedom's song,
> Balm of the bruised heart, man's chief felicity,
> Brother of quiet death, when life is too, too long;
> A comedy it is, and now a history.
> What is not sleep unto the feeble mind?
> It easeth him that toils, and him that's sorry;
> It makes the deaf to hear; to see, the blind.
> Ungentle sleep, thou helpest all but me!
> For when I sleep my soul is vexed most.
> It is Fidessa that doth master thee;
> If she approach, alas, thy power is lost.
> But here she is! See how he runs amain!
> I fear at night he will not come again.

Barnes addresses his sonnet to night instead of to sleep (No. LXXXIII), but, in the third and fourth lines, falls into the ejaculatory style which mars so much of his work:

> Dark night! Black image of my foul despair,
> With grievous fancies, cease to vex my soul
> With pain, sore smart, hot fires, cold fears, long care!
> (Too much, alas, this ceaseless stone to roll.)

The final lines of the sonnet give, nevertheless, the gist of many laments of the sleepless lover:

> Wishing the noon to me were silent night;
> And shades nocturnal turned to daylight.

Drayton, in 1594, addressed a sonnet (No. XLV) to night instead of to sleep,[14] but made certain changes: Sidney's "baiting place of wit" becomes the "inne of care," Daniel's "day's disdain" is the "day's burning fire." The sonnet, by its comparison of night with death, maintains a consistently serious tone too rarely present in Drayton:

Blacke pythchy Night, companyon of my woe,
The Inne of Care, the Nurse of drery sorrow,
Why lengthnest thou thy darkest howres so,
Still to prolong my long tyme lookt-for morrow?
Thou Sable shadow, Image of dispayre,
Portraite of hell, the ayres black mourning weed,
Recorder of Reuenge, remembrancer of care,
The shadow and the vaile of euery sinfull deed.
Death like to thee, so lyue thou still in death,
The graue of ioy, prison of dayes delight.
Let heauens withdraw their sweet Ambrozian breath,
Nor Moone nor stars lend thee their shining light;
   For thou alone renew'st that olde desire,
   Which still torments me in dayes burning fire.

A beautiful version of this apostrophe to sleep appeared, too, in 1616 in the poems of William Drummond of Hawthornden. The sonnet begins:

Sleep, Silence' child, sweet father of soft rest,
Prince whose approach peace to all mortals brings.

But the sonneteers were not alone in making use of this theme.[15] The dramatist John Fletcher appropriated the sonnet phraseology in a lyric beginning "Care-charming sleep, thou easer of all woes."[16] Dowland's *First Book of Songs or Airs* (1597) has a song beginning "Come, heavy sleep, the image of true death." Descriptions of sleep such as these give the real significance to two famous passages in Shakespeare, neither of them, of course, having anything to do with the theme of love. One is the famous soliloquy in *Henry IV*, Part II, in which the king, unable to sleep, says in part:

How many thousands of my poorest subjects
Are at this hour asleep! O Sleep! O Gentle Sleep,
Nature's soft nurse, how have I frighted thee
That thou no more wilt weigh my eyelids down
And steep my senses in forgetfulness?
               (Act III, scene 1, ll. 3–7)

The other is an equally famous passage from *Macbeth* (Act II, scene 2, ll. 37–40):

> Sleep that knits up the ravell'd sleave of care,
> The death of each day's life, sore labour's bath,
> Balm of hurt minds, great nature's second course,
> Chief nourisher in life's feast.

These apostrophes to sleep cause some of the briefer descriptions and more conventional sonnets on the theme to seem more platitudinous than not. Sidney and Spenser, however, have, near the end of their sequences, grave, well-sustained sonnets setting forth sleeplessness as resulting from the sorrows of absence.[17] No poet so often used the theme of the sleeplessness of the lover as does Sidney, or so often made the sonnet narrative turn upon it. He writes to his bed, as had Petrarch; and of morning, not night, bringing rest to him.[18] His verse is written because he cannot sleep. He refers twice to the fact that the image of Stella appears to him in his dreams—once presented by the god of love, once by Morpheus.[19] Griffin (No. XIV) imitates Sidney here, but represents the image of Fidessa as being brought to him by nature instead of by Morpheus. Daniel (No. XV), in his customary fashion of merely stating a conceit without developing it, merely says: "If I have wept the day and sighed the night." Drayton (No. XXXVII) laments that night brings separation; Smith (No. XXXVII) shows the disastrous effects of the loss of sleep by saying he is dying from lack of it.

The theme of sleep is also sometimes a lament upon the sadness of awakening to reality.[20] Unconscious humor is present in Linche's account of a dream of drowning in a pond of grief. He rather enjoys the prospect of death until his mouth fills with the flood. Then he cries out for help, and Diella struggles so hard to pull him from the water that he awakes—to wish he had slept on and perished in the pool (No. XXIV). The sixteenth sonnet of Daniel presents in two lines the poet's desire not to awaken to reality:

> Happy in sleep; waking, content to languish;
> Embracing clouds by night; in day time mourn.

Several poets, however, present the theme of sleeplessness merely as a general manifestation of the grief and fidelity of the lover.[21]

Shakespeare's sonnets upon sleep and the one upon dreams are admittedly less striking in imagery than the passages from *Henry IV* and *Macbeth* already quoted, yet deserve close reading. A citation of them here may close the discussion of this phase of the sonneteer's themes: Nos. XXVII and XXVIII show that night and day alike bring no rest to the weary poet. The first poem concludes:

> Lo, thus, by day my limbs, by night my mind,
> For thee and for myself no quiet find.

The succeeding one is similar:

> But day doth daily draw my sorrows longer,
> And night doth nightly make grief's strength seem stronger.

The best of the group presents the poet's unhappiness arising from doubts concerning Will's love for him (No. LXI):

> Is it thy will thy image should keep open
> My heavy eyelids to the weary night?
> Dost thou desire my slumbers should be broken,
> While shadows like to thee do mock my sight?
>
> .   .   .
>
> Oh, no, thy love, though much, is not so great:
> It is my love that keeps mine eyes awake;
> Mine own true love that doth my rest defeat,
> To play the watchman ever for thy sake:
>   For thee watch I whilst thou doth wake elsewhere,
>   From me far off, with others all too near.

In still another example, dreams of Will prevent his sleep (No. XLIII):

> All days are nights to see till I see thee,
> And nights bring days when dreams do show thee me.

MEDIEVAL CONCEITS OF THE HEART

Ah, what a trifle is a heart
If once into love's hands it come!
DONNE, "THE BROKEN HEART"

HAD Shakespeare alone employed conceits derived from the medieval conventions which purport to describe the state of the poet's heart, his versions of them would alone make it profitable to consider them in some detail. Other sonneteers, however, do make use of them in a manner which is sometimes effective, sometimes merely clever or ingenious, yet attractive in its very medieval stiffness and precision.

One of these medieval conventions is exemplified in Shakespeare's Sonnet XLVI:

> Mine eye and heart are at a mortal war,
> How to divide the conquest of thy sight;
> Mine eye my heart thy picture's sight would bar,
> My heart mine eye the freedom of that right.
> My heart doth plead that thou in him dost lie,
> A closet never pierced with crystal eyes,
> But the defendant doth that plea deny,
> And says in him thy fair appearance lies.
> To 'cide this title is impanneled
> A quest of thought, all tenants to the heart;
> And by their verdict is determined
> The clear eye's moiety and the dear heart's part:
> As thus; mine eye's due is thine outward part,
> And my heart's right thine inward love of heart.

This conceit of a debate between the poet's eye and heart to determine the responsibility for his woes came in part from the classical convention of the eyes as the cause of love, in part from the medieval taste for debates. The belief that love passed through the eye to the heart was, as Hanford shows,[22] a popular one established largely by the romances of Chrétien de Troyes. A passage in *Cligés* (ll. 695 ff.) contains all the elements needed for a formal debate between the heart and eye; later writers needed only to "complete the personification of the heart and eye to make them carry on the dispute themselves, a step which, in view of the popularity of similar debates, was natural and easy." [23] Theological debates such as that of the *Body and Soul* gave a mold for amatory material; on the other hand, the theological *Disputatio inter cor et oculum* may have gained suggestions in regard to its form from Chrétien or from some other secular poet.

Hanford states that a formal debate between the Heart and Eye to determine the guilt for the poet's woe is first found in the allegory of the Court of Love in Huon de Meri's *Le Tornoiment de l'antéchrit* (? 1235):

In the course of the battle between the allegorical hosts of good and evil, Venus aims a shaft at Chastity. It misses its mark, but enters the author's eye and wounds his heart. He is succored by Esperance and others, and brings his case before the court "which renders justice to all lovers," in order to determine whether his Heart, the Goddess, or his Eyes are to blame for his mischance. The judge exonerates Venus who was aiming at another, and accuses the Eyes. The latter excuse themselves on the ground that they do nothing without the Heart's command. At this point Reason appears and decides the case against the Heart.[24]

Later debates of this nature are present in works such as the French *Debat du cuer et de l'oeil,* the sonnets of Petrarch which present dialogues between the poet and his eyes and heart,[25] and the *Salu d'amours,* of Philippe de Remi. The accusation and trial in the *Salu d'amours,* which represents the poet's heart as locked up in prison, may have come, Neilson thinks, from the instance in the *Romance of the Rose* in which the poet's heart is locked with a key.[26] There is in Petrarch (*Canzone* VII, Part II), moreover, the notable instance of love and the poet pleading their cases before reason. Two of the earliest appearances of the theme in England seem to be Gascoigne's "At Beauty's Bar as I Did Stand," a poem no doubt reflecting Petrarch's debate between love and the poet; and a poem in *The Poor Knight His Pallace of Private Pleasure,* where Justice and Judgment plead at Beauty's bar.

From this general background, then, sprang the conceits found in the English sonnet cycles. Sidney follows this tradition, although faintly, in Sonnet LXXIII, when he describes Stella's lips as being the judges in the case against the poet for his theft of a kiss:

> . . . she makes her wrath appear
> In Beauty's throne. See now! who dares come near
> Those scarlet judges, threat'ning bloody pain?

Constable seems to imitate Sidney directly (Dec. IV, No. 6):

> Your lips, in scarlet clad, my Judges be,
> Pronouncing sentence of eternal "No."

The conceit appears, too, as the theme of another sonnet of Constable (Dec. VI, No. 7): "My Heart, mine eye accuseth of his death." Watson's version (No. XX) begins, "My heart accus'd mine eies"; Drayton's (No. XXXIII), "Whilst yet mine eyes so surfeit with delight/My woeful Heart (imprisoned in my breast)." The sonnet of Shakespeare quoted at the beginning of this section differs in having the jury empanelled and in deciding the extent of the guilt of both eye and heart.[27] A second sonnet continuing the theme (No. XLVII) has no English parallel, for it describes a truce arranged between the heart and eye and the good turns each does for the other.

A second conventional conceit for describing the state of the poet's heart is familiar from Sidney's charming lyric:

> My true-love hath my heart, and I have his,
> By just exchange one for the other given:
> I hold his dear, and mine he cannot miss,
> There never was a bargain better driven.
> My true-love hath my heart, and I have his.
>
> His heart in me keeps him and me in one,
> My heart in him his thoughts and senses guides,

He loves my heart, for once it was his own,
I cherish his because in me it bides.
My true-love hath my heart, and I have his.

Shakespeare's Sonnet XXII gives great beauty to this convention:

. . . For all that beauty that doth cover thee
Is but the seemly raiment of my heart,
Which in thy breast doth live, as thine in me:
How can I then be elder than thou art?
O, therefore, love, be of thyself so wary
As I, not for myself, but for thee will;
Bearing thy heart, which I will keep so chary
As tender nurse her babe from faring ill.
    Presume not on thy heart when mine is slain;
    Thou gavest me thine, not to give back again.

Again, Shakespeare's image is that of the poet who, going on a journey, locks up all his treasures (No. XLVIII):

. . . But thou; to whom my jewels trifles are,
Most worthy comfort, now my greatest grief,
Thou, best of dearest and mine only care,
Art left the prey of every vulgar thief.
Thee have I not lock'd up in any chest,
Save where thou art not, though I feel thou art
Within the gentle closure of my breast,
From whence at pleasure thou mayst come and part;
    And even thence thou wilt be stol'n, I fear,
    For truth proves thievish for a prize so dear.

The same convention is the implied and underlying motif in the sonnets in which Shakespeare identifies himself and his actions with those of Will, as when (in No. XXXVII) he enjoys vicariously the beauty, birth, wealth, and wit of his friend; and when he says in Sonnet XL:

Take all my loves, my love, yea, take them all;
What hast thou then more than thou hadst before? . . .
All mine was thine before thou hadst this more.

Even the sonnet on Will's conquest of the Dark Lady (No. XLII), beginning "That thou hast her, it is not all my grief," is to be explained by this conception of the fusion of identities. The sonnet concludes thus:

> But here's the joy: my friend and I are one;
> Sweet flattery! then she loves but me alone.

This conceit of the exchange of hearts [28] is sometimes combined with and is hardly distinguishable from a third medieval convention of the state of the poet's heart, its migration to that of the lady. Petrarch himself had treated this motif simply; he once orders his heart to return to Laura, but finds it has never left her; and, again, commends it for remaining with her.[29] By the time of the English cycles, however, the conceit had become a complete narrative presented in legal phraseology. Watson combines it with the conceit of the debate between the heart and eye in a series of five sonnets (Nos. XVII–XXI): [30] The heart tells how it has escaped from the lady as one escaping slaughter, how it has "fought the lady in court and country," and how the lady has scorned the tears of the poet and his fellow thralls. The forgiving poet then receives his heart, with its thousand wounds, again into his breast, where it conspires "for to abhorre her." The poet is punished by love, however, who says that eyes should ever weep and heart ever groan. At this point (No. XX), the usual heart-and-eye accusation and sentence of grief is introduced:

> My heart accus'd mine eies and was offended
> Vowing the cause was in mine eies aspiring
> Mine eies affirmed my heart might well amend it . . .
> Heart said that love did enter at the eies . . .

Finally, fortune, "forwearied" by the poet's moans, permits him an opportunity to plead his case before the lady, but, since he is tongue-tied and dazed in her presence, he is unable to make his plea.

The extent to which Barnes used this conceit in *Parthenophil*

and Parthenophe appears to have gone unnoticed. The first sixteen sonnets and four of the madrigals of his sequence form, however, a loosely connected narrative based upon it, with returns to
the motif in the twentieth, forty-seventh, and sixty-fifth sonnets.
The narrative, related mainly in law terms obscure to the modern reader,[31] requires a brief summary—but with no attempt to
explain the law terms! Parthenophil, seeking to prevent his heart
(personified as a young boy) from fleeing to a maiden named
Laya,[32] confines it in prisons of neglect walled in by solitary
studies. But his heart, that is, the lad, steals the keys (sight, hearing, touch) and escapes to Laya, who guards it closely until a
courtier richer than Parthenophil appears. Then the neglected
heart manages to free itself—"unyoked himself and closely 'scaped
away"—and flees to Parthenophe to ask that she plead with
Parthenophil for its pardon. Parthenophil at first plans to make
sure of his heart by fastening it with chains and fetters of reason, but, after securing Parthenophe's love as bond if it default,
it is set free.

The traitorous heart, however, then flees to Parthenophe and
gives itself over to her service. The poet demands of her why
she, his bail, has armed his heart for "another start." "Tush," she
answers, "before he go I'll be his bail at last, and doubt it not!"
Yet when the lover calls upon her for the mortgage of his love,
he discovers that she has treacherously passed it off by deed of
gift, so that his only recourse is to mourn his heart's departure
and lament his wounded, heart-less state. Nor has Parthenophe
cherished his heart—she treated it, indeed, with complete indifference. Why had she betrayed him after he had had her sum-
moned to the court of steadfast love? With what sophistry she
has done it! Nature should enact better laws for the protection of
mankind:

> That those which do true meaning falsify
> Making such bargains as were precontractit,

> Should forfeit freelege of love's tenancy
> To th' plaintiff grieved, if he exact it.
>   (Mad. II)

In despair from the assaults of her beauty, the poet resolves to find flaws in it. His efforts, however, end with increased praise of her beauty, for not even Zeuxis had been able to paint her portrait. To whom, then, can the poet complain of the injury done him with "right's injustice and unkind restraint"? Laments in these unpoetic law terms continue with unabated zeal in the twentieth sonnet. Then other conceits, including a series of twelve sonnets on the signs of the zodiac, intervene; but Sonnet XLVII returns to the theme—"Give me my Heart! For no man liveth Heartless!" Lastly, in No. LXV is another brief statement:

> O that I had no heart! As I have none,
> (For thou mine heart's full spirit hast possessed!)

Daniel likewise uses legal phrasing in three sonnets presenting this conceit: one shows his heart as being pursued by Delia's eyes and as fleeing to the sanctuary of her bosom where he hopes his "faith of privilege," signed with blood and three years' witness, will protect it. Yet, although Delia knows well his love and grief, she slays his heart. It is useless for the poet to appeal to the law for aid, for "ladies and tyrants never laws respecteth" (No. XXVI). Again, he describes his heart as being sacrificed to Delia: his eyes, the agents of his heart, entreat relief; his verse, the advocate of his love, follows closely the process of the case; and, if justice could prevail, should have won the case (No. VIII). The third sonnet, found only in the 1591 and 1592 editions (No. VIII), relates the poet's efforts to stop the passage of his heart after it had been betrayed by Delia's voice.

The medieval lover employed, however, still other conventional "heart" conceits for presenting his fidelity to the lady: Her image was engraved or painted or carved in his heart; and the heart itself was a temple where this image was worshiped. Of the origin of the first of these conceits, Hutton says:

Another commonplace of amatory poetry is the theme, Love has sculptured—or painted—my lady's image in my heart. Meleager has it for the whole thought of an epigram . . . centuries later it still serves Paul the Silentiary . . . Petrarch has this conceit at least twice (Canz. 13. 35 and Son. 75. 5–6). Boiardo has it . . . Ariosto more than once employs it; Bembo uses it; and, in a word, it is the common property of all sonneteers in every language.[33]

The brevity of some of these examples listed by Hutton from the *Greek Anthology* permits their quotation as a basis for comparison.[34] The epigram of Meleager says: "Within my heart Love himself fashioned sweet-spoken Heliodora, soul of my soul." That of Paulus is: "The image of me that Love stamped in the hot depths of thy heart thou dost now, alas! as I never dreamt, disown; but I have the picture of thy beauty engraved on my soul." Petrarch's *canzone,* in Nott's translation, says:

> Some power appears to trace
> Within me Laura's face.

His sonnet lines (MacGregor's translation) are:

> But the bright face which in my heart profound
> Is stamped, and seen wher'er I turn my eyes.

Sidney's use of this conceit is not remarkable, yet the sonnets employing it are interesting in comparison with the work of his followers, for at least it avoids their exaggerations: He foresees that virtue itself will fall in love with Stella's image in his heart; Stella's image is the source from which Morpheus steals his gold and gems and is the reward offered Morpheus if he will bring sleep to the poet.[35] Greville's *Caelica* has as its third poem a lyric with the refrain as follows:

> If in my heart all nymphs else be defaced,
> Honour the shrine where you alone are placed!

The sonneteers succeeding Sidney appear, however, to have thought that their fidelity was in proportion to the hyperbole they could muster for themes. Watson tells (Nos. XLV–XLVI) the sad outcome of showing the image in his heart to the unfeeling lady, with the hope that she would be affected by the sight. Seeing her image, however, "so sweetly framed" in his bleeding heart, she immediately demands its return and gives the poet no sympathy. Finding that she cannot take the picture without also accepting the poet's heart, she turns her face and chooses to go without the image. Watson returns to the theme near the end of the cycle and states that he still carries the picture of her fiery darting eyes in his "grieved mind."

Fletcher and Constable give the conceit unusual versions based upon foreign sources. Fletcher warns Licia that if she does not place his heart with her own that he will reveal to the world her naked image painted there (No. VI); Constable says love had painted Diana's image in his heart merely as a target so that he could shoot at him (Dec. II, No. 2).[36] Constable also alludes to the eyes as the windows through which Diana could, if she would only look, see herself painted in bloody colors (Dec. I, No. 5). The unknown author of *Zepheria* assures the equally unknown Zepheria that her image will survive eternally in his verse (No. XIV):

> No! Never shall that face, so fair depainted
> Within the love-limned tablet of mine heart
> Emblemished be! defaced! or unsainted!
> Till death shall blot it with his pencil dart!
>   Yet, then, in these limned lines ennobled more
>   Thou shalt survive, richer accomplished than before!

Daniel (No. XIII), comparing himself to Pygmalion, carved on his heart "the goodliest shape that the world's eye admires." The originality of Shakespeare's sonnets is seen here, as elsewhere, only when his treatment of the conventional conceits is compared with that of his contemporaries: the image his eye has painted in his heart is framed by his body. It is there hung in the shop window of his bosom, where the sun delights to look through the windows of his heart (his eyes) in order to gaze in upon it (No. XXIV).[37]

When the conceit of the image engraved in the heart is carried further, the heart is sometimes worshiped as a shrine or temple for the image enshrined there. Sidney merely requests in two lines (No. XL) that Stella would not destroy the heart which is her temple. Daniel, more ambitious, in one instance represents Delia as being in "thought's temple, sainted"; and, again, as being in the turret of her pride and watching the sack of the temple where her name was honored (Nos. XV, XLII). Constable, still more ingenious, invokes the aid of supernatural forces and compares his heart's temple to a temple of Mohammed (Dec. IV, No. 4). Percy proves his fealty by shedding tears—"huge drops of tears with large eruptions"—upon Coelia's ivory shrine and by offering, twice a day, sacrifices of sighs and psalms of invocations (No. IV). Drayton's version is that of his heart as a hallowed temple in which Idea is a vestal virgin. His holy thoughts are the vestal flame, her eyes the sun which lights the fire (No. XXX). Drayton writes, also, of his bosom as too poor a shrine for the rich relic of her dear remembrance (No. LVII).

Spenser alone lends plausibility to a description of the temple within the heart. His sonnet (No. XXII) may therefore serve as the last illustration here of this convention. It may be noted in passing that the sonnet is also an excellent instance of Renaissance inconsistency in its blending of paganism and Christianity, goddess and saint.[38]

> This holy season, fit to fast and pray,
>   Men to devotion ought to be inclined:
> Therefore, I likewise, on so holy day,
>   For my sweet saint some service fit will find.
> Her temple fair is built within my mind,
>   In which her glorious image placed is,

On which my thoughts do day and night attend
Like sacred priests that never think amiss!
There I to her, as th' author of my bliss,
Will build an altar to appease her ire;
And on the same my heart will sacrifice,
Burning in flames of pure and chaste desire:
    The which vouchsafe, O goddess, to accept,
    Amongst thy dearest relics to be kept.

WASTING IN DESPAIR

THE LITERATURE of the sixteenth century was still remarkably close in spirit to the medieval codes of love which held that the symptoms of true love included sighs and tears, despair and imminent death. One no longer encounters, to be sure, instances of "reeling and writhing and fainting in coils," as Lowes describes the conduct of the characters in Machaut; [39] but, even so, it must be remembered that the professed humility and abjectness of the medieval lover disappeared from English literature only after the seventeenth century. Wyatt had, of course, once expressed a protest in "Farewell, Love, and all thy laws forever," [40] but this note of rebellion is rare enough in the sixteenth century for Cavalier verse such as Suckling's "Why so pale and wan, fond lover" to be a refreshing and salutary check to the notion that looking ill would win the lady when looking well could not and that being mute would prevail when speaking did not. The Elizabethan sonneteers wrote rather less of paleness and dumbness than of other physical manifestations of fidelity in love; yet, even so, the medieval codes with their Ovidian analogies are only too well represented in their work.

A discussion here, however, of all the sighs and tears, despair and impending death of any sonneteer would be a gratuitous performance.[41] Sighs, tears, despair, particularly impending death seem far less lugubrious in the romances of Chrétien de Troyes and in the works of Dante and Petrarch than in the verse of the

Elizabethan poets. In England the situation is not that of sonneteers an unconscionable time a-dying from wanhope and despair, but rather that of poets expending unconscionable energy
in describing the subject in the only manner known to them. To
be sure, the search for new bottles for old wine brought to light
some very strange bottles, but that is scarcely surprising. The
problems confronting the poets as craftsmen were those of the
choice of conceits for showing the volume of sighs and the depth
of despair or for calling loudly upon death in the comfortable assurance that the call would go unheard.

And Sidney—how did the young courtier turn these conventional themes to his own use in seeking favor at the hands of
Penelope Devereux, married to the rich Lord Rich? For one
thing, he invested them with a greater variety of mood than
does any one of his followers; for another, he touched them more
deftly than any other poet by inserting them into contemporary
contexts. He once protests, in bantering vein, because Stella bestows her pity upon the unknown lovers of a tale she read, yet
refuses it to him even when she sees in his beclouded stormy face
the very face of woe itself (No. XLV). Twice he exclaims against
having to rejoice in his own pain: Stella sings so sweetly the
songs he writes of his grief—in "the thoroughest words, fit for
woe's self to groan"—that he can do no other (Nos. LVII–
LVIII).⁴²

Lightness of touch in Sidney comes, too, from restraint. A line
or two is often the extent of a concept developed by other poets to
the length of the entire sonnet. One sonnet (No. LXII), for example, begins:

> Late tired with woe, even ready for to pine
> With rage of love, I called my love unkind.

Sonnet LXI, really about the behavior required of him by Stella,
disposes in two lines of four separate Petrarchan manifestations
of love:

Oft with true sighs, oft with uncalled tears,
Now with slow words, now with dumb eloquence,
I Stella's eyes assailed, invade her ears.

Again, he refers to his woe by saying that he wishes his muse,
who had long drunk his tears, to enjoy "nectar of mirth" after
Stella has admitted her love for him, but is warned by the muse
that wise silence is the best music for bliss (No. LXX).

His mood ranges from that in the sonnets on his distress at
having vexed Stella (Nos. LXXXVI and XCIII) to those recording the deeper pain of separation. Sighs and sorrows are the
theme of No. XCV—sighs which are his best friends because
they do not desert him. When the "iron laws of duty" cause him
to part from Stella, he wept over her sighs, tears, and sad words,
yet "swam in joy" at these evidences of her affection (No.
LXXXVII). In more serious vein, he describes the horrors with
which the silence of the night paint woe's black face (No. XCIV):

Grief! find the words! For thou hast made my brain
So dark with misty vapours, which arise
From out thy heavy mould, that inbent eyes
Can scarce discern the shape of mine own pain.

Even more serious is his sonnet (No. CVIII) on despair ending:

Most rude Despair, my daily unbidden guest,
Clips straight my wings, straight wraps me in his night.
And makes me then bow down my head, and say,
"Ah what does Phoebus' gold that wretch avail,
Whom iron doors do keep from use of day?"
So strangely, alas, thy works in me prevail:
That in my woes for thee, thou art my joy;
And in my joys for thee, my only annoy.

Few, if any, of Sidney's followers exercised his restraint in the
use of these themes. Conceits describing sighs and tears, despair
and death, are mere padding in the hands of some writers,[43] but,
in others, notably Constable, Fletcher, and Griffin, are the re-
curring motif which gives a semblance of unity and purpose to

the cycles.[44] Then, too, as might be expected, the writers of pastoral sonnets—Lodge, Smith, and Watson [45]—make extravagant use of them. Nowhere, however, is the poet's weeping so nearly what Tennyson would have termed idle tears rather than those coming from the depth of some divine despair as it is in Watson's *The Tears of Fancie or Love Disdained*. The pastoral narrative makes it so difficult to distinguish between the versions that only a few examples will suffice: The poet's tears water the grass and make the trees grow; they form wells; floods of them drown his heart; his smoky sighs are like seas that are never calm; he will die from disdain—and so on through most of the sixty sonnets of the cycle. Other works of this period in England indicate that titles containing the word *tears* were generally reserved for serious subjects—Spenser's *The Teares of the Muses,* Nash's *Christ's Tears over Jerusalem,* Gervaise Markham's *Tears of the Beloved* [the lamentation of St. John], Robert Southwell's *Mary Magdalen's Funeral Tears,* and so forth. Later sequences abound in allusions to tears, but, in all likelihood, such sonnets were not inspired by *The Tears of Fancie.* It may be observed in passing that several poets describe tears in the terms (from alchemy) of distillation.[46] The best example is Shakespeare's No. CXIX:

> What potions have I drunk of Siren tears
> Distill'd from limbechs foul as hell within.

Other sequences, especially those of Barnes and Drayton, and, at times, even that of Spenser, are marred by hyperbole in the versions of these conceits. Barnes writes accounts such as the following: [47] Whether he sues with sighs or complains with tears, nothing will soften Parthenophe's heart. The fountains of his tears reveal the torments in which he dwells; the tears that wash his cheeks are endless; his sighs are the smoke from the fiery pain in his heart; the four elements combine in a fearful and wonderful manner against him. A river in full tide flows from his face. The extent of his sincerity in longing for death may be gauged by the sonnet (No. LXXX) which bequeaths each phase of his grief to some element in nature. The poem begins:

> Long-wished-for death! sent by my mistress' doom;
> Hold! Take thy prisoner, full resolved to die!

The hyperbole which characterizes such themes in Drayton's sonnets results from his desire for variety in style. The 1602 edition says, in Sonnet XII:

> As other men, so I myself, do muse
> Why in this sort I wrest invention so?
> And why these giddy metaphors I use,
> Leaving the path the greater part do go?

The sonnets after the 1594 "Ideas Mirrour" show technical improvements, to be sure, but little advance in the matter of sincerity of tone or the consistency of metaphors. A case in question is a sonnet (No. VII, which first appeared in 1599) beginning "Love, in a humour, played the prodigal." Watson's *Hecacompathia* (No. XLII) may have given him the initial idea of love inviting guests to a banquet. Constable, one supposes, furnishes a further hint (Dec. I, No. 6) when he writes of "a glutton eye, with tears drunk every night," or Drayton may even have had in mind a line in Sidney (No. LXX) which says that his muse had often drunk his tears. Drayton, however, "wresting invention," represents love (that is, Cupid), as inviting the poet's senses to a banquet at which he drinks only the poet's tears and eats only his sighs, and then, in his drunkenness, as slaying his guest. Even such a sonnet as that called "Love's Lunacy" in the 1594 edition (No. XLI in later editions), representing the poet as railing and raving in his grief like a bedlamite, is to be preferred to one (No. XXV) of 1599 in which he considers sending his verses to Scotland, where his sighs are to thaw the frozen seas, and to Ireland, where the bards who hear his lines will be enabled to calm the stiff-necked rebels. Or, for that matter, to the sonnet of 1599 (No. LIV) which terms his sonnets the dreary abstracts of his woe: smoked by his sighs, blotted by his tears, they are offered as incense to Idea. If poems such as these are really meant to represent any real feeling of Drayton for Anne Goodere, they seem truly, as Lamb says of certain of Milton's sonnets, to set forth love in a strange fashion.

Spenser, too, often recounts his sighs and tears in a manner sufficiently illustrated here by two sonnets: one says that he plays a tragic role on the stage of life but is rewarded with laughter, and another, that he fries in love and longs for death.[48] Daniel's descriptions are plaintive rather than extravagant and are one of the reasons for thinking that his sonnets are addressed to someone higher in rank than he.[49]

Shakespeare's poems which employ such ideas are poles apart from the ordinary Elizabethan sonnet. No. LXVI begins: "Tired with all these, for restful death I cry." Nothing in Drayton or Spenser equals Shakespeare's No. CXXXIII:

> Beshrew that heart that makes my heart to groan
> For that deep wound it gives my friend and me!
> Is't not enough to torture me alone
> But slave to slavery my sweet'st friend must be?

He does not represent love or his muse as drinking his tears; instead, he says (No. CXIX):

> What potions have I drunk of Siren tears
> Distill'd from limbechs foul as hell within;
> Applying fears to hopes and hopes to fears,
> Still losing when I saw myself to win!

The last of these distressing Petrarchan symptoms of love to be mentioned is that of the conflicting, contrary feelings evoked by the emotion of love. Few later versions, however, of the conceit surpass Wyatt's Petrarchan translation which begins:

> I find no peace, and all my warre is done:
> I feare, and hope: I burne and frese like yse.

I flye aloft, yet can I not arise:
And nought I haue, and all the worlde I season.

[i. e., *seize on*.]

Lodge, who wrote three sonnets of this kind, has one which comes through Ronsard: [50]

I hope and fear, I pray and hold my peace,
Now freeze my thoughts and straight they fry again.

. . .

This likes me most that leaves me discontent,

Barnes (No. XXXI) expresses in ejaculatory half-lines the contrarieties he endures: "I burn, yet am I cold! I am a cold, yet burn!" Fletcher's Sonnets VIII and XXXI belong to this group; Constable begins one sonnet (Dec. IV, No. 1), "Needs must I leave, and yet needs must I love" and another (Dec. VI, No. 2), "To live in hell, and heaven to behold." Drayton's No. XIX, "To Humour," uses this method of showing the indecision of the lady who will neither love nor hate, nor yet give up the poet. His Sonnet XXVI, "To Despair," is really to Hope; his No. LXII, "When first I ended, then I first began," is one technically of the most carefully worked-out sonnets written on this theme. Tofte (Pt. I, No. 34) turns these contrarieties into cold chilly frost and fiery flaming smoke; into freezing ice that became a burning flame.

Spenser has a sonnet (No. XXX) beginning "My love is like to ice, and I to fire." He employs the idea as an undertone in Nos. XXXII and XLVII, and, in No. XLII, says that the love that torments him is pleasing in his extremest pain and that the more his sorrow increases, the more he loves and embraces his bane. In none of these, however, is there the spirited, humorous note found in Sidney (No. LX) of the "fierce love and lovely hate" he endures:

Then some good body tell me how I do!
Whose presence, absence; absence, presence is:
Blessed is my curse, and cursed is my bliss.[51]

THE THEME OF ABSENCE

FEW SONNETS in the Elizabethan sequences give the reader a more definite conviction that he can distinguish fact from simulation and reality from a mere imitation than those on the theme of absence. Sidney's final sonnets of the 1591 edition, as well as those first printed in 1598, have convincing circumstances of time and place; Spenser's separation from the lady of the *Amoretti* can hardly, one feels, be merely a conventional Petrarchan ending. If Shakespeare's sorrow at his absences from his friend Will "be error and upon us proved," then, one feels, no man ever wrote down his own experience. But, in reality, we cannot be sure and must keep the doubt in mind.

It is well enough, too, to recall a statement or two made in the introductory chapter of this study: Petrarch's sonnets written after the death of Laura have no parallels in the English cycles under discussion, for none of the English poets laments the death of the loved one. The cycles of Sidney and of Spenser close with sonnets on the sadness of separation, but most of the cycles have no such conclusive ending; they merely come to a close with a plea for the pity of the lady, while that of Tofte actually has a happy ending. Petrarch wrote sonnets before the death of Laura, however, on the sorrows of temporary partings and absences, and it was to these phases of his cycle that his English imitators turned. Daniel, for instance, writes sonnets during a visit in Italy (Nos. XLVII–XLVIII), and Tofte signs many poems with the names of Italian cities from which they purport to be sent. *Zepheria* has a sonnet anticipating the sorrows of separation; Lodge and Griffin treat the theme as one part of the contrary passions endured by a lover.[52] Greville has several poems in different meters which employ conventional phrases yet are typically his own philosophical adaptations.[53]

Sidney's sonnets on this theme of absence are usually so specific

and realistic that they must surely disturb the commentators who
consider the cycle solely a product of literary convention and as
having no autobiographical reality. Sidney gives a characteristically witty version (No. LVI) in a remonstrance against patience in absence:

> Fie, school of Patience, fie! Your lesson is
> Far, far too long to learn it without book.
> What, a whole week without one piece of look?

At another time, he protests in impetuous fashion to an uncom-
municative friend who merely says that he left Stella well (No.
XCII):

> Be your words made, good sir, of Indian ware,
> That you allow me them by so small rate?
> Or do you cutted Spartan's imitate?
> Or do you mean my tender ears to spare?

The poet demands explicit details: [54]

> I would know whether she sit or walk?
> How clothed? how waited on? sighed she or smiled?
> Whereof? with whom? how often did she talk?
> With what pastime Time's journey she beguiled?
> If her lips deigned to sweeten my poor name?

Sidney's cycle gives a definite conviction of reality in that he
often refers to the reasons for his absence from Stella. Although
these allusions are, unfortunately, not clear today, they appear to
be messages that would be clear enough to the recipient of the
sonnets: "Honour's cruel might" (No. XCI) may be either a personal or a political matter; "iron laws of duty" (No. LXXXVII)
and "this great cause which needs both use and art" (No. CVII)
must surely refer to duties imposed by his sovereign. Different
absences seem to be recorded in his references to the ladies who
seek to cheer him in his absences from Stella.[55] Again, he says
that he has been "thence, thence, so far thence" that almost no
spark of comfort has dared come to the "dungeon dark" where

"rigour's exile locks up all my sense" (No. CIV). Another absence is self-imposed:[56]

> Finding those beams, which I must ever love,
> To mar my mind; and with my hurt, to please;
> I deemed it best some absence for to prove
> If further place might further me to ease.

Perhaps some time elapsed between the writing of the cycle proper and that of the sonnets published in 1598 by his sister, including that in which he states that the stars "with their strange course" have forced him to leave his beloved. Absence is there compared to death:[57]

> Oft have I mused, but now at length I find
> Why those that die, men say, "they do depart."
> Depart! A word so gentle, to my mind,
> Weakly did seem to paint death's ugly dart.
> But now the stars with their strange course do bind
> Me one to leave, with whom I leave my heart:
> I hear a cry of spirits, faint and blind,
> That parting thus, my chiefest part I part.

Others of his sonnets on absence use his favorite figure of Stella as the star that gives him light; when that star is removed, his light is withdrawn.[58] Among these is the last sonnet of the 1591 edition (No. CVIII, on despair).

Spenser's sonnets on absence include those already mentioned in connection with the theme of night and sleep. He turned to his own use, too, Petrarch's comparison of the lost fawn and, in his closing sonnets, of the bird lamenting its mate—sonnets which will be mentioned more fully in the following section of this part on similes drawn from natural history. In another sonnet on absence (No. LII) he compares himself to a prisoner to pain who wishes no joy or pleasure to come to him, only "sudden dumps, and dreary sad disdain" of all the world's gladness. Last but one of his sonnets is a comparison of absence to darkness lighted only by "beholding the Idæa plain."

The English sonnet had indeed traveled a long way from its Tudor beginnings of Petrarchan translations when it could produce poems such as Shakespeare's Sonnet XCVIII:

> From you have I been absent in the spring,
> When proud-pied April, dressed in all his trim,
> Hath put a spirit of youth in everything . . .
> Yet seemed it winter still, and, you away,
> As with your shadow I with these did play.

Then, too, there is Shakespeare's famous comparison of absence to winter (No. XCVII):

> How like a winter hath my absence been
> From thee, the pleasure of the fleeting year!
> What freezings have I felt, what dark days seen!
> What old December's bareness everywhere!

Nothing in the other sequences parallels the two Shakespearean sonnets comparing the poet to a slave in his unhappiness at the unexplained absences of Will. No. LVII says:

> Being your slave, what should I do but tend
> Upon the hours and times of your desire? . . .
> Nor dare I chide the world-without-end hour
> Whilst I, my sovereign, watch the clock for you,
> Nor think the bitterness of absence sour
> When you have bid your servant once adieu;
> Nor dare I question with my jealous thought
> Where you may be, or your affairs suppose . . .

No. LVIII also shows the poet's enslavement to the whims of Will:

> I am to wait, though waiting so be hell,
> Nor blame your pleasure, be it ill or well.

Nor is there an Elizabethan parallel for Sonnet CXIII. When he is absent from Will, his sadness makes him oblivious to his surroundings:

> Since I left you mine eye is in my mind
> And that which governs me to go about

Doth part his function and is partly blind . . .
For it no form delivers to the heart
Of bird, of flower, or shape which it doth latch . . .

CONVENTIONAL COMPARISONS

SLEEPLESSNESS, weeping, the vagaries of a runaway heart, and the pangs of absence were by no means the Petrarchist's only means of revealing the sorrows of his unrequited love. He adapted as well to his own needs and circumstances comparisons from natural history, mythology, and everyday life: his state was that of a trapped bird or ship lost at sea; his sufferings were greater than those of Prometheus and Acteon. Few aspects of Elizabethan verse better illustrate the fact that Renaissance imitation meant individual expression of themes sanctioned by usage than do such sonnets.

The convention of using beast similes to set forth the state of the lover and of the unhappiness caused by his unrequited love is a derivation from Provençal rather than from early Italian verse, for the early Italian bestiaries used animal similes only to illustrate the spiritual life.[59] Definite sources cannot be pointed out, for, as Garver states, the influence of Provençal verse made itself felt through oral, not written, sources until the middle of the twelfth century.[60] About that time manuscript collections of Provençal verse began to be available in Italy and Italian imitations of them increased. Giacomo da Lentino, Pier delle Vigne, and the other Sicilians use figures drawn from the phoenix, panther, basilisk, dragon, eagle, peacock, lion, swan, salamander, and butterfly. All but four of these comparisons are found in Provençal verse. Among the early Italian poets the most influential ones in carrying on these comparisons were Guittone D'Arezzo and Dante da Maiano. Petrarch often uses such similes, among them those of a moth, stag, fish, faun, fox, and several birds. Many, particularly those in which after the death of Laura he compares himself to a bird mourning its mate, are of great beauty.

Such similes are a commonplace in later literature. In the English cycles, however, Sidney's infrequent use of them—he has fewer than any other English sonneteer—recalls his prose protests against the extravagant use of them in "certain printed discourses" [*Euphues,* perhaps]. The well-known passage from the *Defense of Poesie* is as follows:

Now for similitudes, in certain printed discourses, I think all Herbarists, all stories of Beasts, Foules, and Fishes, are rifled up, that they come in multitudes, to waite upon any of our conceits; which certainly is as absurd a surfeit to the ears as is possible.

One of Sidney's most beautiful sonnets, however, is based upon the term from falconry of "seeling" the eyes of a bird, or taming it by stitching up its eyelids with a thread tied behind its head. A seeled dove, Sidney says, is neither free nor yet "to service bound," and, although it flies high in the air trying to gain help for itself, it falls at last from exhaustion. So he himself has received his own hurt, with neither "leave to live nor doom to die," neither "held in evil nor suffered to be sound":

> But with his wings of fancies, up he goes
> To high conceits whose fruits are oft but small,
> Till wounded, blind and wearied spirit lose
> Both force to fly, and knowledge where to fall.
> O happy dove, if she no bondage tried!
> More happy I, might I in bondage 'bide! [61]

The *Arcadia,* it may be noted in passing, also refers to a seeled dove, "who, the blinder she was, the higher she strave." [62]

The comparisons drawn from birds provide even the minor sonneteers with the themes of some of their best sonnets and are the sources of some of the lines freest from affectation. A mere versifier such as Linche writes in Sonnet XXVI:

> Look, as a bird sore bruised with a blow
> (lately dividing notes most sweetly singing)

To hear her fellows, how in tunes they flow,
  doth droop and pine, as though her knell were ringing.

Again, Linche's comparison is (No. XXII):

Look, as a bird through sweetness of the call
Doth clean forget the fowler's guileful trap.

Griffin, another mere versifier, thus expresses (No. XXVI) this conceit of the trapped bird:

The silly bird that hastes unto the net,
  And flutters to and fro till she be taken,
Doth look some food or succor there to get,
  But loseth life: so much is she mistaken! . . .
These did through folly perish all and die:
And, though I know it, even so do I!

When the minor poets are consistent and pleasing in such comparisons, we might reasonably expect distinguished verse from so great a poet as Spenser. Unfortunately, however, his work here is particularly indebted to foreign sources and is at times almost wholly translation, yet, even so, these translations and adaptations are striking and sometimes of genuine beauty: No. LXXIII, from Tasso,[63] tells how the poet's heart flies to the lady as a bird flies to the food it desires. She is to "encage" the heart, or bird, gently, so that it will learn to be her thrall and to sing her praises. No. LXV, which has several analogues, among them Tebaldeo,[64] is of the caged bird which enjoys its captivity. Since Spenser reverses the usual comparison and makes it apply to the lady instead of to himself,[65] Renwick suggests that Spenser thus makes the sonnet allude to marriage: [66]

The doubt which ye misdeem, fair love, is vain,
That fondly fear to lose your liberty . . .
The gentle bird feels no captivity
Within her cage, but sings, and feeds her fill . . .

Petrarch's final sonnet of the bird mourning its mate has its finest English counterpart in Spenser:

Like as the culver, on the bared bough,
Sits mourning for the absence of her mate;
And, in her songs, sends many a wishful vow
For his return that seems to linger late:
So I alone, now left disconsolate,
Mourn to myself the absence of my love;
And, wandering here and there all desolate,
Seek with my plaints to match that mournful dove.

Shakespeare refers to birds only twice in his sonnets. One (No. CII) is a comparison to the song of the nightingale: as Philomel sometimes withholds her song lest it lose its appeal, so he too withholds his verse so that his love may be strengthened, though "more weak in seeming." The other (No. XXIX) is one of his justly famous comparisons to the skylark—a bird, it may be observed, specified by no other sonneteer. The simile here is less striking, perhaps, than the image in the lyric "Hark, Hark the Lark," but it is the best expression in a sonnet of a comparison to a bird:

Haply I think on thee, and then my state,
Like to the lark at break of day arising
From sullen earth, sings hymns at heaven's gate.

As a matter of fact, almost the only sonnet allusions to a specific bird are those to the phoenix.[67] This comparison, however, although variously adapted, produced no very satisfactory results. The immortality of the bird is the aspect of the story which appealed to Daniel and Fletcher: Daniel hopes that his verse, phoenix-like, will make Delia live anew (No. XXXIII);[68] Fletcher professes to wish to rise again, phoenix-like, from the fire of his love (No. XV). Other poets base their comparisons upon the fire in which the phoenix burns: Lodge (No. XXV), compares himself to the phoenix in love's fire; Smith burns, he professes, like the phoenix in a fire of sighs and tears (No. XXIII); and Drayton compares his life to a phoenix in the fire of his soul (1594, No. XXXII). Also, as Petrarch compared Laura to the phoenix, Sidney alludes to Stella (No. XCII) as "Phoenix Stella," and Drayton compares Idea to the bird (No. XVI).

These comparisons with birds were, naturally, commonplace or conventional at times, as when Constable compares Diana's golden hair to the net which ensnared him, a bird already taken who needed no net to be caught (Dec. II, No. 8); and when Tofte compares himself to a caged bird depending upon his captor for food (Pt. I, No. 36). Hyperbole, too, is found in Drayton's involved figure describing his love as an eaglet which is born within his breast and sent forth into the air to prove its kingliness (No. LVI) and in Tofte's comparison of himself as "Beauty's buzzard" caught in Cupid's snare (Pt. I, No. 9).

The conventional comparisons of the poet's state which are drawn from natural history include many figures based upon animals. Some of the most consistent and poetic ones are the personifications of the thoughts of the poet as hounds. Both Daniel and Griffin use this simile and compare themselves to Acteon. Sidney, incidentally, has a charming lyric in the *Arcadia* beginning "My thoughts are sheep which I both guide and serve." Daniel's version (No. V) is: "My thoughts, like hounds, pursue me to my death." Lodge (No. XXXI) writes: "My hounds are thoughts, and rage, despairing, blind." Griffin (No. VIII) thus states the same idea:

> These breed such thoughts as set my heart on fire
> And like fell hounds, pursue me to my death.

With these figures may be compared a passage in *Twelfth Night* (Act I, scene 1, ll. 21–23) substituting *desires* for *thoughts:*

> That instant was I burned into a hart,
> And my desires, like fell and cruel hounds,
> E'er since pursue me.

Other comparisons, the best, perhaps, of this group, are based upon figures of the hunt. Word play is skillfully presented in Drayton's sonnet comparing his heart to a hart which comes to gaze at Diana's eyes and is shot with Cupid's arrow,[69] and in Watson's comparison of his heart to a hart pursued by hounds (No. LVII). Several poets make use of comparisons of a wounded or frightened deer,[70] yet none is in any way comparable to Spenser's adaptation from Petrarch of the lost fawn (No. LXXVIII): [71]

> Lacking my love, I go from place to place,
> Like a young fawn, that late hath lost the hind.

Spenser has a fine sonnet (No. LXVII), moreover, of the gentle deer which allows itself to be captured by the tired huntsman after the hunt has ended: [72]

> Like as a huntsman after weary chase,
> Seeing the game from him escap'd away,
> Sits down to rest him in some shady place,
> With panting hounds beguiled of their prey:
> So, after long pursuit and vain assay,
> When I all weary had the chase forsook,
> The gentle deer returned the self-same way,
> Thinking to quench her thirst at the next brook:
> There she, beholding me with milder look,
> Sought not to fly, but fearless still did bide
> Till I in hand her yet half trembling took,
> And with her own goodwill her firmly tied.
> Strange thing, me seemed, to see a beast so wild,
> So goodly won, with her own will beguil'd.

Spenser also wrote a brief, forceful comparison of himself to a steed: after the long race that he has run through Faeryland, "half foredone" with its six books, he asks leave to rest and gain new breath (No. LXXX):

> Then, as a steed refreshed after toil,
> Out of my prison I will break anew;
> And stoutly will that second work assoil
> With strong endeavour and attention due.

The brief miscellaneous similes comparing the lover to a salamander, gnat, fly, spider, scorpion, boar, or mole [73] may be illustrated by the difference in taste shown in the work of Sidney and Drayton: the darkness endured by the mole gives Sidney an analogy for his own state when the light of Stella's presence is withdrawn; [74] Drayton writes "yet with the mole I creep into the earth" (No. LXII). The same figure shows, too, how Tofte (Pt. II, No. 2) could distort an image—Laura, the "mole of love," is urged to keep her bright eyes underground! One other of these general comparisons may be mentioned. Perhaps the most abject comparison in the cycles is that of Griffin (No. XXVII) of himself to a worm—"thy fellow worm," yet in even a worse state than it, because the worm enjoys its sun while the poet lacks his. All this, apparently, merely because Sidney (No. XCVIII) had written that at dawn his eyes only wink and do not open for spite that even worms have their sun while he lacks his.

The conventional images drawn from classical sources are, when compared with those drawn from natural history, either disappointingly stiff and unyielding or filled with hyperbole.[75] Fortunately, they are rather infrequent and usually allude briefly to the poet's hardship as equalling or surpassing that of Atlas, Ixion, or others.[76] Lodge, for example, says (No. III): "In fancy's world an Atlas have I been." And Sidney (No. LI) writes:

> But find some Hercules to bear (instead
> Of Atlas tired) your wisdom's heavenly sway.

Drayton alludes to his turning upon the wheel with Ixion (No. XL); Watson and Barnes affirm that gazing upon the lady is like gazing upon Medusa. Drayton, for once plausible and consistent, says (No. XLV):

> Whilst I, like Orpheus, sing to trees and stones.
> Which with my plaint seem yet with pity moved;
> Kinder than she whom I so long have loved.

The story of Leander illustrates the inept manner in which these comparisons were utilized at greater length: Daniel professes that he will be able to forget his wounds and grief if Delia will waft him, her "Leander striving in these waves," to her eyes as a happy convoy to a holy land (No. XLI). The author of *Zepheria* states that since Zepheria has not sent the rays of light from her eyes to aid him as Hero aided "arm-finned" Leander, he, her poor Leander, is drowned in the deep (No. VIII). Griffin (No. XIII) compares himself to Leander struggling in vain in the waves; Smith (No. XVII) promises to undertake to swim "ocean seas" if Chloris will pity him. Fletcher has two sonnets on Charon,[77] one of them saying that since Licia's coldness is such that she will fill the Styx with ice, Charon will be unable to ferry her across unless he will allow the poet to come along: if he is allowed to gaze at Licia, he will blow upon the ice sighs so hot that they will melt it.

The images derived from the story of Prometheus appear to have acquired their hyperbole in chronological fashion. Sidney (No. XIV) does not mention Prometheus by name, but says merely that the pain in his heart is a "fiercer gripe" than that which seized "him who first stole down the fire." Daniel (No. XV) speaks of a "vulture-gnawen heart." Barnes stole fire, he says, not as Prometheus did, from heaven, but from the eyes of Parthenophe, and, as punishment, he has been chained to the rock of her hard heart and is tortured by the vulture despair (No. LXI). Constable writes of stealing living fire from the beauty of Diana so that his verse may live. As punishment, however, he is bound to her feet in chains of love where, like poor Prometheus, he fries in "scalding fire" in the brightness of her beauty (Dec. V, No. 10). Tofte characteristically carries the image beyond all plausibility: He has stolen fire from Laura, his heaven above; the heat warms his dying spirit, but his punishment is far greater than that of Prometheus, for thousands of vultures gnaw upon his heart (Pt. I, No. 8). Drayton (No. XIV) reverses the figure and has the theft committed by Idea, a greater thief than Prometheus. He stole only fire, yet Idea, who stole virtue, honor, wit, and beauty from heaven's store, goes unpunished.

A few of these classical comparisons are worked out carefully enough to be reasonably convincing. Daniel, for example (No. XIII), compared his unhappiness in trying to win the lady's flinty heart to the happiness of Pygmalion, who worked merely upon stone. Spenser (No. XLIV) describes his mental conflict by saying he cannot quiet his warring feelings as Orpheus had conquered the quarreling peers of Greece. Comparisons of the poets to any one of several objects or persons of everyday life are, however, more often characterized by skill than are those to classical personages. A tree beaten by storm, a pine destroyed by winter,[78] a seafarer or a shipwrecked mariner,[79] or, in the Petrarchan manner, a ship lost at sea because the stars which should have guided it—the lady's eyes, of course—are hidden, are comparisons which are often clothed in a semblance of reality. Sometimes a couplet serves for this last comparison, as in Watson's figure of a mastless ship (No. LIII), but more often an entire sonnet is given to it, as in Spenser's fine sonnet (No. XXXIV) of the lodestar of his life which will shine again when the storm is past.[80] Daniel, too, describes the manner in which Delia's eyes have falsely lured his boat to destruction.[81]

The outstanding characteristic—or weakness, perhaps—of these images drawn from ships is the allegory which sets forth the central idea of the lady's eyes as the cause of the shipwreck. Lodge writes (No. XI) that his frail, earthly bark, guided by reason, is filled with waves of love. Barnes complains of feeble anchors, faint-hearted pilots, of fortune's ballast, and a voyage that will not be worth "two chips," for his "thoughts-drowned mariners" press toward the whirlpool of "grief's endless glut" (No. XXI). Again, Barnes compares his heart to a ship never free from danger (No. LXXXII). Drayton (1594, No. XXXIV) terms his soul the barque of sorrow, left to the mercy of the winds and waves, floating to the fair islands of the lady's eyes.

Here, too, we may observe the manner in which one minor English poet imitated another. Barnes writes of the fear that his thoughts' swift pinnace might suffer from the hard rock of Parthenophe's heart. If the pinnace were shipwrecked, she might feel remorse, but it would then be too late to aid him (No. XCI):

> Now when thy mercies all been banished
> And blown upon thine hard rock's ruthless shelf;
> My soul in sighs is spent and vanished.
> Be pitiful, alas! and take remorse!
> Thy beauty too much practiseth his force!

In *Zepheria* (No. XXXIX, imitating Barnes) the hopes of the author embarked, safely enough, upon Zepheria's calm smiles. The voyage, however, seems to have been disastrous—certainly the poet's diction leaves the reader stranded:

> Now, on the shelf of her brows' proud disdain
> A harbour, where they looked for asile,
> The pilot who, 'fore now, did expect rain,
> His bark in seas are all ydrenched, alack the while!
> Tell if, at least, she all, through fear, excordiate
> Command thee not to peace, ere thou exordiate!

Shakespeare draws his famous metaphors from nature or from daily life,[82] rarely from the figures echoing the conventions of the Middle Ages. For example, his friend Will effects his thoughts as food does life or as showers do the ground (No. LXXV). Again, his delight in Will is like that of a decrepit father in his active child (No. XXXVII). He compares himself, too, to a rich man who unlocks his treasures rarely that he may enjoy them the more (No. LII); and, in his unhappiness in waiting for Will, twice compares himself to a slave (Nos. LVII–LVIII).

The two Shakespearean sonnets which do contain conventional images have comparisons derived from ships, and both refer to the "rival" poet. The first (No. LXXX) compares his own "saucy bark"—his verse—to that of his rival: his boat is worthless, he feels, while that of his rival is "of tall building and of goodly pride." The second allusion (No. LXXXVI), of only two lines, is the basis of much of the discussion, none of which has a place

here, of the identity of the rival poet who won the affections of
Will:

> Was it the proud full sail of his great verse,
> Bound for the prize of all too precious you?

THE "MIRROR" CONCEIT

THE TWO sonnets of Petrarch in which he inveighs against
Laura's mirror because it makes her disregard him [83] give
later Petrarchists a favorite conceit for expressing the woes caused
by the lady's disregard of the poet. Daniel's thirty-second sonnet
furnishes the aspects of the conceit imitated in England: [84]

> Why doth my mistress credit so her glass,
> Gazing her beauty, deigned her by the skies
> And does not rather look on him, alas,
> Whose state best shows the force of murdering eyes? . . .
> Then leave your glass and gaze yourself on me!
> That mirror shows the power of your face.

Spenser follows the convention closely in one quatrain (No.
XLV):

> Leave, lady, in your glass of crystal clean
> Your goodly self for evermore to view,
> And in myself, my inward self, I mean,
> Most lively like behold your semblance true.

The image in his heart is dimmed and distorted, however, by
the sorrow caused by the cruelty of the lady; and, if she will see
herself plainly reflected in the mirror of his heart, she must remove the cause which darkens her beams.

Griffin uses this conceit with great literalness (No. XXXIII):
His face, the mirror for Fidessa's image, reveals her cruelty. If he
could spare her the humiliation of having that cruelty known to
the world, he would pluck out his silver hairs, wash the wrinkles
from his face, and live as "closely immured" as if he were dead.

He cannot hide, however, what is already known: "I have been seen, and have no face but one!" Linche (No. XXIII) likewise makes a plea for pity because of his unhappy state:

> If thou wouldst look, this my tear-stained face,
>   dreary and wan, far differing from what it was,
> Would well reveal my most tormentful case,
>   and show thy Fair, my Grief as in a glass.

Tofte's *Laura* is the only sonnet cycle where this conceit secures for the poet a favorable reply (Pt. III, No. 17). The poet asks that Laura no longer seek to see her beauty reflected in the water, but see it in his face. Her response is a radical departure from the Petrarchan convention:

> . . . when she answered blive,
> "And thou, my Love! say, Dost thou likewise wish
> To see thyself in one that is alive?
> Then in this breast, look where thine image is!
>   Love shall alike in both our bodies rest;
>   Bear thou me in thine eyes; I'll thee in breast!"

There is a second cheerful version in Tofte (Pt. III, No. 25) of Laura's having broken her mirror. The poet bids her look upon his heart, and she is content in having a new glass for the broken one.

The "mirror" conceit serves, however, a more important purpose for the poet in that his verse, more often than his face, is described as the place in which the lady could see his love reflected. Sidney, in a dialogue with himself concerning his reasons for writing, makes a brief allusion (No. XXXIV) which is natural and appropriate:

> Come, let me write. "And to what end?" To ease
> A burdened heart. "How can words ease, which are
> The glasses of thy daily vexing care?"

Watson has this figure in mind in his thirty-second sonnet: the lady, having consented to look into the well made by his tears of fancy, sees her beauty reflected, but, instead of shedding the tears of pity the poet has longed for, is so puffed up with pride that she will not shed a tear even if he dies.

Barnes (No. I) turns the conceit into a compliment to the lady —his verse is the "true speaking glass" not only of her beauty but of his grief. Constable, echoing Sidney, paints his woes in verse that Diana may see her beauty's praise in "glasses of his pain"; Diana is to read the verses thus: "None loves like he! that is, 'None fair like me.'" (Dec. II, No. 1) He says, too, that since she has not been content with "vulgar breath-mirrors," that is, verbal praise, his pen has made her admired by all (Dec. V, No. 5). Griffin's "doleful verse" causes Fidessa to take up the glass (his verse) to see his love, but, having seen herself "in bloody colours cruelly depainted," her prisoner on his knees pleading for grace, she breaks the mirror, and thus the poet loses his labor (No. XIX). Other uses of the mirror conceit were merely to represent the beauty of the lady as the mirror of womankind or of true chastity, a name often applied in the Middle Ages to the Virgin; [85] and to refer to her eyes as the mirror of the lover's "mazed heart." [86]

The "Eternizing" Conceit

THE FINAL sets of themes by means of which the baleful effects of love were set forth are the conventional explanations and justifications for the writing of the sequences themselves. In one guise or another, all the sonnets are pleas for pity from the lady. Sometimes the plea is stated in a forthright request in an introductory or prefatory sonnet and then repeated at intervals throughout the sequence. At other times it is disguised in sonnets professing that the poet writes, not on his own initiative, but at the mandate of the god of love. Most frequently the poet feels that compassion is due him because of the devotion he has shown in celebrating or making immortal the beauty of the lady. This so-called "eternizing" conceit called forth some of the finest sonnets of the age in the versions written by Daniel, Spenser, and Shakespeare.

The first of these conventional protestations, that of the introductory sonnets stating the poet's desire for pity from the lady, is nowhere so spirited as in Sidney's first sonnet:

> Loving in truth, and fain in verse my love to show,
> That she, dear she, might take some pleasure of my pain,
> Pleasure might cause her read, reading might make her know,
> Knowledge might pity win, and pity grace obtain;
> I sought fit words to paint the blackest face of woe.

Constable affects, on the other hand, the exaggerated humility of the medieval lover:

> Resolved to love, unworthy to obtain,
> I do not favor crave; but humble wise,
> To thee my sighs in verse I sacrifice,
> Only some pity, and no help to gain.

Lodge (No. III) says that his "moan-clad muse" cries out for mercy from one in whom all gifts of Nature are implanted except that of pity. Griffin says, among other things, that his verse is a plea for his heart. Several poets give variety to the fancy by offering advice to the manner in which the cycles should conduct themselves if they ever actually come into the hands of the lady.[87]

If, however, the plea for pity or the revelation of the writer's despair is presented within the sequence rather than at the beginning, the poet usually says that he will continue to unburden his heart, even though he is unheard. Sidney presents the conceit in a dialogue so skillfully written that it deserves a careful reading (No. XXXIV):

> Come, let me write. "And to what end?" To ease
> A burthened heart. "How can words ease, which are
> The glasses of thy daily vexing care?"

Oft, cruel fights well pictured forth do please.
"Art not ashamed to publish thy disease?"
Nay, that may breed my fame. It is so rare.
"But will not wise men think thy words fond ware?"
Then be they close, and so none shall displease.
"What idler thing than speak and not be heard?"
What harder thing than smart and not to speak?
"Peace, foolish wit!" With wit, my wit is marred.
Thus write I, while I doubt to write; and wreak
My harms on ink's poor loss. Perhaps some find
Stella's great powers that so confuse my mind.

Barnes explains that he writes, not because he is heard, but because the writing tires his heart and helps destroy it (No. LIII). Fletcher (No. XXXVI) writes, he says, because he must, although both speech and silence give pain; Daniel (No. VII) says that his degraded hopes force him to "groan out griefs"; Constable sings his sad elegies because Diana flies from him as from misfortune (Dec. V, No. 6) and because she will continue to disdain him unless he speaks and complains (Dec. VII, No. 7).

The poet's writing is often against his will. Sidney (No. XIX) says:

My best wits still their own disgrace invent.
My very ink turns straight to Stella's name;
And yet my words, as them my pen doth frame,
Advise themselves that they are vainly spent.

Barnes (No. XII), in his intention to forget Parthenophe, begins writing of her:

And . . . methinks it's such a sin
As I take pen and paper for to write
Thee to forget, that leaving, I begin!

Sidney several times employs the convention of writing at the dictation or command of love. In No. L he professes the inadequacy of his words, even though written "according to my lord love's own behest"; yet, since he cannot choose but write, he lets the words stand because they bear Stella's name. Nos. III, XXVIII, and XC stress the fact that, if his verse should win fame, he himself deserves no credit.[88] No. XC says:

> For nothing from my wit or will doth flow:
> Since all my words, thy beauty doth indite;
> And love doth hold my hand and makes me write.

This convention of writing at Love's dictation occurs elsewhere. One of the better sonnets (No. XXXI) of Drayton's 1594 edition seems based upon Sidney's dialogue with himself (No. XXXIV) and tells of the strife between Love and Reason over the matter of Drayton's writing:

> Sitting alone, Loue bids me goe and write;
> Reason plucks backe, commaunding me to stay.

Shakespeare, who brought forth a large number of sonnets upon his reasons for writing, twice represents himself as the copying scribe. The first sonnet (No. LXXIX) says:

> Yet what of thee thy poet doth invent
> He robs thee of, and pays it thee again.
> He lends thee virtue, and he stole that word
> For thy behavior; beauty doth he give,
> And found it in thy cheek . . .

The other (No. LXXXIV) says that lean penury dwells in a pen that does not lend some glory to its subject, yet he who writes of Will should do no more than copy what is written there, lest he mar what nature made so clear.

Many of the "writing" conventions profess to reveal the poet's anguish because the lady scorns the tribute of his verse.[89] Others stress the effect that her disfavor—or, very occasionally, her favor —has upon the skill with which the poet writes.[90] Always, however, the beloved is the muse which inspires his verse.[91] The most conventional of all the protestations about writing, the poet's intent to celebrate the beauty of the lady, is also turned into a plea for favor or grace.[92] Such sonnets occur in works dedicated to noble patrons, as those of Daniel and Constable, but, since the minor sonneteers are by no means backward in claiming great beauty for the ladies celebrated in their sequences, the same conceits appear in *Zepheria, Laura, Chloris,* and *The Tears of Fancie.*[93]

The better sonnets upon the theme of writing are those which profess to render the beloved one immortal. This "eternizing" conceit is familiar from Shakespeare's extensive use of it, as in the following lines:

> But thy eternal summer shall not fade
> Nor lose possession of that fair thou owest;
> Nor shall Death brag thou wander'st in his shade,
> When in eternal lines to time thou grow'st:
>   So long as men can breathe or eyes can see,
>   So long lives this, and this gives life to thee.
>
> (No. XVIII)

Sir Sidney Lee has written so extensively both of the origins of this theme (tracing it through Pindar, Sappho, Cicero, Horace, Virgil, Propertius, and Ovid, with Ronsard as the immediate inspiration of the English) and of its use by Shakespeare [94] that mention need be made only of the sonnets other than those of Shakespeare. Sidney not only wrote no "eternizing" sonnets, but he criticized in the *Defense of Poesy* his contemporaries who claimed that their verse would make one immortal. Watson merely says (No. XXXIII) that, since women "droope when as they thinke their faire must die" but enjoy having their beauty exalted by fame's shrill trumpet, he has extolled the lady's beauty. (The lady, however, to whom *The Tears of Fancie* is written—if, indeed, it is written to one—does not have even a conventional name such as Delia or Diana.) Fletcher says (No. L):

> And if my tongue eternize can your praise,
> Or silly speech increase your worthy fame;
> If aught I can, to heaven your worth can raise,
> The age to come shall wonder at the same.

Constable asks for aid in writing that his praise may make Diana live (Dec. II, No. 10) and hopes that at some time he may be able to achieve a higher strain (Dec. VIII, No. 4):

> When reintombing from oblivious ages
> In better stanzas her surviving wonder,
> I may opposed against the monster-rages
> That part desert and excellence asunder;
> That she, though coy, may yet survive to see
> Her beauty's wonder lives again in me.

Seven of Daniel's sonnets are upon this theme.[95] A brief summary will show something of the variety he gives the image: after Delia's beauty yields to the tyrant Time and the flower which so long has fed her pride fades, then his verse is to recall to her what she once was, and, phoenix-like, to make her live anew. When she is old, she is to take the picture of her that is in his verse and see the gifts God and nature lent her, for her beauty will there be kept for posterity. As Laura's name is immortalized by Petrarch, so Delia's memory will not die while the poet's verse is read. She must not grieve that he has revealed to the world how fair she is, for she will live in his verse as if she were engraved in marble, unburied in these lines which entomb her eyes. Fame which cannot be destroyed is conferred by the eternal annals of a happy pen, and therefore she will live in his verses. His verses to her are trophies erected to fortify her name against age and time's consuming rage. His muse desires no fame other than that resulting from eternizing her beauty; he writes only of the Avon where she dwells.

Daniel's preoccupation with this conceit is perhaps to be accounted for by the fact that the dedication of his verse to the Countess of Pembroke caused many of the usual themes of love to be unsuited to his purposes. Drayton, too, wrote many "eternizing" sonnets—some for each edition of his work. The 1594 "Ideas Mirrour" states that his muse is the trumpet of Idea's fame (No. IV), yet, later (No. XLIII), the poet asks why his pen should strive to immortalize the name of one who scorns him. The 1599 edition contains two more sonnets (Nos. XLIII–XLIV) on the theme. One shows the difficulties of trying to eternize her fame: while his pen strives to keep her name from oblivion and the grave, her indifference causes his youth to perish; yet, although his body dies, the best part of him will have been saved. The second sonnet describes his verse as a trophy to her living fame: since she scorns his verse, his bosom will be the hearse wherein the world will entomb her name. In 1605 he speaks of the reward sought in his verse (No. XLVII):

> I in the circuit for the laurel strove,
> Where the full praise, I freely must confess,
> In heat of blood, a modest mind might move.
> With shouts and claps at every little pause,
> When the proud Round on every side hath rung,
> Sadly I sit, unmoved with the applause,
> As though to me it nothing did belong.
> No public glory vainly I pursue:
> All that I seek is to eternize you!

Lastly, in 1619, he gives an account (No. VI) of the many paltry, foolish, painted women now "troubling every street in coaches" who will soon be forgotten, yet her name will live in his verse. Queens will be glad to live upon the alms of her superfluous praise; virgins and matrons will grieve that they have never seen her.

Spenser likewise employs this theme, nowhere so notably as in the famous Sonnet LXXV, an account of his writing his lady's name upon the strand. The waves wash it away, and he writes it a second time. The lady then says that it is in vain to seek to immortalize so mortal a thing, that the memory of her name will likewise pass away. The poet, however, assures her that it will live in his verse and that their love will outlast death itself. Again, Spenser says his verse is vowed to eternity and is a trophy erected to her name (No. LXIX). Finally, he states that if the lady will accept him as her thrall, he will be able to raise her name with fame's trumpet and to fill the world with her praise (No. XXIX).

No matter how preoccupied the sonneteers were, however, with eternizing the name of the lady, they usually wrote with a wary eye upon their contemporary fame. Sidney, to be sure, disclaims both in Sonnet XC and in the *Defense of Poesy* against any right to the name of poet. The more professional poets, however, desired fame, and frankly admitted that such was their aim in writing. Barnabe Barnes is obviously bidding for renown when he adds to his cycle six sonnets to members of the nobility. Smith, dedicating his work to Spenser, begs for kindness to his "weak-penned muse" who tries to fly before her feathers have reached their full perfection; Fletcher's first sonnet admits that it was his wish to be a poet.

The eternizing sonnets of Daniel and Constable [96] intimate that their verses did actually give them contemporary renown. The author of *Zepheria,* however, considers that "untombing" his griefs is honorable indeed in comparison with the aim of the poets who sell the lady's praises as "mercenary writ" to the press. Daniel and Smith indicate their desire for readers who are capable of comprehending the pain recorded in their verse.[97]

Drayton reveals more aspects of the professional poet than any other sonneteer. Even in 1594 (No. XLII) he wrote, perhaps partly as a conventional gesture, but evidently with some truth:

> Some men there be which like my method well,
> And much commend the strangeness of my vein.
> Some say I have a passing pleasing strain,
> Some say that in my humour I excel.

In 1602 he again comments upon the reception of his verse: the critics who say that it proves he is not in love should not judge him too harshly, for, although he "trifles loosely in this sort," he does it as a laugh at fortune, "as in jest to die" (No. XXIV). Drayton's address to the reader in the 1599 edition assures him that no "far-fetched sigh" will ever wound his breast, no tear be

wrung from his eye, no "Ah me's" ever dress his "whining sonnets." Yet his cycle continually belies such statements. In 1599
he wrote:

> My muse is rightly of the English strain
> That cannot long one fashion entertain.

Yet no English sonneteer so often rewrote and re-edited his verse
as did Drayton, and for a quarter of a century he was faithful to
his "Divine Idea," whether she was Mistress Anne Goodere or
merely poetic renown.

The conventional manifestations of love and the portrayal of its
effect upon the poet are thus a part of the background for the
Elizabethan sonnet sequences. The ideas of Ovid, elevated by
chivalry and Platonism and expanded by generations of romanc-
ers and lyricists, provided the common fund of poetic concepts
for later poets. Although the Elizabethan versions sometimes reveal an alacrity in sinking, others are distinguished and beautiful.

THE SONNET LADY

The Conventional Idea of Beauty

THE Petrarchist adapted to his own use not only the conventional themes which enabled him to set forth his love and to analyze his woes but also those which enabled him to describe the beauty of the lady to whom he addressed his verse. For Petrarch's *Canzoniere* expresses at the same time the poet's Platonic belief that Laura's beauty leads to the contemplation of the heavenly good and his very mundane appreciation of that beauty. Every aspect of it is described with so much grace and skill that one need not wonder at the number of imitators who tried to draw Ulysses's bow.

Laura's golden hair, for instance, is described in sonnet after sonnet, comparison after comparison. Her eyes are described in many entire sonnets and three entire canzoni. They are brighter than the sun; absence from them is the darkness of night; they lead the poet to contemplate heaven, for they are the source of his every good. Described dozens of times as *begli occhi,* they are also, more specifically, *occhi lucenti, occhi leggiadri, occhi soavi, occhi sereni,* and *occhi beati.* Laura's appearance upon specific occasions is described—her green gown, her gay apparel, the pearls and chaplets worn in her golden hair. Her voice, her smile, her brow, lips, and teeth, her sighs and tears—hardly a detail is not celebrated time and again.

After the death of Laura, the poet represents her as an angel surrounded by heavenly splendor. She awaits the poet's coming and beckons him to her; she appears to him in a vision and endeavors to console him. This latter half of Petrarch's work, the part marked by the strongest feeling and the most convincing emotion, is, however, without imitation in the English sonneteers under consideration because, as it has already been said, none wrote to a loved one who had died. Most of Petrarch's followers, moreover, use the images of *saint* and *angel* only in the manner of Petrarch's early sonnets as indicating merely superlative grace and beauty.

Dante, on the other hand, had had no need to describe Beatrice in the *Vita nuova* by means of so specific a set of figures as those used by Petrarch for Laura. Although Beatrice is described as having worn in her childhood a red robe and as being "this youngest of the angels," her gentleness and beauty and their effect upon the poet are the things chiefly shown. After her death, she became an angel surrounded by heavenly splendor:

> Beyond the sphere which spreads to widest space
> Now soars the sigh that my heart sends above:
> A new perception born of grieving Love
> Guideth it upward the untrodden ways.
> When it hath reach'd unto the end, and stays,
> It sees a lady round whom splendours move
> In homage; till, by the great light thereof
> Abash'd, the pilgrim spirit stands at gaze.
> It sees her such, that when it tells me this
> Which it hath seen, I understand it not,
> It hath a speech so subtle and so fine.
> And yet I know its voice within my thought
> Often remembereth me of Beatrice:
> So that I understand it, ladies mine.[1]

Yet, although Petrarch's *Canzoniere* was the pattern for all later sonneteers who celebrated the beauty of a lady, the figures of comparisons he used were those which earlier Italian poets had drawn from the storehouse of their Provençal inheritance of poetic ideas. Similarity in theme between the Provençal and Sicilian poets is shown in this as in the other aspects of their verse. Gaspary says, in part, with regard to this analogy:

Der Preis der Dame, die Schilderung ihrer Schönheit und ihres Werthes geschieht in allgemeinen Ausdrücken; alle trefflichen Eigenschaften sind in ihr, Anmuth, Liebreiz, Verständigkeit und feine Sitte; sie wird die Blume und der Spiegel der Frauen genannt. . . . Sie ist das Musterbild der anderen Frauen, an dem sie sehen, wie sie sich zu benehmen haben. . . . Dergleichen Ausdrücke kehren unendlich oft wieder; die italienischen Dichter nennen ihre Dame besonders häufig *rosa, rosa aulente, rosa fresca, rosa colorita, rosa di maggio,* u.s.w. . . . Oder man sagt von ihr, sie übertreffe die lieblichsten Frauen, wie die Rose die anderen Blumen . . . Die Dame gleicht dem Morgenstern . . . ihr Antlitz gleicht der leuchtenden Sonnenscheibe; sie glänzt schöner als Edelsteine.[2]

Provençal poetry had not, however, contributed the most characteristic and significant quality of the work of Dante and Petrarch, the idealization of the beauty and goodness of the lady, for that idealization is never present in Provençal verse.[3] It comes, instead, from the early Italian poets. Cavalcanti, Cino da Pistoia, Guinicelli, and others had indeed been strongly influenced by conventional poetry, yet Moseley shows that they had an aversion for stock comparisons, and that the few which they adopted from the Provençals were used "either in a peculiar sense or in a simple but perfectly suitable sense. They never drag in a comparison for the sake of using it." [4] Sonnets, as a part of the *dolce stil* verse, thus came to be greatly elevated in tone by the worship of the beauty and goodness of the lady.

Yet the kind of blonde beauty celebrated by the Provençals was that afterward celebrated in Italy, England, and France as ideal. This conception, gained from Chrétien de Troyes and passed on to the Italians is, moreover, celebrated in classical verse from the time of Homer, whose heroes and heroines, gods and goddesses, are usually presented as golden-haired and who are so described by later Greek writers despite the fact that the Greeks of the classical period had dark hair and eyes.[5] The same type of beauty is later celebrated in Propertius, Horace, Vergil, and Ovid; and Ovid, as has been said, influenced Chrétien. "All the ladies in the Arthurian stories of Chrétien of Troyes," says Ogle, "are blondes with golden hair, with brows whiter than marble or ivory, with bosoms whiter than snow, with countenances 'where the rose covereth the lily.'" [6] In Italian poetry, blonde beauty is sung in the verse of Cavalcanti, Guinicelli, Ariosto, Boccaccio, and others.[7] Petrarch's Laura conforms to this type with the exception that she seems to have had dark eyes. Chaucer's Emily and Virginia, Lydgate's blonde gods and goddesses, and Hawes's La Belle Pucel are further examples of this conception of beauty.

It must therefore be accepted as almost inevitable that all the ladies in the sixteenth-century novels, plays, and sonnets should look very much alike indeed and show the same characteristics. The images used to describe them had so long been the stock in trade of English writers since Chaucer [8] that in 1578 Barnabe Rich thus satirized them: [9]

If he [the poet] be learned, and that he be able to write a verse, then his penne must plie to paint his maistresse prayse; she must then be a *Pallas* for her witte, a *Diana* for her chastitie, a *Venus* for her face, then shee shall be praysed by proportion: first her Haires are wires of golde, her Cheekes are made of Lilies and red Roses, her Browes be arches, her eyes Saphires, her looks lightnings, her mouth Corall . . .

The sonneteers, it is true, often heighten these conventional descriptions, and the modern reader is prone to consider them "taffeta phrases and silken terms precise" even when the language itself is felicitous and some variety is shown in handling the enveloping conceits. Yet such descriptive sonnets were apparently entirely to the taste of an age well-trained in bestowing extravagant, if expedient, adulation upon an aging and exacting queen. It is, incidentally, rather odd that very few sonnets to Elizabeth herself are known to us. The most dignified of the surviving ones are among the poems of Fulke Greville's *Caelica,* especially his "Under a throne I saw a virgin sit." But, from the tributes to her in other types of verse, it is not hard to conjecture the mixture of flattery and obsequiousness in such offerings. Essex, we are told by Sir Robert Wotton, "once chose to evaporate his thoughts in a sonnet (being his common way) to be sung before the Queen, as it was by one Hales, in whose voice she took some pleasure." [10] Unfortunately, however, for the point in question, the two lines quoted from the "sonnet" of Essex indicate that it was a song about his apprehensions concerning his own place in the sun rather than the flattery of the queen which might have helped his cause.

The modern reader who cavils at the insincerity he senses in the sonnet descriptions of beauty must be reminded, too, of another Elizabethan point of view before he utterly condemns the poet for comparing the sonnet lady so often to gem or queen, saint or angel—the social value of the sonnet, as Professor Fletcher so happily expresses it in a phrase unlocking many such a tribute, as "a strictly legal currency for all compliment." [11] The sonnet was legal currency, moreover, for tributes not only to one's equals but also to one's superiors. A glance at the names of the noble patrons to whom the sequences were dedicated will remind us that Daniel, Lodge, Constable, Fletcher, Barnes, and Tofte used their verse, as Bolingbroke his thanks to Harry Percy, as the "exchequer of the poor." Drayton, Smith, and Griffin dedicated their work to a favorite poet or patron without varying appreciably in tone the descriptions of the paragons celebrated as Fidessa or Chloris or Divine Idea.[12] Sidney's verse, on the contrary, has none of this obsequious humility, for Lady Rich was his social equal and the sonnets were not written to pay off or to gain a patron. The ubiquitous dedicatory sonnets and occasional tributes such as Drayton's "Bright Star of Beauty" (to the "Lady L.S."), Alexander Craig's sonnets to Lady Rich and others in his *Amorose Songes, Sonets, and Elegies,* and the many poems of John Davies of Hereford to his pupils and patrons,[13] usually set forth the wildest extravagances at the poet's command.

Before, however, we consider these conventional descriptions in the sonnets themselves, it is of considerable interest to observe the treatment they receive at Shakespeare's hands. For, although both the plays and sonnets contain many striking descriptions of conventional beauty, Shakespeare seems to have recognized fully their limitations and to have satirized them even while employing them.[14] In *Love's Labour's Lost,* for example, Berowne scoffs at

Rosaline's "velvet brows" and "two pitchballs stuck in her face for eyes" (Act III, scene 1, l. 198). Rosaline herself, whose dark complexion matched her "pitchball" eyes, ruefully admits later on, after Berowne had completely changed front, that were his "numberings" of her true, she would be the "fairest goddess on the ground," for he compared her to "twenty thousand fairs."

Satire seems implied, too, in *Twelfth Night* in Shakespeare's avoidance of a detailed description of Olivia. Orsino is too concerned with analyzing his woes to say more than that Olivia attracts his soul "as a miracle and queen of gems that nature pranks her in." No description is forthcoming from the dazed Sebastian, while Caesario, more concerned than anyone else, merely admits summarily that Olivia is the "nonpareil of beauty" and reproaches her for leaving no copy of that beauty to the world. Olivia quickly dispenses with even this brief praise by promising to bequeath each feature in her will: "*Item,* two lips, indifferent red; *Item,* two grey eyes with lids to them; *Item,* one neck, one chin, and so forth" (Act I, scene 5, ll. 266–68).

Familiar enough is the burlesquing speech in *Midsummer's Night's Dream* of Thisbe over the body of Pyramus which misapplies the customary descriptive epithets in the anti-Petrarchistic manner as lily lips, cherry nose, yellow cowslip cheeks, and eyes green as leeks. Earlier in the same play (Act III, scene 2, ll. 137–44), however, Demetrius had thus addressed Helena:

> O Helen! goddess, nymph, perfect, divine!
> To what, my love, shall I compare thine eyne?
> Crystal is muddy. O! how ripe in show
> Thy lips, those kissing cherries, tempting grow;
> That pure congealed white, high Taurus' snow,
> Fann'd with the eastern wind, turns to a crow
> When thou hold'st up thy hand. O! let me kiss
> This princess of pure white, this seal of bliss.

Sarcastic enough are the jibes of Mercutio when he attempts to conjure up Romeo's presence by calling upon Rosaline's bright eye, scarlet lips, and so on. Even more pointed is the satire in the familiar prose passage (Act II, scene 4, ll. 40–46) beginning:

Now is he for the numbers that Petrarch flowed in; Laura to his lady was a kitchen-wench . . . Dido a dowdy; Cleopatra a gipsy; Helen and Hero hildings and harlots; Thisbe a grey eye or so, but not to the purpose.

Not only do the plays, however, satirize the conventional description of beauty. The "Dark Lady" of the sonnets, whatever her identity, called forth several anti-Petrarchist sonnets, among them the famous No. CXXX:

> My mistress' eyes are nothing like the sun;
> Coral is far more red than her lips' red;
> If snow be white, why then her breasts are dun,
> If hairs be wires, black wires grow on her head.
> I have seen roses damask'd, red and white,
> But no such roses see I in her cheeks;
> And in some perfume is there more delight
> Than in the breath that from my mistress reeks.[15]
> I love to hear her speak, yet well I know
> That music hath a far more pleasing sound:
> I grant I never saw a goddess go,
> My mistress, when she walks, treads on the ground:
>> And yet, by heaven, I think my love as rare
>> As any she belied with false compare.

The Dark Lady presents a strange appearance indeed among the galaxy of Elizabethan sonnet beauties. She merits one distinction, however, that of freeing at least one cycle from the meaningless phraseology employed by most of the poets of the day.

It will not be supposed that the conventional descriptions of beauty produced many sonnets of remarkable beauty or great distinction. The English versions are sometimes all but indistinguishable, for, after all, blonde hair, roses in the cheeks, and the like, can be described in only a fairly limited number of ways. Yet the English phrasing is sometimes pleasing, the language connotative. The color of the hair, for example, is a matter of the choice of adjectives or adjectival phrases. Fair hair, yellow gold, golden wires, crisped wire, hairs of angels' gold, amber-colored tresses, threads of beaten gold, buds of marjorum, hair like the marigold, hair paler than gold, hair like burnished gold —so run some of the phrasings.[16] The hair itself is sometimes described in classical terms as a golden snare,[17] or, in imitation of Petrarch, as golden hair blowing in the wind.[18] The gold of the hair, too, is sometimes regarded as the coin of the realm. Constable so treats it in a sonnet on the seven deadly sins in which his covetous eye, because of its love for gold, cannot remove itself from Diana's fair hair (Dec. I, No. 6). Again, Constable writes of Diana's hair as gold that could be used to pay the soldiers of the Fifth Monarchy (Dec. IV, No. 2). Tofte (Pt. I, No. 16) wishes to exchange Laura's hair for golden coin.

Still another method of describing the lady's hair was to include it in the "eternizing" conceit foretelling the eventual decay of the lady's beauty. Daniel writes that the golden hair of Delia will change to silver wires (No. XXXIII) and that the winter snows will come to it (Nos. XXXVI–XXXVII).[19] Drayton, in 1619 (No. VIII), professes to regret that he will not see Idea when she is old so that he may have the spiteful pleasure of reading to her the verse she now ignores which praises her beauty. He foresees, with Elizabethan exuberance, the perils of old age: her eyes will be two loopholes, her cheeks lean and sunken, her nose and chin will meet, no teeth will remain, and her "dainty hair, so curled and crisped now," will be "like grizzled moss upon some aged tree." Lodge and Smith write, in almost identical phrasing (based upon Ronsard) of the nymph combing locks of yellow gold that put to shame the "curled wire" of the dewy roseate morn.[20] A commonplace compliment was to regard the lady's hair as purer or more valuable than gold.[21]

Comparisons of hair to golden wires had appeared in England as early as Lydgate, and are to be found in *The King's Quair,* in Henryson, Lyndsay, and Gascoigne.[22] Kathleen Lea, observing that the critics have noted with pain the frequent use of this comparison, says:

It is possible that from the art of painting and the goldsmith craft of Italy, perhaps even from the fashions of the age, Elizabethans in their appreciation of hair were conscious of a latent suggestion which is now lost for us in this common conceit.[23]

She notes particularly Leonardo da Vinci's custom of painting hair as thread upon thread of fine gold or bronze. Miss Lea's suggestion may be true for the Elizabethan age, yet the influence of Italian paintings upon Lydgate and the Scots, for example, seems problematical. Sonnet allusions to the hair as golden wire are, moreover, far less numerous than those merely to the golden color of the hair,[24] and the convention is no doubt remembered today largely because of Shakespeare's "If hairs be wires, black wires grow on her head."

Fair hair, however, is only one aspect of the blonde beauty a sonneteer was more or less under contract to glorify. The white hand is in itself a distinct literary convention.[25] Brows, when mentioned, are usually Cupid's bows. Lips are coral, ruby, cherry; the sonnet descriptions of Stella's, for example, range from that of her "sweet swelling lip"—an almost perfect description, by the way, of the only known portrait of Lady Rich—to that of her as the nymph of the garden guarding the cherry tree with fruit surpassing that of the Hebrides. One recalls first, however, a madrigal rather than a sonnet as the epitome of this convention—Campion's "Cherry Ripe." The method of writing such descriptions is often that of cataloguing the features in the manner used in *Twelfth Night* by Olivia in describing herself to Caesario—another literary convention known in England since Chaucer.[26] Such sonnets usually list the conventional phrases with little or no expansion, and the variety lies in the enveloping conceit rather than in the statement of the details themselves. Sidney, for instance, itemizes Stella's beauty in sonnets such as those describing the court of Virtue, the weapons of Cupid, the image presented by Morpheus, and the effects of illness.[27] He, Barnes, and Constable all describe the beauty of the lady as the colors of coats-of-arms.[28] The four directions, the four elements, the planets, the garden of Eden, echoes, gems, goddesses, flowers, saints—any springboard would serve,[29] and the method was used so often that Sir John Davies attacked it in a "gulling" sonnet beginning:

> Mine eye, mine ear, my will, my wit, my heart
> Did see, did hear, did like, discern, did love
> Her face, her speech, her fashion, judgments, art.

The presence of this set of descriptive images in the sonnets and elsewhere in Elizabethan verse is more understandable if we recall the antiquity of this tradition. Ogle says that in Greek literature the redness of cheek and lip is infrequently mentioned, yet is sometimes described as "porphyreus."[30] The Greeks did not use the combination of roses and lilies, but they did describe the skin as lily white. The Latin poets, evidently translating "porphyreus" as "purpureus," often write of the coloring of the face and lips as roses and lilies.[31] The Italian poets rarely employ these figures in combination, and Petrarch never uses them. In England, however, several examples are found despite Sidney's protest in Sonnet XV against the poets who drag every flower, sweet or not, into their comparisons of the lady. Sidney even uses the comparison himself in a rather poor sonnet (No. C) beginning:

> O tears! no tears but rain from beauties skies,
> Making those lilies and those roses grow.

Lodge also describes the face of Phillis as "showers of rose and lilies" (No. XXXVII), while Fletcher (No. LII) writes:

> O rose and lilies! in a field most fair,
> Where modest white doth make the red seem pale.

Constable, in one version (Dec. I, No. 9),[32] says:

> My Lady's presence makes the Roses red
> Because to see her lips they blush for shame.
> The Lily's leaves, for envy, pale became.

In another (Dec. I, No. 10), he refers to roses and lilies in the enumeration sonnet already mentioned which describes Diana's beauty as a coat of arms. Tofte (Pt. II, No. 16) states that Laura has the colors of the rose and of the lily in her beauty. Barnes, more than any other poet, employs this combination in describing the lady, but he rarely, if ever, raises it above mediocrity.[33] Campion's lyric,

> There is a garden in her face
> Where roses and white lilies grow

is probably better than any sonnet inspired by this convention.

The numerous sonnet comparisons of the lady to flowers cannot be said to possess great significance or to express remarkable depths of feeling, nor, except in Shakespeare, does a sonnet version compare with the stanza in Ben Jonson's "Hymn to Charis" beginning:

> Have you seen but a bright lily grow
> Before rude hands have touched it?

Yet such sonnets, or lines or phrases from them, sometimes have beauty enough to remind us that these comparisons were far less threadbare in the Elizabethan age than they are today. Instances range from Lodge's brief comparison of Phillis to the lily and amaranthus (No. XXVIII) to Griffin's entire sonnet "Fair is my love that feeds among the lilies" (No. XXXVII), reminiscent of the Song of Solomon.

The favorite sonnet comparison here is that of the rose. Historically, different factors contribute to the popularity of the figure. First, the poets of Provence had used it frequently, and this meant that it was often used in early Italian poetry. Next, the flower, because of the *Romance of the Rose,*—and no doubt, too, because of the Wars of the Roses—had especial significance to the Middle Ages and to the Renaissance. The English sonneteers sometimes limited themselves to brief decorative phrases —Barnes' "sweet beauty's rose" and "sweet damask rosebud,"

Shakespeare's "beauty's rose," and Lodge's "primrose of love's garden." At other times a few lines are given to the figure. Daniel has a sonnet (No. XXXIV) beginning:

> Look, Delia! how we 'steem the half-blown rose,
> (The image of thy blush, and summer's honour)
> Whilst, in her tender green, she doth inclose
> The pure sweet beauty Time bestows upon her.

The classical *purpureus* is evident, as Ogle notes, in phrasings of Barnes. One instance is in Sonnet XLV:

> Sweet Beauty's rose! in whose fair purple leaves
> Love's Queen, in richest ornament doth lie.

Another instance is in Madrigal 18: "My prickless rosebud veils his purple leaves."

Again, comparisons of the lady to flowers are sometimes incorporated in descriptions meant primarily to display her blonde beauty, as in the accounts of flowers which give their color or perfume to the lady, of flowers which take theirs from her, and of the lady whose beauty or perfume exceeds those of the flowers.[34] In reality such comparisons are present in the cycles in smaller numbers than might be expected: Barnes recounts how Parthenophe lends her beauty to Venus that she may take it as a gift to sick Flora; Constable shows how all the flowers take their color, perfume, and life from Diana; Lodge writes of the hundred thousand flowers springing from the beauty of Phillis.[35] Spenser lists flowers (roses, gilly-flowers, "bell-amoures," pinks, columbines, lilies, and jasmines) which have odors that cannot equal the perfume of the lady (No. LXIV).[36] Shakespeare uses this comparison in No. XCIX. The third line, it will be noticed, also reflects the classical *purpureus*:

> The forward violet thus did I chide:
> Sweet thief, whence didst thou steal thy sweet that smells,
> If not from my love's breath? The purple pride
> Which on thy soft cheek for complexion dwells

In my love's veins thou hast too grossly dyed.
The lily I condemned for thy hand,
And buds of marjoram had stol'n thy hair;
The roses fearfully on thorns did stand,
One blushing shame, another white despair,
A third, nor red nor white, had stol'n of both,
And to his robbery had annex'd thy breath;
But, for his theft, in pride of all his growth
A vengeful canker eat him up to death.
        More flowers I noted, yet I none could see
        But sweet or colour it had stol'n from thee.

Shakespeare writes, too, in No. XCVIII:

Nor did I wonder at the lily's white
Nor praise the deep vermilion in the rose;
They were but sweet, but figures of delight
Drawn after you, you pattern of all those.

Comparisons of the beauty of flowers are, in other instances, sometimes a part of the sonnets on the *carpe diem* theme of earthly beauty that will fade [37] and of the descriptions of the loss of beauty during the lady's illness.[38] The age-old comparisons with the springtime or the flowers of spring are surprisingly infrequent:[39] Spenser writes that as the spring is ready to receive new flowers, so the lady, a flower, is to prepare herself "new love to entertain" (No. IV). Lodge's first sonnet describes Phillis as one whose singing to her flocks makes winter in the valleys turn to spring. His thirtieth sonnet, so similar to the famous Shakespearean "Shall I compare thee to a summer's day," begins:

I do compare unto thy youthly clear,
Which always bides within thy flow'ring prime,
The month of April, that bedews our clime.

The beautiful Shakespearean "Shall I compare thee to a summer's day," "From you have I been absent in the spring," and "How like a winter hath my absence been" have, it need not be said, more than enough beauty to recompense the reader for any ineptitudes in other cycles of figures comparing the lady to flowers or seasons.

SUN AND STARS

WHEN Shakespeare was confronted with reality in describing the Dark Lady, it is not surprising that the first line of his anti-Petrarchistic sonnet CXXX should be a boast that her eyes are "nothing like the sun," for the most commonplace comparison of his day was that of eyes as sun or stars. Before listing examples of these sonnet descriptions, however, we may gratify our curiosity as to the color of the eyes of the various personages, real or hypothetical, to whom the sequences are addressed.

Shakespeare once describes the eyes of the Dark Lady as raven black (No. CXXVII). Another Shakespearean description offers an interesting parallel with lines by Sidney. Sidney's seventh sonnet ends:

> . . . she, minding Love should be
> Placed ever there, gave him this mourning weed
> To honour all their deaths, which for her bleed.

Shakespeare's No. CXXXII reads:

> Thine eyes I love, and they, as pitying we,
> Knowing thy heart torments me with disdain,
> Have put on black and loving mourners be,
> Looking with pretty ruth upon my pain.

The fact that Stella had black eyes is eagerly seized upon by those who profess to find only conventional echoes in Sidney's work, for the probability is that Petrarch's Laura also had black, or at least dark, eyes.[40] Yet, since Lady Rich is elsewhere described as having "black sparkling eyes," [41] Sidney appears to have combined truth with convention. Tofte's Laura is the only other lady with black eyes.

Spenser writes (No. XV), on the other hand, of blue eyes: "If sapphires, lo, her eyes be sapphires plain." [42] Barnes twice mentions that the eyes of Parthenophe took their color from violets (Nos. LVIII and XCVI). For the rest, no specific color is given. The other sonneteers either describe the sparkling clearness of the eyes merely as diamond or crystal [43] or explain the force of their beauty or power over the poet. When this idea is developed, the power of the eyes is that of a heavenly body over an earthly one, ruling its motions, giving light, guiding it through shipwreck, or, in Platonic fashion, reflecting heavenly beauty through the eyes of the beloved and thereby leading the poet to contemplate heavenly love.

The comparison of the eye to a star has, as Ogle shows, a classical origin.[44] Descriptions of the lady herself as sun, moon, or stars were frequent in classical literature, as in Sappho, Theocritus, and Meleager; but the first instance Ogle notes which compares the eye, not the lady, to a sun or star is in Propertius. Ogle infers, however, from descriptions in Ovid, that the figure had been used earlier (as in Callimachus). The conceit is common in Latin literature, especially in Ovid, and, as Moseley shows, is also present in Provençal and early Italian verse. Petrarch used it, as did Lorenzo de Medici, Tasso, and Sannazaro; and during the Renaissance it continued to be favored in Italy,[45] France, Spain, and England. So familiar, indeed, is this theme in all types of sixteenth-century English verse that we need remind ourselves of only one instance outside the sonnets, that from *Romeo and Juliet* (Act II, scene 2, ll. 3, 14-17):

> It is the east, and Juliet is the sun! . . .
> Two of the fairest stars in all the heaven
> Having some business, do entreat her eyes
> To twinkle in their spheres till they return.

No other sonnet cycle is so permeated with the concept of the power of the lady's eye as the giver of light as is Sidney's *Astrophel and Stella,* literally star-lover and star.[46] It gives the cycle much of its unity. The first allusions, however, to Stella's eyes contain no comparisons to stars; they merely show their power: her eyes shine upon Stella's cheek like the morning sun upon snow, they are the windows of the soul, they are able to conquer Reason at a glance.[47] Sidney first mentions in Sonnet XXVI the power of Stella as a star over him as an earth-born mortal— "dusty wits" who scorn astrology think the stars exist only to "spangle the black weeds of night," but he knows that nature does nothing in vain and that the two stars in Stella's face rule him in the manner in which heavenly bodies rule earthly ones.

In one sonnet (No. XLVIII) Stella's eyes are described specially as the morning stars. In others, the influence is that of a planet rather than a star: Stella's eyes make his tempests clear; she "thundered disdains and lightnings of disgrace" upon him.[48] Then, too, the narrative is sometimes carried forward by the motif of the power of the eye: one tournament is won and another almost lost because Stella has looked on. The first of these tournament sonnets, the famous No. XLI, ends:

> . . . The true cause is,
> Stella lookt on, and from her heavenly face
> Sent forth the beams which made so fair my race.

In the second, he recounts how he almost lost the battle because Cupid, angry at seeing his slave Astrophel in the uniform of Mars, compels him to gaze upon Stella (No. LIII):

> Who, hard by, made a window send forth light:
> My heart then quaked, then dazzled were mine eyes,
> One hand forgot to rule, th'other to fight.
> Nor trumpets' sound I heard: nor friendly cries;
> My foe came on, and beat the air for me:
> Till that her blush taught me my shame to see.

His confusion in Stella's presence is again set forth by means of an enumeration of the subjects of conversation which the beams of her eyes prevent him from hearing (No. LI). When he wishes to inform us that Stella has begun to return his love, his words are that her eyes send him beams of bliss (No. LXVI); when he wishes to convey the fact that she is angry, he does it by expressing the hope that his punishment will not come from her blest eyes, for "no doom should make once heaven become his hell"—that is, that which was once heaven (No. LXXXVI).

The first mention of Stella's eyes as light giving is a very conventional one which declares that death from the "majesty of sacred lights oppressing mortal sense" will be a triumph (No. XLII). Again, Stella is the planet of his light—"light of my life, and life of my desire" (No. LXVIII); the inward sun that shines in her eyes is virtue (No. LXXI). The image of Stella as the sun giving light appears in two decidedly inferior sonnets (Nos. LXXVI–LXXVII) in hexameters which may have been written earlier than the others of the cycle. The first says Stella's absence leaves him benumbed with cold, and her appearance is at first like the coming of Aurora, although later her looks burn him and no wind or shade can cool him.[49] The second of these hexameter sonnets contains only one line on the point in hand: "Those looks! whose beams be joy, whose motion is delight." No. LXXXVIII, on absence, refers to the mists of absence as eclipsing the light of the sun. The poet then turns to memory, the bliss of solitude:

> My orphan sense flies to the inward sight
> Where memory sets forth the beams of love.

Absence is several times presented as night, as in Sonnet LXXXIX:[50]

> Now that of absence the most irksome night
> With darkest shade, doth overcome my day;

> Since Stella's eyes wont to give me my day,
> Leaving my hemisphere, leave me in night.

Sidney returns in two sonnets not published in the 1591 editions of *Astrophel and Stella* [51] to the theme of the influence of the stars upon the earth-born mortal. The first, "Finding those beams," states that he has voluntarily removed himself from the power of the beams which mar his mind and are pleased with his hurt; henceforth he must live, like a mole, in darkness. The other, "Oft have I mused," one of the finest sonnets Sidney ever wrote, makes no allusion to Stella as a star but affirms that the stars in their strange course have caused the absence from her which he considers worse than death.

Although the sonneteers who follow Sidney often compare the eyes of the lady to stars or show the influence of the stars upon the mortal, none executes them with the skill or motivation of Sidney. The best of the conceits still to be considered are adaptations from Petrarch's sonnet which professes that the lady's eyes are stars that, if withheld, bring shipwreck to the poet's barque.[52] Wyatt, it will be remembered, translating this sonnet as "My galley, charged with forgetfulness," rendered the conceit as "The stars be hid that led me to this pain." Watson's version is in No. LIII:

> The Lampe whose light should lead my ship about
> Is placed upon my Mistres heavenlie face.

Daniel (No. XII of the 1591 edition) writes:

> The twin lights which my hapless course did show
> Hard by th'inconstant sands of false relief
> Were two bright stars which led my view apart.

With these may be compared Spenser's thirty-fourth sonnet:

> So I, whose star, that wont with her bright ray
> Me to direct, with clouds is over-cast,
> Do wander now, in darkness and dismay.

Shakespeare probably refers to this familiar figure in a line in
Sonnet CXVI which says that love

> . . . is the star to every wandering bark
> Whose worth's unknown, although his height be taken.

Finally, there are many brief sonnet allusions which compare
the lady to a star. Watson's version is "My loves bright shining
beeautie like the starre"; Fletcher's, "Are those two stars, her
eyes, my life's light, gone?" and "Eyes, like stars that twinkle in
the night." [53] Constable, in one line, compares Diana to sun,
moon, star, saint, and shrine (Dec. VI, No. 1). Daniel, translating Du Bellay, writes (No. XXVIII):

> Oft do I marvel, whether Delia's eyes
> Are eyes, or else two radiant stars that shine.

Drayton (No. IV) addresses the "Lady L.S." [54] as "bright star of
beauty"; Griffin (No. XXXIX) terms Fidessa's eyes the brightest
stars the heavens hold; and Smith (No. II) speaks of the bright
crystal beams and star-bright eyes of Chloris. Barnes (No. LVII)
alludes to the graces like stars that encamp in the face of Parthenophe, and, in another instance (No. XCV), writes of Sidney's Stella as a star:

> Thou bright beam-spreading Love's thrice happy Star!
> Th' Arcadian Shepherd's Astrophel's clear guide! . . .
> Star of all stars! fair favoured night's chief pride! . . .
> Of two clear stars, outsparkling Planets all!
> For stars, her beauty's arrow-bearers be!
> Then be the subjects, and superior, she!

Comparisons, however, of the lady to the sun outnumber those
to stars. The glory of the sun was not only a less astronomical
and therefore a more easily handled figure but also one probably
considered as a greater compliment to the lady. These comparisons—often mere phrases or lines describing the lady's brightness
as comparable to or exceeding that of the sun and her smile as
sunbright [55]—are so often decorations more tinsel than gilt that

it is small wonder that Shakespeare boasted that his Dark Lady had eyes "nothing like the sun." Other poets sometimes secure variety by making a planet the figure of comparison.[56] Usually, however, the lady is said to be fairer than the sun or to give the light of day. Some of the versions from Constable's *Diana* show a minor poet's inability to give life to such comparisons:[57] Diana's heavenly eyes draw the poet upward and cause him to shun base desires. He flatters the sun, not Diana, in comparing her to it. She is the "sun of suns, light of lights"; at night, though he feels the heat of the sun, he misses its light. He reproaches the sun for flying from him:

> Fair sun! if thou would have me praise your light,
> When night approacheth, wherefore do you fly?
>
> (Dec. II, No. 10)

Comparing Diana to sun and moon, star and saint, he says that "one sun unto my life's day gives true light" and that "one sun transfix'd hath burnt my heart outright." (Dec. VI, No. 1)

Constable, however, is at least never obscure. Barnabe Barnes, on the other hand, often distorts a figure beyond plausibility or good taste. Sonnet XXII begins by saying that the vestal fires of Parthenophe's heart create two suns for him, and ends by describing the serious case of sunburn he acquired in gazing upon those suns:[58]

> On it till I was sunburnt, did I gaze
> Which with a fervent agony possessed me;
> Then did I sweat, and swelt; mine eyes daze
> Till that a burning fever had oppressed me
> Which made me faint. No physic hath repressed me,
> For I try all. Yet, for to make me sound,
> Ay me, no grass, nor physic may be found!

Sonnet XXIV, presumably carrying over from the preceding sonnet the figure of a dial, perhaps some form of sundial, says:

> These mine heart-eating eyes do never gaze
> Upon thy sun's harmonious marble wheels

But from these eyes, through force of thy sun's blaze
Rain tears continual . . .

The many images of the sun included in Barnes's series of sonnets on the zodiac (Nos. XXXII-XLIII) need not be dwelt upon
here.[59] Another instance, however, of the realism he sought to
inject into his themes is in Sonnet CII, where he calls upon all
the bored young gallants who would "be touched fain with an
amorous fit" to gaze upon Parthenophe, his sun. Any who could
gaze upon such brilliance dry-eyed will be declared eagles because of their eyes, bears and tigers because of their hard hearts.
More reasonable consistency and better taste are shown in Sonnet XCVIII, beginning "The sun my lady's beauty represents."
The pun in Sonnet XLVI, the "pierce-eye piercing eye," upon
the name *Percy,* is one of the reasons for assuming that some
member of this noble family is the Parthenophe to whom the
poems are addressed.[60]

Drayton and Spenser illustrate, on the other hand, the use
which the major sonneteers make of comparisons of the lady to
sun and stars. Drayton usually incorporates his allusions within
sonnets on other themes, as those on the phoenix and on the
fires of the vestal virgins as being lighted by the lady's eyes. One
of the better sonnets (No. LV) concludes with the lines:

> Those eyes to my heart shining ever bright
> When darkness hath obscured each other light.

Especially satisfactory, however, as lacking the hyperbole that
mars so much of Drayton's imagery is Sonnet XLIII:

> Why should your fair eyes, with such sovereign grace,
> Disperse their rays on every vulgar spirit,
> Whilst I in darkness, in the self-same place,
> Get not one glance to recompense my merit?
> So doth the plowman gaze the wandering star,
> And only rest contented with the light
> That never learned what constellations are

Beyond the bent of his unknowing sight. . . .
Heavens are not kind to them that know them most!

Spenser, like Petrarch, usually stresses the ennobling, that is, Platonic, influence of the lady upon the poet and the power of her eyes to elevate him to higher things.[61] No. III, for example, describes her beauty as

> The light whereof hath kindled heavenly fire
> In my frail spirit, by her from baseness raised;
> That, being now with her huge brightness dazed
> Base thing I can no more endure to view.

Yet Sonnet LXXII is anti-Platonic [62]—the poet's spirit, "clogged with burden of mortality," wishes an earthly, not heavenly reward; and it flies to earth rather than to heaven after spying the beauty which resembles heaven's glory. Then, too, Spenser, like Sidney, describes absence as darkness because he is removed from his sun. His two final sonnets rank among his best-sustained verse. No. LXXXVII says in part:

> Since I have lack'd the comfort of that light
> The which was wont to lead my thoughts astray,
> I wander as in darkness of the night,
> Afraid of every danger's least dismay.

His last sonnet concludes with the same figure:

> Dark is my day, while her fair light I miss,
> And dead my life that wants such lively bliss.

Spenser achieves notable originality in a poem (No. IX) which sums up all the conventional comparisons of the eyes of a lady. The originality lies not in the rejection of all the customary comparisons as unworthy, but in the religious note in the last lines:

> Long-while I sought to what I might compare
> Those powerful eyes, which lighten my dark spright;
> Yet find I naught on earth to which I dare
> Resemble th'image of their goodly light.
> Not to the Sun; for they do shine by night;

Nor to the Moon; for they are changed never;
Nor to the Stars; for they have purer sight;
Nor to the Fire; for they consume not ever;
Nor to the Lightning; for they still persever;
Nor to the Diamond; for they are more tender;
Nor unto Crystal; for nought may them sever;
Nor unto Glass; such baseness mought offend her.
　Then to the Maker self they likest be,
　Whose light doth lighten all that here we see.

Miscellaneous Comparisons

PRAISING a lady by comparing her to a gem, a goddess, a saint, or, forsooth, to an angel, was one of the oldest of literary conventions. The average Elizabethan poet, however, who made occasional use of these comparisons obviously did not regard them as trite or threadbare. One suspects, too, that the well-read Elizabethan gentlewoman might have noted the omission of any of the customary set of compliments and might not have greatly fancied "originality" that emphasized the poet's singularity more than her own preëminence. Since most of the sonnet comparisons of this group are used in the customary and obvious meanings of the figures, they require little more than an enumeration.

To give a new turn to a comparison of the lady to a gem would indeed have been a notable feat, for the figure is at least as old as Solomon's statement that woman is fairer than rubies. The earliest sonneteer, Giacomo, employs this conceit in the sonnet quoted on page 31 of this work. In the English cycles such comparisons range from a phrase of mere embroidery to an entire sonnet. Yet, perhaps because the conceit offers so few possible combinations and variations, such sonnets are comparatively few, and the conceit is not included in Shakespeare's black list in Sonnet CXXX. In Sidney (No. XXIV), Stella is the "richest

gem of love and life," and again she is described in the statement that not even the Indies hold such ivory, rubies, pearls,
and gold (No. XXXII). Barnes (No. XLVIII) likewise asserts
that no other nation holds such gems as those contained in England in the beauty of Parthenophe; and Daniel has a sonnet
(No. XIX) beginning:

> Restore thy treasures to the golden ore . . .
> And to the Orient do thy pearls remove!
> Yield thy hands' pride unto the ivory white!

Fletcher (No. LII) describes the pearls enclosed in the pale ivory
of Licia's face; Spenser says that, although the lady in herself
contains "all this world's riches that may be found"—sapphire
eyes, ruby lips, golden locks, an ivory forehead, teeth like pearls,
hands of silver sheen—her mind is more valuable than any of
these (No. XV).[63] Smith, protesting that some poets compare
their loves to a goldsmith's shop, says that Chloris imitates only
herself, not the gems of India (No. XVIII); Tofte often compares Laura to pearls and other jewels.[64] Shakespeare (No.
CXXXI) gives brief but satisfactory expression to the conceit:

> For well thou know'st to my dear doting heart
> Thou art the fairest and most precious jewel.

Comparisons of the sonnet lady to goddesses, even to gods,
were, like other classical themes, of great interest to Elizabethan
writers. Shakespeare, who satirized these comparisons in *Love's
Labour's Lost* as "pure, pure idolatry," [65] was alone among the
sonneteers in his anti-Petrarchistic realism:

> I grant I never saw a goddess go;
> My mistress, when she walks, treads on the ground.

So, alas, do the earth-born goddesses of the sonnets. Sometimes a
single feature of the beauty of a goddess satisfies the poet—the
blush of Aurora [66] or the chastity of Diana (Daniel, No. V).
There are even a few general references such as Drayton's "god-

dess" (No. XLI), Daniel's "laughter-loving goddess" (No. X), and Percy's "my goddess" (Nos. I, II, V). Sidney once carries forward the narrative of his sequence by the implications of a line in Sonnet XXXIII, "No lovely Paris made thy Helen his"; Spenser illustrates the treatment given him by the lady by comparing her to Penelope and to Pandora (Nos. XXIII–XXIV).

The function, however, of these allusions to the deities was usually the purely descriptive one of revealing the more-than-mortal fairness of the lady rather than the furthering of a narrative and the lady's beauty is usually accounted for as being a gift from the gods and the goddesses, as being stolen from them, or as surpassing the beauty of the deities.[67] It could even cause a goddess to shed tears of jealous rage.[68] Fletcher makes interesting and surprisingly extensive use of such comparisons. Taking the sonnets in numerical order, the comparisons of Licia to a goddess are as follows: The infant Cupid mistakes Licia for his mother Venus (No. II). The deities, beholding the beauty of Licia, wonder why Jove does not come down to earth to woo her. His previous "matches" with mortals are, in comparison, but "bloomless buds, too base to make compare" (No. III). Venus, angry that Cupid was slave to Licia, freed him and made the poet thrall to the maiden, and the poet then says that Licia, not Venus, is the goddess (No. V). Love weeps because Licia stole his weapons while he slept, but Venus reassures him that they will be returned since her beauty is so great that she will not need them (No. IX). A painter mistakenly painted love as a boy— had he wished to paint it in its true character as a maid, a goddess, and a queen, he would have painted it as Licia (No. X). Licia surpasses in beauty Venus, Juno, and Minerva (No. XI). Licia shines fairer than Phoebus (No. XV). He calls Licia, Venus, but begs that she not be angry at the comparison, since she is more chaste than Venus (No. XXII). When Licia lay dying, Death came for his prey, but was so abashed at the beauty of Licia that he grants her immortality as a goddess (No. XXIV).

Licia's eyes can bring either calm or storm at sea; Neptune has no power over her (No. XXIX). When (No. XXX) her hair blows in the wind,

> Diana-like she looks, but yet more bold:
> Cruel in chase, more chaste, and yet more fair.

A spider, going into Licia's house, could not build her web there, for she mistook Licia for Minerva (No. XLVIII). Each phase of her beauty was given by a god or a goddess (No. LI).

Turning to another type of comparison, we encounter a few instances in which the lady is described as a warrior. These Petrarchan borrowings are usually found in the sonnets (discussed in Part I) of Sidney and the others who represent the lady's heart as a citadel.[69] Only one group of comparisons, therefore, will be given any comment here—those in which Spenser makes a plea for peace with the lady. These allusions, as it was noted in the introductory chapter, lead Garrod to conclude that they are word plays upon the name *Pease* and that the sonnets are to Elizabeth Boyle, whom he believes to have been the widow of a Tristam Pease at the time of Spenser's marriage to her.[70] Although one's first impulse may be to dismiss the implications of such word play as far-fetched, the idea is certainly consistent with the recurrence of the word and with the tone given by such phrases as the "fair cruel" and the "cruel fair one" (Nos. XLIX and LIII).

The sonnet description of the lady as being a queen was originally no far-fetched compliment when bestowed by a chivalric poet or troubadour whose patroness might indeed be a queen or one who possessed some kind of sovereign power. Nor were the sonneteers the only sixteenth-century poets who dispensed this kind of flattery with lavish hands. The sonnet lady is described as queen of love or beauty, summer, or earthly delights; more modestly, even merely as queen.[71] Drayton's Idea is queen of the Ankor River (No. LIII). Fletcher, using the theme of content which is the subject of Dyer's "My mind to me a kingdom is,"

Greene's "Sweet are the thoughts that savor of content," and
Barnes's sonnet "Ah, sweet content," writes that he would scorn
crowns and kingdoms for Licia (No. XII). Fletcher describes
the manner in which Licia, queen-like, keeps her world in awe
(No. LI), and in which love fills his mind with treason against
his sovereign (No. XXXVII).[72] Constable compares Diana to a
queen by calling her the sweet sovereign of many subjects who is
asked to rule the Fifth Monarchy (Dec. IV, No. 2). Several poets
describe the lady as queen of the poet's heart or soul.[73] Stella is
the princess both of beauty and of all the powers life bestows
upon the poet; [74] Griffin (No. XXXI) designates these powers:

> Tongue, heart, eyes, lips, hands, breath, arms, feet,
> Consent to do true homage to your queen!

Spenser and Drayton both mention the power of the sovereign
beauty of the lady.[75]

Descriptions of the lady as a saint result not only from the
medieval adulation of a patroness and the Platonic worship of
beauty in women—the religion of beauty in women, as Professor Fletcher describes it—but also from the medieval cult of the
worship of the Virgin. Yet the fact that all the Elizabethan sonneteers under discussion apply the name of saint to the ladies
honored rarely means idealized innate goodness; it is merely
that such tributes were a part of the traditional sonnet vocabulary.
The requirements of Barnes, for example, were certainly easy of
attainment (No. XXVIII): [76]

> Then if thou be but human, grant some pity!
> Or if a saint? Sweet mercies are their meeds!
> Fair, lovely, chaste, sweet-spoken, learned, witty,
> These make thee saint-like, and these, saints befit:
> But thine hard heart makes all these graces weeds!

The descriptions of the lady as a saint are sometimes a part of
an "echo" [77] sonnet, sometimes a mere phrase such as "heavenly
saint," "fair saint," "a saint's cruel mind," one "sacred on earth,

designed a saint above." Or, if the conceit describes the lady's image as being worshiped in the temple of the poet's heart,[78] as in Spenser and Constable, emphasis is laid upon the worship due a saint.

Spenser (No. LXI) alone [79] approaches the truer Platonic worship of the lady as a saint because of her innate goodness and says that she derives her qualities from heaven:

> The glorious image of the Maker's beauty,
> My sovereign saint, the idol of my thought,
> Dare not henceforth, above the bounds of duty,
> T'accuse of pride, or rashly blame for aught.
> For being, as she is, divinely wrought,
> And of the brood of Angels heavenly born;
> And with the crew of blessed saints upbrought,
> Each of which did her with their rifts adorn;
> The bud of joy, the blossom of the morn,
> The beam of light, whom mortal eyes admire;
> What reason is it then but she should scorn
> Base things, that to her love too bold aspire?
>   Such heavenly forms ought rather worshipped be,
>   Than dare be lov'd by men of mean degree.

This poem contains, also, the best sonnet expression of the angelic nature of the lady, for such allusions are usually to the earthly beauty or to the undefined excellencies of the lady rather than to any quality derived from divine goodness.[80] In Sonnet LXXIX Spenser again refers to this quality as implying a heavenly origin of the beauty that will not fade—the gentle wit and virtuous mind which are true beauty and which show that she is divine:

> Deriv'd from that fair Spirit, from whom all true
> And perfect beauty did at first proceed:
> He only fair, and what He fair hath made,
> All other fair, like flowers, untimely fade.

His Sonnet XVII describes the "glorious portrait of that angel's face" which was made to amaze weak men's confused skill.

Opprobrium, however, was often the fate of the sonnet lady, for it is hardly to be expected that the poet endured all his misery without a few feeble protests. The line of descent of these images is that of the other images mentioned. Flint is the favorite epithet for her heart, but stone, steel, and marble give the poets a semblance of variety.[81] She is also often compared to various animals. The term "tiger's heart" seems reasonably strong language;[82] Spenser, however, calls his lady a lion, a lioness, a cockatrice, a leech, and a panther;[83] Smith compares Chloris to a scorpion; and Tofte, Laura to the basilisk.[84] Word play on the poet's own name is Griffin's contribution (No. XXXIX) when he says that the lady bears the mind of a "griffon." Sidney nowhere uses such comparisons in a derogatory sense; on the contrary, he protests in his third sonnet against the poets who so use them:

> Or with strange similes enrich each line
> Of herbs or beasts which Inde or Afric hold.

He once refers, however, in a complimentary manner to Stella as his young dove (No. LXIII).[85]

Descriptions of eyes as sun or stars, crystal or diamond, of the lady as a gem or a flower, a goddess or an angel, were too firmly established in the language of all poets to cease entirely with the sonnet vogue. The old order gradually gave way to greater realism, yet such comparisons occur in the seventeenth century in poetry ranging from Milton's Italian sonnets to the verse of Lovelace, Carew, and Suckling, and as late as the nineteenth century in that of Keats, whose "nymph of the downward smile and sidelong glance"—the Miss Wylie who was afterward the wife of his brother George—wandered in "labyrinths of sweet utterance," in a "trance of sober thoughts," and spared the flowers in her "mazy dance." Keats also writes, and five years after the event, of a lady seen casually at Vauxhall whose beauty tangled him in its web: he is ensnared by the ungloving of her hand; he cannot look upon the midnight sky without remembering her eyes; he cannot behold the rose that his soul does not take flight to her cheek.

The decline of the sonnet vogue, however, gradually decreased the use of such conventional comparisons, for a sonnet cycle, by its very nature, was the chief depository for them. Distinction in using these conceits was all but impossible in the sixteenth century, yet Sidney and Spenser achieved it in a few instances. The other sonneteers sometimes have beauty of phrase, but the search for new combinations often leads, here as elsewhere, to hyperbole and unpoetic comparisons. To only one sonneteer was given the insight and perception to avoid the empty echoes of an earlier era: Shakespeare's Dark Lady, it may be repeated, merits at least the distinction of freeing one sonnet sequence from the conventional description employed by most of the English poets of her day.

CONCLUSION

SUCH, in reasonably complete detail, is the conventional language of a Petrarchan sequence of love sonnets, the sonneteer's "precious tablet of rare conceits"; and such is the nature of the versions produced by the Elizabethan poets. Some of them may never be popular again in English verse; their bright day is done. Of doubtful value as a source of autobiographical information, they nevertheless provide in themselves a basis of understanding closer than any other to the point of view of both the Elizabethan reader and the Elizabethan writer, and, if the sequences are to be read today with comprehension, they require greater consideration than is usually bestowed upon them. The sonneteer, to be sure, did not draw up the table of his conceits in the conscious manner necessarily employed in this discussion, yet some plan, however informal, must have guided his selection, some cycle or cycles have been used as the models for his Petrarchan imitation.

Let us, then, sum up the conceits according to the division of material which has arbitrarily been used in this discussion. First, there was the portrayal of the theme of love. The Elizabethan manner is so different from that of today that many of these sonnets now seem, as Carroll says of his *Alice,*

> Like pilgrim's wither'd wreath of flowers
> Pluck'd in a far-off land.

Yet, to the Elizabethan the portrayal of love in the classical manner as the exploits of the god Cupid was taken for granted. Love is usually described, as in Petrarch's *Canzoniere,* as a stern, vindictive little tyrant: a heritage from the Latin poets who had repressed love as a god who dwelt in the eyes, face, or breast of the lady as well as in the heart of the poet; who carried on a cruel warfare against him by shooting arrows from the lady's eyes or by besieging his heart as a fort; who tricked him with snares and tortured him with the fires of love. This conception of love as a tiny god appeared rather infrequently in England before Wyatt,

Surrey, and the other Tudor poets, for Chaucer and his imitators employed in the main a composite conception evolved in the Middle Ages which gave love the powers of a cruel deity, a feudal overlord, and a god worshiped according to the ecclesiastical customs of the age. Once established, however, the Ovidian conception dominated Elizabethan literature.

But the sonneteer also made use of another and older conception of the guises and appearance of love—one derived from the Greek literature of the Alexandrian period, but almost unknown to later ages until the Renaissance recovery and publication of works such as the *Greek Anthology* and the *Anacreontea*. This conception represents love not only as an unescapable tyrant, but also as a tiny, insouciant, Puckish child. He gained access to the poet's heart by the ruse of seeking refuge on a stormy night. His fugitive state was variously accounted for, but most of the narratives relating it end with an account of his setting fire to his lodging and then laughing gleefully at his host's discomfiture. All the sonnet descriptions derived from the Alexandrian tradition show Love as having the merry, irresponsible nature of a child or very small boy. This conception, appearing in England only a few times before the sonnet vogue, as in Spenser, Greene, and Watson, forms an important part of the cycles of Sidney, Greville, Fletcher, Barnes, and Drayton. Echoes of it also appear in other cycles, even in Shakespeare. All in all, these light, gay accounts of Cupid are today the most readable phases of the sonnet presentation of love; but it is clear that the Ovidian conception remained the Elizabethan's basic and favorite device.

The second of the arbitrary divisions employed here of the sonneteer's material is the group of themes which enabled the poet to set forth the effect of his love upon his mental and physical state. These aspects of Petrarch's work also take us back to Ovid, this time to the description of the effects of love as set forth in the *Ars amatoria*. Ovid's sensual conception of the nature of love was greatly elevated, however, in the Middle Ages by an infusion of Platonism and chivalric idealism. Petrarch's love for Laura is therefore at once Platonic and mundane; and, so, in varying degrees, is that of his imitators for the persons to whom they address their verse. The influence of Ovid's portrayal of the effects of love had been strengthened rather than diminished, however, during the Middle Ages, because codes of love imitating the *Ars amatoria* helped to crystallize the already-conventional notions of the behavior of the lover. In brief, the lover who was dumb in the presence of the lady and out of his wits when absent from her, who was pale and sleepless, who sighed, wept, and longed for death, who compared himself to many things and analyzed carefully both the state of his heart and his reasons for writing of it was for centuries the central figure of romance and lyric verse of all types. The sixteenth-century romances and dramas made this concept so familiar that the sonnets must have been thoroughly to the taste of the Elizabethan age.

The English sonnets written on these themes range from the most charming to the most lugubrious of Elizabethan verse. The poems on absence and sleep are often beautiful. The conceits describing the state of the poet's heart are ingenious, technically interesting, even though they now seem an artificial means of revealing an unhappy state of mind. These conceits of the heart include the debate between the heart and eye to determine which was guilty of causing the poet's unhappiness, the exchange of hearts and the migration of the heart, the engraving of the image of the lady upon the heart itself, and the heart as the sanctuary where that image is worshiped. Descriptions abound of the sighing, dying lover, yet his state seems no more critical than that of the lovers in other types of verse of that day. Many conceits were employed in describing his woes: figures from natural history, particularly the hound, deer, and birds; from everyday life, especially of ships and trees; and from personages of classical literature, such as Prometheus and Leander. The "mirror" conceit was also a means of revealing the poet's despair, but was less useful than the conceits belonging to the various conventional reasons for writing verse: the sonnets themselves are usually put forth as being in one form or another a plea for pity deserved because of the sufferings endured or of the service he has rendered in celebrating or "eternizing" the beauty of the beloved. Nor is it without interest to observe the various comments which bear upon the poet's desire or lack of desire for contemporary fame. Of these "writing" sonnets, the ones best liked today are those which profess to "eternize" the fame or beauty of the lady—or, in Shakespeare's verse, the beauty and goodness of Will. The various conceits revealing the anatomy of the poet's melancholy are today among the most interesting phases of the sonnet cycles.

The third and last division of the conventional material of the cycles is that given over to the description of the beauty of the lady. The ideal type of blonde beauty has been traced to Homer; certainly it dominates for centuries the literature of Italy, France, and England. Aside from portraying every detail of the blonde beauty of this ideal conception—rejected outright by Shakespeare when the Dark Lady appeared—the poets concerned themselves chiefly with showing the power or beauty of the lady by comparing her to a star or to the sun. Other comparisons, however, were almost obligatory: the lady was a flower—or the flowers stole their beauty from her—a gem, a goddess, a saint, or an angel. The lady's heart was hard as flint, stone, or steel. Such sonnets are rarely distinguished by great originality, but two points are worth noting—the infrequency with which Sidney uses such themes and the beauty which Spenser gives his translations and adaptations of them.

This stock taking of the themes of the English sequences which grow out of the Petrarchan pattern raises the question of the possible differences between the English sequences and the *Canzoniere*. A few general differences are immediately apparent. First, the fact can hardly be over-stressed that no English sonneteer under discussion wrote his sequence to a loved one lost to him by death, and thus, as it has been said several times, the most deeply moving parts of Petrarch, the sonnets presaging and lamenting Laura's death, are without imitation in England, although Drummond wrote such sonnets in Scotland. Many of the themes of the first half of the *Canzoniere* reappear, to be sure, in the second, particularly when Petrarch describes his grief, but there his sadness and longing transform them.

Other differences between the work of Petrarch and that of the English sonneteers arise in part from the matter of scope and length. Compared with the *Canzoniere,* the longest English sequence is short. For one thing, the *Canzoniere,* as published from the Vatican manuscript, includes the occasional sonnets and friendship poems already referred to,[2] whereas such verse is usually not included within the English sequences. Constable and Fletcher each insert a sonnet addressed to their patrons; Spenser has one addressed to Bryskett; Barnes one to Sidney's Stella; and Sidney three to unnamed friends. With these exceptions, such verse is occasional. For another thing, the English poets produced only one, or at best a few, versions of many of the themes appearing several times each in Petrarch. Sidney, for example, has three sonnets with puns upon the name "Rich"; Petrarch has a dozen or more punning upon the word "laurel." Few of Petrarch's themes fail to reappear, however, in some form or context in the Elizabethan era.

This matter of scope, however, accounts for a more significant difference between the *Canzoniere* and the English cycles. The *Canzoniere* covers a period of more than twenty years, and this passage of time gives both a variety of mood and deepening of tone and a more specific narrative quality than is found elsewhere. Spenser rather vaguely alludes to the length of time that had passed since he met the lady, and Sidney several times says that he fell in love with Stella when it was too late; but such casual references in no way parallel the time element in Petrarch or the note of conviction and sincerity growing out of it. Last and most important difference of all is the quality in the *Canzoniere* of immediacy which may, to some degree at least, be attributed to its scope. The English sequences seem vague and inadequate in the face of Petrarch's description of the specific hour, day, and place of his meeting with Laura, of the anniversaries of this meeting, of the times and places of parting and reunion,[3] of her green robes,[4] and of all the other details of her appearance. His mention of definite places, such as Vaucluse and the Po, is imitated in England only in Sidney's description of Stella on the Thames and in the obscure allusions of Drayton and Daniel to the rivers near which Delia and Idea live.

The last point of comparison between the English sonnets and those of Petrarch is one in no way connected with the length of the sequences. It is the difference in attitudes toward love. Petrarch often expresses religious misgivings over the distractions which Laura causes him and prays that all his love may be given to heavenly things. More immediate doubts seem not to have troubled him, and his renunciation of love came long years after Laura's death. With the exception of one or two sonnets in Shakespeare, especially No. CLII, only one English sequence reflects a mood of doubt over the probity of the writer's course, perhaps because they were usually tributes to patrons. Yet, in the one instance of this kind, the English sequence is rather different from the Italian. Sir Philip Sidney, sixteenth-century Protestant courtier, idealist, and philosopher, was fully aware of what was at stake because he loved the wife of Lord Rich, yet for a time he regretted only that he had no more to lose for her than his good name and his place at court. Stella herself, if we may believe the story in the sonnets, held him to a more fortunate course, and, in time, he was able to write his sonnets of renunciation, especially "Leave me, O love which reachest but to dust." This problem is touched upon in the appendix to this study.

Finally, it may be asked what effect the analysis here set forth

can have upon the evaluations of the style of the sequences themselves. Although the motive has been primarily to provide the
basis for eclectic judgments by listing the conceits under their
respective headings, a few opinions concerning style may nevertheless be ventured.

This analysis reveals, first of all, some aspects of the greatness
of Shakespeare when he makes use of conventional material. His
sequence as a whole recalls the statement of the late Professor
A. H. Thorndike that hardly in the great tragedies themselves is
there clearer proof of his supremacy in thought and language.[5]
This analysis reveals, also, the excellence of Sidney's *Astrophel
and Stella*. The sequence deserves to be better known—the entire sequence, not merely the half-dozen sonnets in the antholo-
gies. For, with the exception of Shakespeare's sonnets, most of
Sidney's versions of the themes of the Petrarchan pattern surpass
those of his contemporaries, even of Spenser, in individuality,
spirited feeling, artistic judgment, and lyric quality. Whatever
the provenance of the original idea, he, more than any other,
makes it completely his own.

Better known, too, should be the verse of Fulke Greville, for
he was not only, as he wrote for his famous epitaph, "servant to
Queen Elizabeth, councellor to King James, and frend to S^r
Philip Sidney"; he was one of the finest sonneteers of his day. His
skillful, original versions of conventional themes lack, it is true,
the range and depth of those of his beloved Sidney, yet they are
not unworthy to stand beside them, and it is fortunate that they
were published even fifty-odd years after they were written.

This analysis of the sonnet conceits also reveals the weaknesses
of the style of Drayton. Good poet though he is, great sonneteer
though he sometimes could be, his sonnets often come off badly
when placed side by side with those of his fellow craftsmen, for his
quest for originality led him to unjustifiable hyperbole. His faults,
however, probably spring from a lack of incentive other than a
desire for poetic renown. Among the other poets, Daniel should

perhaps be mentioned first. His verse, which is pervaded by a gentle longing and mild unhappiness, often has genuine beauty, yet it is so correct, so restrained, so perfect a tribute of poet to patroness, that mediocrity is often the result. As for Constable, so much work remains to be done in the matter of the authenticity of the text that it is impossible to speak definitely of his style. Since, however, he now takes rank as one of the earliest English poets to write a sonnet cycle, his verse deserves careful editing and greater consideration in its relationship to the other verse of his day.

As for the other writers, a few generalizations, none very different from the critical estimates usually bestowed upon them, will suffice. Fletcher makes really remarkable use of the classical material he adapts. Barnes, who also uses classical material, shows some originality, as in his conceits of the migration of the heart; and he has a few good sonnets. He is often obscure, however, because of an ejaculatory style and exaggerated versions of the usual sonnet themes. If the other minor poets who were inspired by *Astrophel and Stella* to attempt Petrarchan sonnet sequences had known Donne's "Canonization," they would no doubt have felt their case well put in that poem:

> And if no piece of chronicle we prove,
>   We'll build in sonnets pretty rooms;
> As well a well-wrought urn becomes
> The greatest ashes, as half-acre tombs,
>   And by these hymns, all shall approve
>   Us canonized for love . . .

APPENDICES

The English Petrarch

THE IDENTITY OF STELLA

S TYLE and craftsmanship, however significant to some, are of less interest to the average reader than the biographical implications in the major sequences. Most, if not all, of Spenser's admirers wish they could know the identity of the person or persons to whom he wrote the *Amoretti* and the relation of the events implied in the sequence to those of his life. Readers of Shakespeare usually formulate their own theories with regard to the identities of "Will" and the "Dark Lady." Sidney's cycle, at once the work of the first of the English Petrarchists and of a heroic figure, has induced a miniature Battle of the Books over the actuality of his love for the person celebrated as Stella and the identity of Stella herself. The professions of reality in that cycle are so convincing that their integrity has somehow been made the test of the worth of the entire sonnet vogue and attacks against the truth of Sidney's professions to reflect discredit upon it as a whole. It may therefore afford a better understanding of that cycle if we observe briefly some of its controversial points. In brief, recent investigations preserve and strengthen the long-established idea that the cycle is, in its larger aspects, an autobiographical account of the poet's love for Penelope Devereux, Lady Rich.

At the outset, however, it must be freely admitted that the reader of Sidney's sonnets has to steer a difficult course between the present-day and Elizabethan points of view. First, he must recall that subjectivity in lyric verse, as we understand the word, was unknown in the sixteenth century. Sidney's sequence is characterized, too, by an impetuosity and variety of mood not present in Petrarch or in the other English sequences. This is understandable, however, when one considers the probable circumstances and impulses prompting the different sonnets and recalls that the poet was not only a grave, gentle personality, but also a complex, many-sided Elizabethan statesman and courtier, a Renaissance novelist who wrote both versions of the *Arcadia*. These aspects of his character as they are reflected in *Astrophel and Stella* are best comprehended by Mona Wilson in her statement that the cycle reveals the "whole nature of the lover, by turns tender, sensual, chivalrous, contemplative, passionate, and playful." [1]

The first charge against Sidney's cycle is Sir Sidney Lee's denial of autobiographical reality in the sonnets because of what he considers their lack of originality. In the preface to his edition of the Elizabethan sonnet cycles he makes the statement that few of Sidney's poetic ideas are his own, few of his "swelling phrases" of his own invention, and that the imitative quality of the cycle destroys "most of the specious pretensions to autobiographical reality which the unwary reader finds in them." [2] These opinions have gained all the more credence in that Lee's edition of the Elizabethan sonnets remains the only one still generally available. His editing and source hunting are indeed invaluable, yet the statements just quoted take little, if any, account of the Renaissance attitude toward imitation. The more extensive researches, therefore, of Janet Scott are gratifying in that they show that his indebtedness was only a little more extensive than Koeppel had already pointed out. Koeppel's conclusions may be quoted: [3]

Sidney hat sich dem mächtigen Einflusse Petrarcas nicht entziehen können, er hat ihm reichlich Tribut gezollt—aber er hat in die alten Schläuche doch so viel des neuen Weines gegossen, dass ihm niemand das Recht bestreiten kann, von sich zu sagen:

> And this I sweare by blackest brooke of hell,
> I am no pickpurse of another's wit.

Miss Scott's own summary of Sidney's indebtedness is:

Nous avons essayé de dégager la part de convention et la part d'originalité dans les sonnets de Sidney, et nous venons de voir que les thèmes et les concetti d'*Astrophel et Stella* sont bien de la Renaissance. On remarquera cependant que nous n'avons pu donner de précisions que pour une douzaine de poèmes environ, c'est-à-dire bien peu de chose si on se souvient qu'*Astrophel et Stella* contient 108 sonnets sans compter les chansons. Sidney n'a pas traduit, et affirmer cela au sujet d'un sonnettiste du XVIe siècle est un sérieux éloge. . . . Ce n'est pas que les thèmes de la plupart des sonnets soient originaux; c'est que le poète a assez de talent pour donner une forme nouvelle à une vieille matière. Les contemporains de Sidney auraient appelé ce talent "originalité," et dans ce sens Sidney est original même dans ses thèmes.[4]

Another recent study of Sidney, that of A. W. Osborn, likewise indicates that Lee overstates the matter of Sidney's indebtedness and that the problem is usually one of analogues rather than of specific borrowings:

On voit donc que l'influence nettement française se borne à quelques traits qu'on saisit par ci par là dans les poésies de Sidney, des traits qui ont été quelquefois si bien remaniés par lui qu'on s'aperçoit à peine de leur origine étrangère, et qu'on peut dire qu'ils sont devenus siens.[5]

The presence of an autobiographical element in *Astrophel and Stella,* then, is not to be discredited by Lee's sweeping allegations concerning Sidney's foreign indebtedness. The poet's own statement that he "looked into his heart and wrote" probably receives its true explanation at the hands of Henry Osborn Taylor when he says that Sidney, looking into his "heart, or mind," found it "stored with love-thoughts and images derived from reading, which had become a part of himself and his musings. He could look into his heart and write, and make use of all its thoughts and sentiments, whatever their provenance." [6] He is indebted to Petrarch in much the same manner that the author of a pastoral poem is indebted to his predecessors or that the writer of a Pindaric ode is indebted to Pindar. Indeed, few things are more noteworthy about Sidney as an Elizabethan poet than his ability to make his themes, whatever their source, completely his own.

The question of originality has not been, however, the only controversial point in regard to Sidney's sonnets. The cycle has sometimes been disparaged as having had no basis in reality, as professing love for "Stella" when little or no such feeling existed, and as addressing a person whose identity is problematical at best. Some points may never be settled, yet modern research produces evidence confirming the early tradition that the poet was for a time in love with a lady unhappily married and that this lady was Penelope Devereux, Lady Rich. The proof rests upon Elizabethan opinion, internal evidence, and the dates of composition of the sonnets. First let us consider the evidence concerning the identity of Stella as Lady Rich.

The most valid objection against accepting this identity of Stella as Lady Rich is Spenser's poem called "Astrophel," a group of obituary poems published in 1595, nine years after Sidney's death, which appears to identify Stella as the poet's wife, Frances Walsingham, daughter of Queen Elizabeth's foreign secretary. The separate poems of "Astrophel" are as follows: the first is by Spenser; the second, usually called the "Doleful Lay of Clorinda," is ostensibly by Sidney's sister, the Countess of Pembroke. The third and fourth are by Lodowick Bryskett, and the fifth is by Mathew Royden. Lastly, there are one each by Sir Walter Raleigh and (presumably) Fulke Greville. The difficulty raised by "Astrophel" has been held to be owing to the facts, first, that the poem is dedicated to Sidney's widow (who had married the Earl of Essex by 1591—perhaps, as Conyers Read suggests, by 1587 [7]) in the single line: "To the Most Beautiful and Virtuous Lady, the Countess of Essex"; and, second, that both the first poem by Bryskett and that by Spenser appear to identify Stella as the poet's wife. Several critics have felt convinced that Spenser would not have had the effrontery to dedicate to Sidney's wife a work celebrating her former husband under the name he had used in praising another lady; also, that in such a poem Spenser and Bryskett would hardly have referred to the poet's love for another or have described her mourning for him; and, lastly, that the Countess of Pembroke would never have contributed to a work which thus appeared to insult her sister-in-law.[8]

Several circumstances, however, must be taken into account in considering the weight to be placed upon "Astrophel" as evidence against the actual autobiography in *Astrophel and Stella*. First of all, Spenser's part in the entire undertaking is by no means clear. Much may be said for Dodge's suggestion that the printer Ponsonby, not Spenser himself,[9] dedicated the work to the Countess of Essex. The single, unsigned line just quoted is different indeed from the longer signed dedications of the *Ruines of Time, The Teares of the Muses, Prosopopoia,* and *Muiopotmos.* There is no reason to assume that Ponsonby would know that the Countess of Essex was not the Stella represented as mourning Sidney's death. For another thing, Spenser may not have planned the entire group of poems in "Astrophel." H. H. Hudson suggests that he may have been responsible for only three of the six elegies: his own, that by the Countess of Pembroke, and one of those by Bryskett. Ponsonby, he says, "seems to have lifted the other three elegies from the *Phoenix Nest* and have appended them."[10]

The two elegies, moreover, in "Astrophel" which seem to identify Stella as the Countess of Essex are largely translations rather than original poems written to express the laments of Spenser and Bryskett themselves. First, Spenser's elegy is closely related to Bion's *Adonis.* Shafer, pointing out that fact, says that some of the resemblances are the more significant in that "one scarcely can help seeing how Spenser has, almost literally, dragged certain of these passages into the poems."[11] Bryskett's first elegy, moreover, is based upon Bernardo Tasso's *Selva nella morte del Signor Aluigi da Gonzaga;* it has even the same arrangement of rhyme as that poem, while "the lament in Bryskett's poem of Sidney's Stella (ll. 93–127) parallels the lament of Gonzaga's 'sister.' "[12] Bryskett's second elegy, referring to Stella in a more general fashion, is paraphrased from Tasso's *Alcippo* and has an even greater proportion of translation. This lack of originality in "Astrophel" should therefore be considered before the work is taken at its face value as a means of discrediting Sidney's verse as reflecting an actual experience of the poet. Nor is it clear that the "Doleful Lay of Clorinda" is actually the work of Sidney's sister. Renwick considers that it is, but Long and Osgood both believe that Spenser himself, not the Countess of Pembroke, wrote the poem.[13] This authorship, of course, would remove one of the stumbling blocks of the poem, although it would not remove the implications in the contributions of Spenser and Bryskett that "Stella" is the poet's wife.[14]

Strangely enough, parallels for some of the circumstances of the nature and the dedication of "Astrophel" held to be impossible if Sidney had been in love with Lady Rich are to be found in a contemporary poem hitherto overlooked in this connection. The critics have said that Spenser would scarcely have had the effrontery to dedicate to Sidney's widow a poem using the name under which he had celebrated another person if Sidney had really been in love with Stella. Yet this is exactly what Thomas Watson had done four years earlier than Spenser's poem, with the added circumstance of pointedly omitting any mention of Stella. The significance lies in the fact that an earlier work *had* mentioned her. In 1591 Watson published a pastoral elegy, *Melioboeus,* written in honor of Sir Francis Walsingham, Lady Sidney's father.[15] The Latin version was dedicated to Walsingham's nephew, the English one to Lady Sidney. Watson explained the pastoral disguises: Sidney is Astrophel, Lady Sidney is Hyale, and so forth. Yet, in 1590, before *Astrophel and Stella* was published, Watson refers in his *Italian Madrigals Englished* both to Astrophel and to Stella in one of the earliest known allusions to Stella. The poem is as follows:

> When first my heedless eyes beheld with pleasure
> In Astrophill both of nature and beauty al the treasure
> In Astrophill, whose worth exceeds al measure,
>   my fawning hart with hot desier surpryzed,
>   wyld me intreat, I might not be dispyzed,
> But gentle Astrophil with looks unfained,
> Before I spake, my praier intertained,
> And smiling said, unless Stella dissembleth,
> Her looks so passionat, my love resembleth.

The implication is clear that Watson knew enough of the circumstances not to confuse the two personalities, for, if Stella and Lady Sidney were one and the same, it is strange that he should have chosen the new name of Hyale for her in a poem celebrating Sidney as "Astrophel."

Watson's poem may perhaps be considered merely as additional evidence of the Platonic nature of Sidney's sonnet cycle in the same way that "Astrophel" is thought to indicate it. Yet, it may, on the other hand, indicate merely that Lady Sidney accepted the poetic fame of her husband as a matter of fact—how can she have done otherwise? As for Lady Rich,[16] she was by 1591, or perhaps even as early as 1587, the sister-in-law of Lady Sidney, and, as contemporary allusions in the *Sidney Papers* and other places prove, they were on the best of terms. Such references also reveal the friendly relations of Sir Robert Sidney's family and Lady Rich, and show that Sir Philip's only child, Elizabeth, later Countess of Rutland, was likewise on friendly terms with Lady Rich. One allusion from the *Diary* of Lady Hoby may be noted as an illustration. (Lady Hoby's first husband had been Lady Rich's brother Walter Devereux, her second, Sidney's younger brother Thomas.) The *Diary* contains for January 8, 1600, the following entry: [17]

After priuatt praier I dined, and, sonne after, I went to walsingams house, wher I saw my lady Rich, my lady a Rutland and my lady walsingame: after I Cam home I was pained in the toothach which Contineued with me 4 days after. . . .

Identifying Stella as Lady Sidney seems an impossibility, not only because of the contemporary evidence against it, but also because of the nature of the sonnets themselves. How could the three sonnets punning upon the name "Rich" be accounted for in sonnets about a Walsingham? Why should Sidney have departed from the Petrarchan pattern by writing of someone lost to him by his own blindness if such were not the case? There is no reason to think that Frances Walsingham would ever have been opposed to a marriage to him. Beginning with the second sonnet, he makes it very clear that he had only his own blindness to blame for his unhappiness. The strongest expression, of course, is in Sonnet XXXIII:

> I might—unhappy word, O me!—I might,
> And then would not, or could not see my bliss . . .
> Heart rent thyself! thou dost thyself but right.
> No lovely Paris made thy Helen his;
> No force, no fraud robbed thee of thy delight;
> No Fortune, of thy fortune author is;
> But to myself, myself did give the blow. . . .

Then, too, the cycle reveals the poet's conflict over the rightness of his course—a conflict rather different in tone, as was said in the last chapter, from Petrarch's ecclesiastical misgivings over Laura. Symonds points out that such sonnets would have no meaning if they were written for a maiden and that they would surely have been inappropriate for Frances Walsingham.[18] Any interpretation of these passages (amply treated by Symonds and others) is, to be sure, bound to be a matter of personal opinion, yet the conflict itself cannot be ignored, even when told in terms of wit and will, reason and virtue.[19] The word "alas" in Sonnet IV is the first intimation: [20]

> Virtue! Alas, now let me take some rest.
> Thou sett'st a bate between my will and wit.

Sonnet X states his failure to fulfill his own ambitions:

> Reason! in faith, thou art well served! that still
> Wouldst brabbling be with Sense and Love in me.
> I rather wisht thee climb the Muses' hill,
> Or reach the fruit of Nature's choicest tree,
> Or seek heaven's course, or heaven's inside to see. . . .

Sonnet XIV, addressed to a friend, would appear to have little significance if the poet felt his course to be above reproach:

> But with your rhubarb words ye must contend
> To grieve me worse in saying "that Desire
> Doth plunge my well-formed soul even in the mire
> Of sinful thoughts, which do in ruin end."

Why should his friend (was it Dyer, ten years his senior, or his shrewd and wary contemporary Greville?) have so advised him if no danger threatened? How can No. XVIII be explained if the poet knew his course to be above reproach? He says:

> My youth doth waste, my knowledge brings forth toys;
> My wit doth strive those passions to defend,
> Which for reward, spoil it with vain annoys.
> I see my course to lose myself doth bend;
> I see, and yet no greater sorrow take,
> Than that I lose no more for Stella's sake.

Again, a friend (the same, or another? Dyer, one feels) had reproached him (No. XXI):

Your words, my friend (right healthful caustics!) blame
My young mind marred, whom love doth windlass so;
That mine own writings (like bad servants) show
My wits quick in vain thoughts; in virtue, lame.
"That Plato I read for nought, but if he tame
Such coltish years; that to my birth I owe
Nobler desires: lest else that friendly foe
Great Expectation, wear a train of shame . . .
Sure you say well! Your wisdom's golden mine
Dig deep with learning's spade! Now tell me this,
Hath this world ought so fair as Stella is?"

The struggle continues [21] until Stella herself, if we are to trust the sonnet narrative, decided the outcome and kept the poet to a safe course. The story ends with Sonnet CVIII, on absence and the despair of separation—Nash, it may be recalled, summed up the story in 1591 as "the prologue Hope, the epilogue Despair." To this Sonnet CVIII we may attribute all the later allusions to the unhappy Astrophel, for the sonnet vogue was almost over in 1598 when the Countess of Pembroke first published the two renunciation sonnets which conclude the story for the modern reader.[22] One of these, "Leave me, O love, which reachest but to dust," would hardly have been written if he had married Stella, and so it seems impossible for her to be Frances Walsingham.

The identification of Stella as Lady Rich instead of Sidney's wife now seems beyond cavil, however, because of a recent discovery which sets aside any doubts raised by Spenser's "Astrophel." Ruth Hughey's discovery at Arundel Castle of a manuscript owned by Sir John Harington brings forward contemporary evidence hitherto unknown in regard to the matter.[23] The manuscript contains, in the handwriting of Sir John, the first sonnet of *Astrophel and Stella* with the heading: "Sonnettes of Sr Philip Sidney to ye Lady Ritch." This also confirms, if confirmation is needed, the pun upon Lady Rich's name in the preface to Sir John Harington's translation of the *Orlando Furioso:* [24]

And our English Petrarke, Sir Philip Sidney . . . often comforteth him selfe in his sonets of Stella, though dispairing to attaine his desire, and (though that tyrant honor still refused) yet the nobilitie, the beautie, the worth, the graciousnesse, and those her other perfections as made him both count her, and call her inestimably rich, makes him in the midst of those his mones reioyce e en in his owne greatest losses.

Lady Rich's later history perhaps has no place here, but some references which have apparently not been heretofore mentioned in any of the accounts of her may be included for their own sake. One is in a letter of Philip Gawdy, who wrote to his brother Sir Bassingbourne Gawdy on November 26, 1605, as follows: [25]

My Lo: Riche and my lady wer dyvorsed uppon fryday was sennight before the hye commysioners, when my L. Archbishop chydd my Lo: Riche very muche and gave my lady great commendacion, telling what an honourable house she was of, and how hardly my Lo: had used her, and in the ende very honourably (or rather gratiously) bade my Lorde Riche go amongst his puritans; thanks be to God, his grace colde not touche my ladye withe that heresye, for hers is *error veniales*. This matter hathe done her somme little good anyway and thers an ende of that matter.

Another reference is to the unhappy end of Lady Penelope. A passage in a letter from Thomas Coke to his brother John, on July 21, 1607, says: [26]

The Lady Rich fell sick, sent for Doctor Layfield, disclaimed her last marriage, sent to her first husband to ask forgiveness, and died penitently.

This comment confirms little-known statements in Robert Johnston's *Historia rerum Britannicarum* (Amsterdam, 1655) to the deaths of both Lady Penelope and her second husband, the Earl of Devonshire.[27] Johnston says:

Unde *Devonius,* qui omnibus ex rebus Voluptatem, quasi Mercedem, exegit, abjectis vitæ hujus blandimentis, in Complexu charrissimæ fæminae, cum laudibus, et lachrimis, Os Manusquè ejus exosculantis, supremum spiritum exantlavit. Illa, Dolore Luctuque confecta, non diu supervixit; Pannis pullis, Vittisquè obsita, Noctu, Interdiu, in Thalami sui angulo, humi jacens. Fælices Ambo, si legitimo fædere junctus esset ardens & constans Amor. Funus, mærore Procerum, et Charitate Plebis, celebratum. Funebria Insignia viti Militares tulere. . . . (p. 420)

The death of Lady Penelope herself is described by Johnston as follows:

Penelope, Essexij Soror, insignis formâ fæmina, cui omnes Corporis, Animiquè dotes contigerant, præter Pudicitiam, in ipsâ curâ, ac meditatione Devonij Conjugis, decessit: in quo ab Adolescentiâ summa fortitudo, eximina virtus, singularis Humanitas fuit; et mansura hæc, nisi infaustum Matrimonium cum alienâ Conjuge contraxisset: Jus Matrimoni castum & legitimum violasset; Nobilissimam familiam disturbasset; ac Sobolem in alieno Matrimonio conceptam, in suam familiam inseruisset, propter Similitudinem Oris, ac totius corporis. Hoc Impudentiæ genus non est ferendum publice, aut privatim, ne latius serpat Contagio mali, traheturquè in Exemplum, contrà Iuris Ecclesiastici rationem. Crediderunt plerique, Penelopen morientem, Filiam, & Natos ejus priori Marito commendasse; ac Prolem suam unicuique tribuisse (p. 443).

THE DATE OF THE SONNETS

ONE question remains to be considered in examining the meaning of the sonnets and their relation to Lady Rich as Stella—the probable dates of their composition. This problem is so complicated by the surreptitious, posthumous publication of the cycle that no agreement is likely to be reached in regard to it. Yet, here again, no evidence has been brought forward which disproves the long-established belief that the sonnets record Sidney's love for Lady Rich. The Sidney critics have agreed that most, if not all, of the sonnets were written after the marriage of Lady Penelope Devereux to Lord Rich. Pollard, Wallace, Mona Wilson, and A. H. Bill think that a few may have appeared before the marriage,[28] whereas Sir Sidney Lee has expressed several different opinions regarding them.[29] Symonds and Courthope are inclined to think that practically all the sonnets were written after the marriage; Fox Bourne merely says they were written between 1580 and 1583.[30]

The dates 1580–81 have hitherto usually been assigned to the composition of the sonnets, partly because this period was thought to follow the marriage of Lady Penelope. That date, however, as we shall see, is probably too early, for the marriage of Penelope Devereux is now known to have come later than was formerly supposed. The marriage was thought to have taken place in the spring of 1581 because of two circumstances. One is the fact that the only extant reference known to it is a letter of March 10, 1581, from Huntington, one guardian of Penelope, to Burghley, another guardian, proposing to arrange the match, and it has been assumed that the marriage took place soon afterward. The second fact is that the eighth lyric in the sonnets refers to May, "then young," and says that Stella's "fair neck a foul yoke bare." This was held to refer to May, 1581, with the rest of the sonnets as coming during the months immediately following.

The actual date of the marriage, however, is the end of October, 1581. An entry in regard to it in the *Household Book* of Lord North for 1581 was noted by Purcell: [31] "Oct. 29. A cup to geve to my Ladie Penelope to hir marriage £11.16s." Purcell is apparently correct in assuming that "Ladie Penelope" is Penelope Devereux because of the kinship of Lord Rich and Lord North, and he notes that the gift is more expensive than that of £10 given that year by Lord North to Queen Elizabeth.

Confirmation of this date of Penelope Devereux's marriage is found in a news-letter of September 18, 1581, from Richard Brakenbury to the Earl of Rutland. The letter, sent from the queen's court at Greenwich, first gives the Earl detailed information concerning political news, then the events of the court itself. Among these items is the fact of the approaching marriage of a maid-in-waiting to Lord Rich. In part, the letter is as follows:

The Lord Chamberlain has not come to the Court since his chaplain died of the plague. My Lady and mistress will be married about Allhallow tide to Lord Rich. Though your Lordship is mindless of beauty, our maids are very fair.[32]

Brakenbury, a gentleman usher in Elizabeth's court,[33] has been found to be accurate in his references to political events, but not enough is known about him to explain why he should refer to Penelope Devereux—or any maid-in-waiting at Court—as "My Lady and mistress." Perhaps the marriage was not performed until October because of the reluctance of Lady Penelope to marry Lord Rich, but, if so, the source of that reluctance seems to have been Charles Blunt, later the Earl of Devonshire and Lady Rich's second husband, instead of Philip Sidney.[34] In any event, the marriage was not performed immediately, as has so often been said in biographical accounts of Sidney. And, if Sidney's cycle was written after her marriage, as it appears to have been from the nature of the sonnets themselves, then they came after November, 1581, and "May, then young" must refer to May, 1582.

Internal evidence, at best inconclusive with regard to dates of composition, is especially hazardous in connection with a composition having a conventional framework. Certain sonnets in *Astrophel and Stella* have nevertheless been thought to refer to specific events which if they could be dated would determine the dates of composition of the cycle.[35] One of these, No. XXX, is thought by Pollard to belong to 1581 and by Wallace to refer to 1580; another, No. XLI, by both Pollard and Wallace to refer to 1581. These dates, it will be noticed, agree with the theory that the cycle was for the most part composed largely after the marriage of Penelope Devereux, believed to have come early in 1581.

Purcell, however, has made the suggestion in his *Sidney's Stella* that Sidney's thirtieth sonnet refers to political events in Europe before 1575, probably of the winter of 1573–74, when Sidney was in Italy, and that, therefore, the sonnets cannot have been written to Penelope Devereux. The events to which Purcell refers seem, however, to belong too little to any one year to make it possible to date the sonnets from them, for the references apply equally well to later dates. Is there, for example, anything in the sonnet which opposes the idea that it was written in 1582?

Sonnet XXX, the theme of which is the poet's abstraction, is as follows:

> Whether the Turkish new moon minded be
> To fill his horns this year on Christian coast?
> How Poles' right king means, without leave of host,
> To warm with ill-made fire, cold Muscovy?
> If French can yet three parts in one agree?
> What now the Dutch in their full diets boast?
> How Holland's hearts—now so good towns be lost—
> Trust in the shade of pleasing Orange tree?
> How Ulster likes of that same golden bit
> Wherewith my father once made it half tame?
> If in the Scotch Court be no welt'ring yet?
> These questions busy wits to me do frame:
> I, cumbered with good manners, answer do;
> But know not how, for still I think on you.

Purcell, taking in turn each allusion of the sonnet, first concludes that only an early date could apply to the affairs of Turkey, for after 1579 England had no reason to fear her movements.[36] Yet Sidney says not "English" but "Christian" coasts, and contemporary allusions in the *Fugger News-Letters*[37] and the *State Papers Foreign*[38] showing that Spain greatly feared the Turks in 1582 make Sidney's reference equally appropriate for that year.

Purcell's second conclusion concerns the affairs of Poland and is based in part upon what he took to be Sidney's opinion that the "Poles *right* king" was Henry of Valois, Duke of Anjou. Sidney, however, appears to refer not to Anjou but to Stephen Bathory. Purcell quotes early letters of Languet to Sidney which show his approval of Anjou, yet he ignores a later one of March, 1578, expressing approval of Bathory:

Everyone praises most highly the wisdom and moderation of Bathori the King of Poland. I am glad that we have in Christendom at least one King who possesses some goodness. The Poles are ill pleased that the Germans speak so highly of him.[39]

Purcell (p. 26) misreads, moreover, Fulke Greville's *Life of Sidney* (p. 83) when he says:

. . . that Sidney did not look wholly with favor upon Bathory is pointed out by Fulke Greville, who reports the following observation by Sidney: "Battorie, that gallant man, but dangerously aspiring King of Poland . . . as busy to encroach upon their marches."

In reality the statement that Bathory is a "gallant man, but dangerously aspiring King of Poland" is Greville's, not Sidney's; and Sidney's comment, which begins after that point, pertains only to the trouble between Bathory and the nobility of Poland. If Poland's "right king" was Stephen Bathory (who lived until 1586) Sidney's sonnet allusion might conceivably apply to any of his expeditions against the Muscovites, for it was not until January, 1582, that he concluded a peace with Ivan the Terrible.[40] Then the death of Ivan soon after gave Bathory "hopes of carrying out a great European scheme of conquering Muscovy and incorporating it with Poland, uniting Poland and Hungary, and driving the Turk from Europe." [41]

Purcell seems, too, to misinterpret a note by Pollard upon Sidney's phrase "without leave of host." Pollard's note ends, "for to take 'host' as meaning the 'Muscovites' seems weak." Purcell continues as if Pollard had said the Muscovites were a weak nation, not that the interpretation of "host" as "Muscovites" seems weak. He then proceeds (pp. 27–28) to show that "the Muscovite was considered no negligible force" in 1573. Pollard, however, seems right in considering "host" as meaning "Muscovite." It may here be observed in passing that no good explanation has hitherto been offered for Sidney's phrase in line four, "warm with ill-made fire." Perhaps there is a clue to it in a chance reference observed in Motley's *The Dutch Republic*. Motley, speaking of Renneberg's attack in 1581 on Steenwyk, says:

He bombarded it with red-hot balls, a new invention introduced five years before by Stephen Bathor, King of Poland, at the siege of Danzig.[42]

Sidney's reference to France is sufficiently explained by Pollard as being the three rival parties of the Huguenots, the intolerant Catholics, and the Politiques, or moderates, who were not in accord until 1589, when Henry IV came to the throne. Sidney's references to Scotland and Ireland both seem too indefinite to permit the dating of a sonnet from them. The words "golden bit" appear to offer no help in dating the poem. (Can it refer somehow to the "cess" tax imposed by Sir Henry Sidney?) In Scotland political agitation, especially in the time of Mary Stuart, was so constant that Sidney's line would fit almost any year. Yet the definition of the word "weltering" in the *New English Dictionary* taken from this sonnet as meaning "unstable condition," "political agitation," and so on, appears to invalidate Pollard's note that the sonnet refers to one specific event, the "turbulent scenes which preceded the Raid of Ruthven" in 1581.[43]

The one safe thing to be said in regard to the date of Sonnet XXX is that "the shade of pleasing Orange tree" must refer to William the Silent and that the sonnet must come before his death in 1584. In the last years of his life the Netherlands lost "good towns" in increasing numbers to the Duke of Parma, in spite of their desperate resort to an alliance with France against Spain. It must be remembered, too, that in January of 1582 Sidney was in Flushing, having been sent by Elizabeth as one of the escorts of Anjou. Here Anjou was received on February 10 with all honors by Orange and the Prince of Épinoy. The country was in the hands of William of Orange from the time of the Oath of Abjuration (July, 1581) against Philip of Spain, until March, 1582, when Anjou became official ruler over all the Netherlands except the provinces of Zealand and Holland, which refused to accept any ruler except William.[44] Even after Anjou's rule began, it was William's task to encourage support of the unpopular Frenchman, "to arrange everything, to organize the army, the court, the government." [45] Meantime, Parma had in 1581 won important towns such as Breda and Tournay (November 30), and while waiting for reinforcements in 1582, "had not been idle, but had been quietly picking up several important cities." [46] He won, among others, Oudenarde, Lier, and Ninove; Ypres was regarded as insecure, and Ghent acknowledged Anjou only in August.[47] In 1583 Parma won even more towns, and by 1584 only nine important cities held out against him.[48]

The historical allusions in the thirtieth sonnet, then, are too indefinite to make it safe to accept Pollard's and Wallace's dating of the sonnet as referring to the first few weeks of 1581 or to 1580. There seems no reason at all to accept Purcell's belief that the sonnet comes before 1575. Likewise uncertain as a means of determining a date for the cycle is the first quatrain of Sonnet XLI:

> Having this day my horse, my hand, my lance,
> Guided so well that I obtained the prize,
> Both by the judgment of the English eyes
> And of some sent from that sweet enemy France.

The lines seem to refer to an event which took place during one of the several visits of the French ambassadors to arrange for the marriage of Anjou to Elizabeth. No record is known of a tournament in which Sidney played a winning part during one of these occasions. There are, however, enough general references to these entertainments to indicate that such an event may indeed have taken place. Anjou's last visit in England was from October, 1581, to February, 1582. Contemporary sources such as the *Fugger News-Letters* report tourneys and diversions in his honor during 1581.[49]

Until facts or allusions are turned up, therefore, which will yield new light upon the date of composition of the sonnets, they may be considered as having been written after the marriage of Lady Penelope Devereux to Lord Rich at the end of October, 1581. Presumably, most of them were written in 1582. The "sincerity," or autobiographical truthfulness, of Sidney's cycle is not disqualified by a lack of originality, for, as his age understood that word, his sonnets were original. As we know from the list of allusions marshaled by H. H. Hudson and confirmed beyond cavil by Miss Hughey's discovery of the Harington Manuscript, the sonnets are addressed to Lady Rich. These allusions and the nature of the sonnets themselves indicate that the poet was for a time in love with her. The sonnet vogue and the legend of the unhappy Astrophel arose from the circumstance that for the Elizabethan sonneteers and readers the story ended with the present Sonnet 108, on separation; later sonnets imply that Sidney got himself in hand and that his renunciation of Stella or Lady Rich was final. The poet's wife is a curiously shadowy person, known chiefly from allusions to the death of Sidney, to the fate of her second husband, Essex, and from facts concerning a son by her third husband, the Earl of Clanrickard.[50] She seems to have had no part in inspiring *Astrophel and Stella*.

Sidney's sequence, the first of importance in England, remains today the most readable Elizabethan sequence except that of Shakespeare. The absence of an obsequious tone, the elements of wit and occasional humor, the great artistry and lyric beauty shown in adapting to personal expression the conventional *concetti* of the Petrarchan pattern, all show that Sidney's contemporaries who termed him the English Petrarch gave praise not ill-bestowed.

TABLE OF CONCEITS

DESCRIPTIONS OF CUPID AS THE GOD OF LOVE

Greek derivatives

Beggar, Cupid as: Barnes, XCIII; Constable, Dec. II, 6 and 7; Drayton, XXIII, XLVIII; Greville, XII; Sidney, LXV

Fowler, Cupid and: Barnes, Mads. III, XXV

Fugitive, Cupid as: Barnes, LXXV, XCIII; Greville, XIII, XXXII, XXXV; Linche, XVIII; Sidney, VIII

Irresponsible child or boy, Cupid as: Drayton, XXII, XXXVI; Fletcher, II, IV, V, IX, XXI; Greville, XII, XIII, XX, XXV, XXVI, XXVIII, XXXII, XXXVII, LXII, LXX, LXXI, LXXXV; Griffin, XIV, XVII, XXII, XLII; Lodge, XXXVI; Shakespeare, CXV, CLI; Sidney, XI, XVII, XXXV, XXXVII, XLVI, LXXIII, CI; Watson, I, VI

Little loves, Cupid accompanied by: Barnes, XXIV; Lodge, XXV; Spenser, XVI

Winged god, Cupid as: Fletcher, XIV; Greville, II, XV, XXVII; Sidney, VIII; Tofte, Pt. III, No. 23; Watson, II, VI

Latin, or Ovidian, derivatives

Abode of Cupid: Constable, Dec. III, No. 1; Dec. IV, No. 1; Dec. VI, No. 5; Dec. VII, No. 3; Daniel, LV; Drayton, II, IV, IX of 1599, XXXIX of 1599; Fletcher, XIII, XXXIX; Griffin, XXIII; Linche, IV; Lodge, XIII, XXXIX; Shakespeare, XXXI, XCIII, CIX; Sidney, VII, XII, XLIII, LXII, LXXXIII; Spenser, LX; Tofte, Pt. III, No. 23; Watson, XXII

Fire, Love as: Barnes, XXVIII, LXXVII, LXXXV–LXXXVII, XCII, C; Constable, Dec. I, Nos. 2, 3, 5, 6; Dec. II, No. 5; Dec. V, Nos. 1, 6, 10; Dec. VI, Nos. 3, 5, 6, 7, 8; Dec. VIII, No. 5; Fletcher, VII, XV, XIX, XXVII, XXIX, XXXIII, XLI, XLIV; Griffin, I, VIII, XI, XXIII, LIX; Linche, I, III, XIV, XXXIV–XXXV; Lodge, II, XXV, XXXV, XXXVII, XXXVIII; Sidney, XVI, XXV, XXVIII, XXXV, LIX, LXVIII, LXXII, LXXX–LXXXI, LXXXIX; Smith, V, XVII, XXIII; Spenser, XXII, XXX; Tofte, Pt. I, Nos. 8, 15, 19, 22, 27, 34; Pt. II, Nos. 12, 17, 29; Pt. III, Nos. 3, 8

Labyrinth or maze, Love as: Barnes, XII, XXVII; Watson, Hec. XVIII, LC, XCV; T. of F., LIII

Warfare, Cupid's against the poet

Darts from the ambush of the lady's eye: Barnes, XXVI, LX, LXII, LXVII, LXXXVII, XCIV; Constable, Dec. IV, 8; VI, 5, 8, 9; Daniel, XIV; Linche, I, XXXVI; Lodge, XIX; Percy, I, II, III, XIV, XVIII; Sidney, II, XX; Smith, XXXIV; Spenser, VIII, X, XII, XVI, LVII; Tofte, Pt. II, No. 4

Heart besieged as citadel by Cupid: Barnes, III, Mad. X; Drayton, XXIX; Linche, VII; Percy, X; Sidney, XII, XXXVI; Smith, XXVII; Spenser, XIV

Love conquered by the lady: Barnes, LIV; Drayton, XXVI of 1599, IV, LXI of 1619; Fletcher, V, VII, IX, XIV; Griffin, XXXII, XLIII; LXII; Linche, XXXIV; Sidney, XLII; Spenser, X; *Zepheria,* XIII

Poet as a slave to Cupid: Barnes, LIV; Sidney, II, XXIX, LIII

Yoke, Love as: Barnes, LXV; Sidney, unnumbered sonnet, "Since shunning pain"; Watson, *Hec.,* I; *T. of F.,* XVII

THE EFFECTS OF LOVE

Absence

Daniel, XLVII–XLVIII; Fletcher, XLIII; Griffin, XVIII; Lodge, XXIV–XXV; Shakespeare, LVII–LVIII, XCVII–XCVIII, CXIII; Sidney, LVI, LXXXVII–LXXXIX, XCI–XCII, XCV, XCVII, CIV, CVI–CVIII; unnumbered sonnets "Finding those beams" and "Oft have I mused"; Spenser, LII, LXXVIII, LXXXVI–LXXXVIII; *Zepheria,* XXX

Comparisons, the conventional ones

Animals (wounded hart, hound, and others): Barnes, XXIV; Daniel, V; Drayton, XXXV of 1594, LXII; Griffin, VIII, XIII, XXVI, XXVII; Linche, XXIII; Lodge, XXXI, XXXVIII; Sidhey, "Finding those beams"; Spenser, XXIII, LVI, LXVII, LXXI, LXXVIII, LXXX; Smith, XIX; Tofte, Pt. III, No. 15; Watson, XLIX, LVII; *Zepheria,* III

Birds (phoenix, falcon, nightingale, and others): Barnes, LVII; Constable, Dec. II, No. 8; Daniel, XXXIII (1591 only); Drayton, XVI, LVI; Fletcher, XV; Griffin, XXVI; Linche, VIII; Lodge, X, XXV, XXVII; Shakespeare, XXIX, CII; Sidney, unnumbered sonnet, "Like as to the dove"; Smith, XXIII, XXXIV; Spenser, LXV, LXXIII, LXXXVIII; Tofte, Pt. I, Nos. 9, 36; Watson, VII, LVIII; *Zepheria,* XXVII

Classical personages (Prometheus, Leander, Acteon and others): Barnes, LXI; Constable, Dec. V, No. 10; Daniel, XIII, XV, XLI; Drayton, Nos. XIV, XL, XLIV, XLV; Fletcher, XLI; Griffin, XIII; Linche, XXV; Lodge, III, XXXIV; Sidney, LI; Smith, XVII; Spenser, XXXV, XLIV; Tofte, Pt. I, Nos. 8, 40; Watson, XXI, XLIX; *Zepheria,* VIII

Objects of everyday life (ship, tree, and so forth): Barnes, XXI, XXIX, LXXXII, XCI; Constable, Dec. IV, No. 3; Daniel, XII of 1591; Drayton, I; Linche, XVII, XX; Lodge, XII; Shakespeare, XXXVII, LII, LVII–LVIII, LXXV, LXXX, LXXXVI; Smith, XXX; Spenser, XXXIV, LVI, LXIII; Watson, III; *Zepheria,* XXXIX

Despair, sighs, tears, and death: Barnes, XIV, XV, XXIV, XXV, XXVII, XXIX, XXX, LIII, LVI, LXI, LXXVII, LXXX, XCIV; Constable, Dec. I, No. 1; Dec. II, No. 4; Dec. III, No. 9; Dec. IV, No. 6; Dec. V, Nos. 3–10;

VII, No. 7; Fletcher, dedicatory sonnet; Griffin, I; Lodge, III; Percy, I; Sidney, I, XXXIV; Spenser, I; Watson, dedicatory sonnet; *Zepheria,* II

His grief caused by the lady's scorn of his verse: Drayton, VIII, XXI, XLV; Griffin, LX; Linche, VI; Percy, III; Sidney, XIX, LV; Spenser, XXXVIII, XLVIII; Smith, V, XIV, XV

His verse inspired by the beloved: Barnes, XVII; Drayton, XXXV, XXXIX; Shakespeare, XXXVIII, LXXVI, LXXVIII–LXXIX, CIII; Sidney, XV, XLIV, LV, LXXIV; Smith, I

The effects of her favor (or disfavor) upon his skill: Constable, Dec. I, No. 1; Daniel, VI–VII, LII; Fletcher, XLVII; Percy, VIII; Sidney, LVII, LVIII, LXX; Smith, III, XLI, XLIV, XLVI; *Zepheria,* XVIII, XXX

The beauty of the beloved the reason for his writing

To celebrate it; Constable, Dec. II, No. 1; Dec. III, No. 9; Dec. IV, No. 1; Dec. V, No. 5; Dec. VI, Nos. 3, 6; Dec. VII, Nos. 4, 5; Daniel, II, XVII, LI; Fletcher, dedicatory sonnet; Lodge, XX; Smith, I, II, XLI; Watson, dedicatory sonnet, XXXIII, LIV; *Zepheria,* II

To "eternize" it; Constable, Dec. II, No. 10; Dec. VIII, No. 4; Daniel, XXXIII, XXXVII–XXXIX, XL, L, LIII; Drayton, IV, VI, XLIV–XLV, XLVII; Fletcher, L; Shakespeare, I–XIX, XXI, XXXII, LV, LX, LXIII, LXV, LXXXI, C–CI, CVII; Spenser, XXIX, LXIX, LXXV

THE SONNET LADY

Blonde beauty

Roses and lilies, features of face catalogued as: Barnes, Mads. 4, 11, 24; Sonnets XXVI, XLVI, LXIV, LXXI, LXXVIII, LXXXV, LXXXIX, XC, XCII, XCVI, XCVIII; Constable, Dec. I, Nos. 9, 10; Dec. VI, No. 4; Dec. VII, No. 1; Daniel, VI; Drayton, VIII, XXIX; Fletcher, V, XXX, LII; Griffin, XXXVII, XXXIX; Linche, III, IV, XXII, XXXI–XXXII; Lodge, VIII, XXII, XXXVII; Percy, XII, XV; Sidney, IX, XII, XIII, XXIX, XXXII, XLIII, LII, LXXVII, C, CII; Smith, XVIII; Spenser, XVII, LV, LXXVI–LXXVII; Tofte, Pt. I, No. 29; Pt. II, No. 16; Watson, XXXI; *Zepheria,* XVII, XXIV, XXXIII, XXXIV

Hair (golden, golden wire, golden snare); Barnes, XIX, XXVI, XLVIII, LVIII, LXVIII, LXXI, LXXXIV, LXXXIX, XCVI; Constable Dec. I, Nos. 6, 9, 10; Dec. II, No. 8; Dec. IV, No. 2; Daniel, XIV, XIX, XXXIII, XXXVI–XXXVII; Drayton, VIII, IV of 1594; Fletcher XXX, LII; Griffin, XXXIX; Linche, III, XVI, XXVII; Lodge, IX, XXII; Percy, XII; Sidney, IX, XII, XIII, XXXII, XCI, CIII; Smith, IX, XXVI; Spenser, XV, XXXVII, LXXIII, LXXXI; Tofte, Pt. I, Nos. 16, 29, 31; Pt. II, Nos. 21, 38; Pt. III, Nos. 6, 14, 16, 25, 35; *Zepheria,* XVII

Comparisons of lady,
  Flowers or the springtime: Barnes, XLV, LVIII–LIX, XCVI, Mads. 18, 20; Constable, Dec. I, No. 9; Dec. IV, No. 10; Daniel, XXXIII–XXXVII, XLV–XLVI; Drayton, VIII; Fletcher, XX, XXVIII; Griffin, XXXVII; Lodge, I, VII, XXVIII, XXX, XXXVII; Shakespeare, XVIII, XCVII–XCVIII; Sidney, CI–CII; Smith, XXXI; Spenser, IV, LXIV, LXX, LXXIX; Tofte, Pt. II, No. 8; *Zepheria,* XVII, XXXIII
  Gem: Barnes, XLVIII; Daniel, XIX; Fletcher, LII; Griffin, XXXIX; Sidney, XXIV, XXXII; Shakespeare, CXXXI; Smith, XVIII; Spenser, XV; Tofte, Pt. I, Nos. 7, 25, 29, 30; Pt. II, Nos. 20, 32; Pt. III, Nos. 12, 14, 35
  Goddess: Barnes, XIX, XXVI, LXIV, LXVIII, LXXI, LXXXV, XCVI, Mad. 18; Constable, Dec. I, Nos. 3, 4; Dec. II, No. 10; Dec. VI, No. 10; Daniel, V, X, XIX; Drayton, IV, XIV, XX, XXXIX, XLI; Fletcher, II, III, V, IX, X, XI, XV, XXII, XXIV, XXIX, XXX, XLVIII, LI; Griffin, XXXIX, LVII; Linche, V; Lodge, IX, XXII, XXXIII; Percy, I, II, V, XI, XIII; Sidney, XXXIII, XLII, LXXVI LXXVII, CII; Smith, IX, XLV; Spenser, XXIII–XXIV; Tofte, Pt. I, Nos. 13, 28, 37; Watson, LV; *Zepheria,* VII, XIII, XXIII
  Queen (love, beauty, the poet's heart or soul, and so forth): Barnes, XLV; Constable, Dec. IV, No. 2; Dec. V, No. 10; Daniel, VIII, X, XVI, XIII; Drayton, L, LIII; Fletcher, III, X, XI, XII, XXXVI, XXXVII, XLIX, LI; Griffin, XXXI, LV; Linche, VI, XXXVI; Lodge, IV, XX; Sidney, XXVIII, CVII; Smith, XII; Spenser, III, LXXII; *Zepheria,* XI, XIII, XXXII
  Saint or angel: Barnes, XXVI, XXVIII, XLIV, LXXXIX; Constable, Dec. VI, No. 1; Daniel, VI; Drayton, XVIII, XX, LIII; Griffin, XXXVI; Linche, XII, XXII, XXX; Lodge, X; Percy, XV; Sidney, LXI; Smith, XXII; Spenser, XVII, XXII, LXI, LXXIX; *Zepheria,* XXXIII
  Star: Barnes, LVII, XCV; Constable, Dec. VI, No. 1; Daniel, XII of 1591; XXVIII; Drayton, IV; Fletcher, XXXVIII, XLIII; Griffin, XXXIX; Sidney, XXVI, XLI, XLII, XLVIII, LI, LIII, LX, LXVI, LXVIII, LXXI, LXXVI–LXXVII, LXXXVI–LXXXIX, XCI, XCVI–XCVII, CVIII; Smith, II; Spenser, XXXIV; Watson, XXXI, LIII
  Sun or planet: Barnes, XXII–XXIV, LXXVIII–LXXIX, XCVIII, CII; Constable, Dec. I, Nos. 2, 7; Dec. II, Nos. 3, 10; Dec. VI, No. 1; Dec. VII, Nos. 1, 3; Daniel, VI, XLVIII; Drayton, XLIII, LV; Fletcher, XV, XXV, XXXVIII; Griffin, II, X; Linche, VIII, IX, XIII, XXXI; Lodge, XIX; Percy, VI; Sidney, LXVIII; Smith, XXXVIII, XLIII; Spenser, III, IX, LX, LXXII, LXXXVII–LXXXVIII; Tofte, Pt. I, Nos. 3, 5, 20, 24; Pt. II, Nos. 4, 15, 24; Pt. III, No. 38; *Zepheria,* XVII, XIX, XXVII, XXXIX.
  Stone, steel, flint, marble: Barnes, XXV, LXXXVII; Daniel, XIII,

NOTES

INTRODUCTION

[1] The most important studies in the field are: R. M. Alden, "The Lyrical Conceit of the Elizabethans," *Studies in Philology*, XIV (1917), 130–53, and M. B. Ogle, "The Classical Origin and Tradition of Literary Conceits," *The American Journal of Philosophy*, XXXIV (1913), 125–53, and "The 'White Hand' as a Literary Conceit," *The Sewanee Review*, XX (1912), 459–69. Other studies are Kathleen Lea's "Conceits," *The Modern Language Review*, XX (1925), 389–407, and the chapter in Sir Sidney Lee's *A Life of William Shakespeare* (pp. 112–28) called "The Borrowed Conceits of the Sonnets." Several general phases of the subject are discussed in Elizabeth Holmes's *Aspects of Elizabethan Imagery* (Oxford, 1929) and in H. W. Wells's *Poetic Imagery* (New York, 1924). Miss C. F. E. Spurgeon's *Shakespeare's Imagery* considers the sonnets only incidentally.

[2] The cycles discussed here are those in Sir Sidney Lee's *Elizabethan Sonnets*, Vols. I and II, since these compose the best of the regular cycles and since Lee's edition is the only one generally available: Sidney's *Astrophel and Stella*, Thomas Watson's *The Tears of Fancie*, Spenser's *Amoretti*, Barnabe Barnes's *Parthenophil and Parthenophe*, Thomas Lodge's *Phillis*, Giles Fletcher's *Licia*, Henry Constable's *Diana*, Samuel Daniel's *Delia*, Michael Drayton's *Idea*, William Percy's *Coelia*, Robert Linche's *Diella*, Bartholomew Griffin's *Fidessa*, William Smith's *Chloris*, the anonymous *Zepheria*, and Robert Tofte's *Laura*. Occasional reference is made to Fulke Greville's *Caelica* and to Shakespeare's *Sonnets*. Collections of irregular verse misnamed sonnets are not considered.

[3] Chaucer, however, had translated one of Petrarch's sonnets in rime royal stanzas in *Troilus and Criseyde* (I, stanzas 58–60). He called it the song of Troilus, "as writ myn auctour called Lollius."

[4] Villey, "Marot et le premier sonnet francais," *Revue d'histoire littéraire de la France*, XXVII (1920), 538–47. Villey states that the earliest French sonnet extant is that of Marot to the Duchess of Ferrara and that the earliest to be printed is one of Marot's of 1538. Patterson, *Three Centuries of French Poetic Theory*, Pt. IV, p. 438, accepts this date. See, however, note 11 below, for some views regarding Saint-Gelais as the earliest sonneteer.

[5] Bullock, "The Genesis of the English Sonnet Form," PMLA, XXXVIII (1923), 729–45, mentioned more fully below in note 19.

[6] Chambers, *Sir Thomas Wyatt and So ne Collected Studies.*

[7] Agnes K. Foxwell so lists them, with the names of the discoverers of their sources, in her edition of Wyatt, Vol. II, Appendix A. The sonnets based on Petrarch are Nos. 1–4, 6, 10–12, 14–18, 20–21, 28–29; the one expanded from Sannazaro is No. 19; those from Serafino, Nos. 8, 22. No. 26

is suggested by Filosseno. The sources of the poems included in Tottel's *Miscellany* are listed by Rollins in his edition of that work.

[8] Koeppel, "Sir Thomas Wyatt und Melin de Saint-Gelais," *Anglia,* XIII (1890), 97–99; Lee, *Elizabethan Sonnets,* I, xxxii; Padelford, *Early Sixteenth Century Lyrics,* pp. 111–112; Samuel Waddington, "Mellin de Saint-Gelais and the Introduction of the Sonnet into France," *Athenæum,* July 11, 1891, p. 64.

[9] Torraca pointed out in 1882 that the sonnet of Saint-Gelais was a translation from Sannazaro; Olmsted, repeating that fact in 1897, stated that both Wyatt and Saint-Gelais had translated Sannazaro. Yet it is to Arthur Tilley that credit for the discovery of the sonnet source is usually given after his independent finding of it in 1902. Cf. Olmsted, *The Sonnet in French Literature,* pp. 22–23, 50; Arthur Tilley, *Modern Language Quarterly,* V (1902), 149. The source in Sannazaro is Sonnet 3, Pt. iii, of the *Rime.*

[10] The question was discussed in the following articles:

Berdan, "The Migrations of a Sonnet," *Modern Language Notes,* XXIII (1908), 33–36. Berdan says that Torraca, not knowing Wyatt's version, thinks Saint-Gelais's sonnet is a modification of Sannazaro. Berdan considers that Saint-Gelais translated Wyatt.

——— "Professor Kastner's Hypothesis," *Modern Language Notes,* XXV (1910), 1–4. Berdan, in his *Early Tudor Poetry* pp. 451–52, restates his belief in the impossibility of the influence Saint-Gelais upon Wyatt.

Kastner, "The Elizabethan Sonneteers and the French Poets," *The Modern Language Review,* III (1908), 273–74. Kastner and Berdan each contributed to "Wyatt and the French Sonneteers," *The Modern Language Review,* IV (1909), 240–53.

[11] Villey, *op. cit.,* p. 545, says that the sonnets of Saint-Gelais came later than 1536: "Or, de ces 13 sonnets pas un n'est antérieur à 1544. On ne serait pas fondé assurément à conclure de là que Mellin de Saint-Gelais n'a pas composé de sonnet avant 1544." Olmsted (*op. cit.,* pp. 20–25), however, believes that Saint-Gelais wrote sonnets earlier than did Marot. Other earlier writers have expressed the same opinion. Max Jasinski, *Histoire du sonnet en France* (Paris, 1903), p. 37, dated the sonnet in France as beginning about 1530. Hugues Vaganay, *Le Sonnet en Italie et en France au XVIe siècle* (Lyons, 1902) holds that Mellin wrote sonnets immediately after his return from Italy in 1518; and Molinier, *Mellin de Saint-Gelays (1490?–1558),* dates certain sonnets of Saint-Gelais as early as 1525 and 1533.

[12] The following sonnets are those for which no sources have been indicated. The numbers are from the Foxwell edition:

No. 5. "Eche man me telleth I chaunge moost my devise." Tottel, No. 46.

No. 7. "Ffarewell Love and all thy lawes for ever." Tottel, No. 99.

No. 9. "There was never ffile: half so well filed." Tottel, No. 39.

No. 13. "Though I my self be bridilled of my mynde." Egerton MS.

No. 23. "Dyvers dothe use as I have hard and kno." Devonshire MS only.

No. 24. "Mye love toke skorne my servise to retaine." Tottel, No. 75.

No. 25. "To rayle or jest ye know I use it not." Devonshire MS only.

No. 27. "You that in love finde lucke and habundance." Tottel, No. 43.

No. 30. "Such is the course that natures kind hath wrought." Tottel, No. 84.

Nos. 31–32. "The flaming sighes that boyle within my brest." Tottel, No. 101.

[13] It may be noted that the rebellion and protest expressed in No. 7 occurs more often in the sixteenth century than is commonly recognized. Tottel's volume, as well as later miscellanies and the works of many poets, includes farewells to or renunciations of love. Watson's *Hecatompathia*, for example, contains many sonnets on the theme. None have, however, the quality to be found in Sidney's final sonnets.

[14] In *The Poems of Henry Howard, Earl of Surrey* (edited by Padelford), Nos. 1, 2, 3, 4, and 6 are from Petrarch, No. 5 from Ariosto, and No. 7 (which may be by Lord Vaux) and No. 8 have ideas drawn from Petrarch. No. 8, however, is largely original.

[15] The numbers used here are from Padelford's edition of Surrey, and do not refer to a consecutive number of sonnets. The sonnets presumably Surrey's own work are:

No. 9. "The fansy which that I haue serued long." Tottel, No. 36.

No. 29. "Ffrom Tuscan cam my ladies worthi race." Tottel, No. 8.

No. 30. "When Windesor walles sustained my wearied arme." Tottel, No. 11.

No. 38. "The greate Macedon, that out of Persy chased." Tottel, No. 29.

No. 40. "Th' Assyryans king—in peas, with fowle desyre." Tottel, No. 32.

No. 44. "In the rude age when scyence was not so rife." Tottel, No. 263.

No. 45. "Dyvers thy death doo dyverslye bemone." Tottel, No. 30.

No. 47. "Norfolk sprang thee, Lambeth holds thee dead." Not in Tottel.

[16] Professor Rollins traces the growth of the story in his edition of Tottel's *Miscellany*, II, 70–75.

[17] Padelford, *op. cit.*, p. 210.

[18] Wyatt twice uses, however, the scheme *cdcd ee* in sestets (Nos. 28 and 29); once uses *cdcc dd* (No. 2); once *bcbc bb* (No. 27); and once *bccb dd* (No. 24). One sonnet with a regular scheme in the manuscript source (Foxwell, No. 26) was incorrectly printed by Tottel (No. 42) as *abba acca deed ff*. See Hanscom's "The Sonnet Forms of Wyatt and Surrey," *Modern Language Notes*, XVI (1901), 274–80.

[19] Bullock, *op. cit.*, pp. 740–43. Bullock believes that Wyatt knew the Italian anthology published in Florence in 1527 called the *Raccolta dei Giunti,* where there are seven sonnets with tercets of *xyy xyy*. Bullock

thinks that Wyatt may have considered the second *x* as a final line of a third quatrain: *xyyx yy*. Five of these sonnets are by Cino da Pistoia and one is by Cavalcanti. All have parallels in Wyatt. Bullock thinks, too, that Wyatt may have known (either in manuscript or from the 1527 printed form) the work of Benedetto Varchi, who also used the form which Wyatt twice employed of new rhymes for the couplet. Varchi has sestet schemes such as *xyyx zz* and *xyxy zz*.

[20] Rollins (Tottel's *Miscellany*, II, 103) notes that Surrey has three sonnets in Tottel with only three rhymes (Nos. 9, 10, and 36) and one (No. 2) with only two rhymes. No. 9 in Tottel is No. 7 in Padelford's edition; No. 10 is No. 1; No. 36 is No. 9; and No. 2 is No. 2.

[21] See Rollins's edition, II, 104. Those of Grimald are Nos. 137, 146, and 156. Those by unknown authors are Nos. 173, 179, 186, 232, and 233. Four have rhyme schemes of five or six rhymes: Nos. 218, 219, 241, and 300.

[22] The influence of the "Surrey" sonnet is traced by Emerson in "Shakespeare's Sonneteering," *Studies in Philology*, XX (1923), 111–36. Emerson wrongly follows Lee, however, in saying that Googe wrote no sonnets and that Byrd's songbooks contain none. Both statements will be noticed later in this chapter.

[23] These are occasional sonnets: one praises the *Aeneid* (No. 137); another (No. 156) is an elegy on a patron; the author of the third, No. 146, sends his heart as a New Year's gift to a lady.

[24] See Rollins's edition, Nos. 173, 179, 186, 218, 219, 232, 233, 241, 300.

[25] *Nugae antiquae* (London, 1804), II, 326, 329.

[26] *Thomas Tusser—1557* (edited by Dorothy Hartley, London, 1931), pp. 47–48.

[27] See Walter Raleigh's reprint of the 1561 edition (London, 1900).

[28] The infrequent writing of sonnets has been attributed to the distrust of things Italianate (G. Gregory Smith, *Elizabethan Critical Essays,* Oxford, 1904, I, xxxvi) and to the inherent difficulty of the form (Rollins, Tottel's *Miscellany*, II, 108). There is no sound explanation for the slow growth of the sonnet in that the technical restrictions of the term *sonnet* were not understood, for the actual sonnets in Tottel's *Miscellany* were infrequently imitated. The popularity of the form in France during this period only adds to the perplexity.

[29] The derivation of the word from *sonare* and the French *sonet* resulted in the association of the word with lyrics and ballads. It should be remembered, however, that some adverse criticism against the sonnet, such as that in William Webbe's *A Discourse of English Poetrie,* is in reality directed against the ballad. (Quoted by G. G. Smith, *op. cit.,* I, 264.) *A Handful of Pleasant Delights* of 1584 consists of broadside ballads, such as "Lady Greensleeves" and "A New Sonet of Pyramus and Thisbie," each "sonet" being "orderly pointed to his proper tune."

Examples of ballads called sonnets are: "A Briefe sonet declaring the lamentation of Beckles," *Ballads and Broadsides* ("Roxburghe Club Publications," CLX 261–62), and "A Doleful Ditty, or Sorrowfull Sonet, of Lord Darly" [Darnley], 1567 ("The Harleian Miscellany," X [1813], 264, probably by Henry Chettle.) "The Harleian Miscellany," (II, 111), also contains a poem called "A penitent sonnet written by the Lord Fitz-Gerald (a great Gamester) a little before his death." Timothy Kendall, for example, misuses the word in his "Sorrowfull Sonet upon the Death of Walter, late Erle of Essex," 1577 (*Flowers of Epigrammes,* "Publications of the Spenser Society," Manchester, 1874, Vol. XV).

[30] A convenient list is given by Sir Sidney Lee in his *Elizabethan Sonnets,* I, cv, note 2. An example interesting because of its reference as early as 1594 to "sugared sonnets" is *Greene's Funerals* (*B. R.; Greene's Newes,* and *R. B.; Greene's Funerals,* edited by McKerrow, London, 1911), Sonnet IX. McKerrow says that this poem is evidence that Meres did not mean to attribute any special excellence to Shakespeare's sonnets by calling them "sugared." "Sugred invention" is the phrase in Sidney's *Defense of Poesy* for describing the love in Heliodorus of Theagenes and Chariclea. James I, in a sonnet on a translation of Petrarch's *Triumphs,* says that Petrarch raised a pillar to his name "in toungue Italique in a sugred stile" (*New Poems by King James I of England,* No. 29). Another instance of the phrase is in Sir John Harington's Epigram XXXVII, where Faustus, censured for liking sonnets, defends himself by saying that their "sugred taste" pleases his "likresse senses," Harington preferring the "salt" of his own epigrams. The *Amoretti* sonnets of Spenser were referred to by the printer Ponsonby as "sweete conceited sonets." Lee points out (*Elizabethan Sonnets,* I, xlvi) that the epithet *sucre* is frequent in French sonnets. The word occurs in England, however, much earlier than the sixteenth century in this sense of "pleasant" or "pleasing." The *New English Dictionary* lists examples from Lydgate, Dunbar, Thomas Usk, and others.

[31] In a dedicatory sonnet by George Bucke for Watson's *Hecatompathia, quatorzain* rhymes with *raigne* and *vaine.* A second example in Watson's book is another prefatory quatorzain by the author himself "unto this his booke of Lovepassions." In the preface of *Astrophel and Stella* Nash speaks of the crazed quatorzains of the poets and rhymers who are to put out their rushlights and send their quatorzains to the chandlers. The title page of the 1594 edition of Constable's *Diana* reads: "The excellent conceitful Sonnets of H. C. Augmented with divers Quatorzains of honourable and learned personages." These poems, however, are all sonnets. Although the title of Drayton's 1594 edition is *Ideas Mirrour; Amours in Quatorzains,* all these poems have fourteen lines except Nos. 15 and 16. Barnabe Barnes, in 1595, likewise speaks of his *Divine Centurie of Spiritual Sonnets* as "an hundreth Quatorzaines."

[32] *The Complete Works of George Gascoigne,* I and II. The earliest printed work of Gascoigne appears to be a sonnet of 1566 commending

"The French Littleton." In 1576 he wrote two such sonnets, one to preface a translation of *Cardanus Comforte,* and another, "a prophetical sonet," for Sir Humphrey Gilbert's *A Discourse of a Discoverie for a New Passage to Cataia.* In the same year, he dedicated the French, the Italian, and the Latin versions of his work called "The Tale of Hemetes the Heremyte" to Queen Elizabeth in a sonnet.

[33] Gascoigne used the sonnet, too, as a "Farewell" in his "Dan Bartholmew of Bath" (I, 124), as an "Epilogismus" in his "Fruits of Fetters" (I, 382), and as an introduction to his translation called *De profundis* (I, 59).

[34] Professor Fletcher has called my attention to the fact that Lope de Vega and other Spanish playwrights use sonnets as soliloquies in their plays.

[35] The *Epitaph* on Gascoigne is appended to Whetstone's *Metrical Life of George Gascoigne* (Bristol, 1815), p. 19. That on the Duke of Bedford (1585) is in *The Mirrour of Treue Honour and Christian Nobility,* in Thomas Park's *Heliconia* (London, 1815), II, 31.

[36] For the sonnet of James on Sidney see *New Poems by King James I of England,* p. 29. James also wrote other "epitaphes," such as that upon Montgomery. For the sonnets of Constable see Park's edition in "The Harleian Miscellany," IX, the division called "Funerall Sonets of the Death of Perticulers."

[37] This Princess of Espinoy or Épinoy is the Christine de Lelaing who, during the absence of her husband, so gallantly defended the city of Tournay against Parma's attack in 1581. According to *La Grande Encyclopédie* (XVI, 91) she died in 1582. Motley's *Dutch Republic,* III, 525–26; *The Calendar of State Papers Foreign,* 1581–82, recount her defense of Tournay.

[38] Quoted from Flügel's article in *Anglia,* XIV (1891–92), 346–62, on the poetry of Queen Elizabeth. Also quoted in Ritson's *Biographia poetica,* (London, 1802), pp. 364–65, and in *The European Magazine,* XIII (June, 1788), 391.

[39] Quoted in *The European Magazine,* XIII (1788). See also notes 68–69, below. A curious later instance (1598) of a series or cycle of these elegiac sonnets is one called *Celestial Elegies* written by Thomas Rogers upon the Countess of Hertford. Fifteen goddesses and the nine muses mourn in as many sonnets. Annotations follow to explain each goddess and each muse. In *A Lamport Garland,* "Roxburghe Club Publications," CIX. For such facts as are known about Thomas Rogers see F. B. Williams, Jr., *Thomas Rogers of Bryanston,* "Harvard Studies and Notes in Philology and Literature," XVI, 253–67.

[40] Howell's *Devises,* to the three daughters of the Earl of Shrewsbury. Perhaps the immediate inspiration of the acrostics was a fifteen-line acrostic poem by Grimald (Tottel, No. 141).

[41] Gascoigne wrote two such sonnets to the "same friend," one from "Excester," one from "Founteine belle eaü in Fraunce" in "commendation of the said house of Fountaine bel' eaü." Gascoigne also wrote a sonnet

to "Zouch late the Lady Greye of Wilton whome the auctor found in a homely house." Three occasional sonnets by Gascoigne were written, too, in a friend's copy of *The Golden Ass* of Apuleius (I, 463–64).

[42] Googe addresses a sonnet to a friend (George Holmedon) complaining of the unhappiness caused by a restless mind. The theme of friendship was often used, as in Churchyard's *Charge*, Howell's *Devises*, and *A Gorgeous Gallery of Gallant Inventions*. For the last-mentioned, see the edition by Rollins, p. 69. Howell also wrote on fortune and sorrow.

[43] *The Complete Works of George Gascoigne*, Vol. I. One was written for Kinwelmarsh on *Audaces fortuna juvat;* seven, in a series, were for Neville on *Sat cito, si sat bene*. These have the interlocking lines often used later in the sequences and seem to have been the first of their kind in England. Gascoigne's influence appears to be the inspiration for a sonnet upon a Latin motto and, as well, for a group of three sonnets with interlocking lines called "A Letter to William Th[ynne]," found in the work of the unknown author of "The Poore Knight, His Pallace of Priuate Pleasure," *English Poetry of 1578–79*, "Roxburghe Club Publications," Vol. LXII.

[44] These two poems appeared in later editions of Spenser's work as "The Visions of Petrarch" and the "Visions of Bellay." See Dodge's edition of Spenser's *Complete Poetical Works*, pp. 764–65, and Jones' *A Spenser Handbook*, pp. 120–25.

[45] See Dodge's edition, pp. 764–65, and Jones, *op. cit.*, pp. 107–10.

[46] Googe, *Eglogs, Epytaphes, and Sonettes*, "Arber Reprints" (London, 1871), p. 95. Googe obviously did not understand the restrictions of the term "sonnet," for poems of every length, including five by his friends, are all called sonnets. These were divided by the publisher into two half lines, a form that misled Sir Sidney Lee and others into saying that Googe wrote no sonnets. The existence, however, of the two regular sonnets was noted by P. N. U. Harting, "The 'Sonnettes' of Barnabe Googe," *English Studies*, XI (1929), 100–102; by Hebel and Hudson, *Poetry of the English Renaissance*, p. 952; and by Hudson in *Modern Language Notes*, XLV (1930), 540–43. Also, they were printed by Hudson in PMLA, XLVIII, 293–94.

[47] Howell's *Devises, op. cit.*, pp. 16, 25, 34, 48. The book also contains a number of didactic sonnets by Howell and his friends.

[48] *The Complete Works of George Gascoigne*, I, 471–72, "Certayne Notes of Instruction Concerning the Making of Verse or Ryme in English": ". . . then have you Sonnets, some thinke that all Poemes (being short) may be called Sonets, as in deede it is a diminutive worde derived of *Sonare*, but yet I can beste allowe to call those Sonets whiche are of fouretene lynes, every line conteyning tenne syllables. The firste twelve do ryme in staves of foure lines by crosse meetre, and the last twoo rhyming togither do conclude the whole. There are Dyzaynes, & Syxaines which are

of ten lines, and of sixe lines, co͞monly used by the French, which some English writers do also terme by the name of Sonettes."

[49] See Bowers, "Notes on Gascoigne's *A Hundreth Sundrie Flowers and The Posies.*" For B. M. Ward's belief that the work is an anthology, with verse by Hatton and others, see his edition of the *Hundreth Sundrie Flowers* (London, 1926). Gascoigne's statements in the second edition, called *Posies,* to the "reverende Divines" and "To the Readers" imply that he wrote many sonnets for others—"For in wanton delightes I helped all men, though in sad earnest I never furthered my selfe any kinde of way" (I, 17).

[50] One was omitted in the 1575 edition of *The Poesies.* Cf. *op. cit.,* I, 496. "G. T.," the nominal editor of *The Hundreth Sundrie Flowers,* says that two sonnets are translations from the Italian, but the statement is omitted in the 1575 edition for that beginning "Love, hope, and death do stirre in me such strife." The other one said in the 1573 edition to be translated is that beginning "The stately dames of rome, their pearls did wear." Three sonnets of this work are in a sequence and are called a "terza sequenza" (pp. 388–89). The mottoes in Gascoigne's work and the involved comment in regard to them need not be entered into here.

[51] The point is not without interest, for it is the only instance in Gascoigne of the word "sonnet" being misapplied. The error probably arises from an original ordering of the manuscript. If "G.T." is really George Turbervile, the heading is understandable, for he consistently misused the word with regard to his own verse. Whatever the source of the error, it occurs both in the 1573 and 1575 editions.

[52] Rollins suggests in his edition of the *Paradise* (p. lxvi) that the sonnet was withdrawn because of its inappropriateness in so grave and sedate a work.

[53] *A Gorgeous Gallery of Gallant Inventions,* pp. 56, 58, 69, 108, 111.

[54] Mentioned more fully in the next chapter.

[55] Foscolo, *Essays on Petrarch,* pp. 90–92, and Tatham, *Francesco Petrarca,* I, 204, believe that Petrarch tested the rhythm of the sonnets and the lyrics of the *Canzoniere* by singing them to his lute. Villani (d. 1405) in his *De illustribus Florentiae civibus* says in regard to it: "His prædictis artibus, ne quidquam suæ deesset disciplinæ, vulgaribus audiis atque sonictis quæ per rhytmos maternâ locutione defluerent, se frequenter immiscuit, in quibus incredibile et ferê angelicam (si sic dicere fas est) dictandi potentiam atque decorem ostendit. Tantâ si quidem dulcedine fluunt, ut ab eorum pronunciatione et sonis gravissimi nesciant abstinere. Doctus insuper lyra mirê cecinit undè labores studii molestioris levabat." (Published by Sade in *Mémoires pour la vie de François Petrárque,* 1764, III, Appendix, 10). Foscolo (*op. cit.,* p. 57) quotes Petrarch's notes to show that he composed with a melody in mind, such as "I must make these two verses over again, singing them (*cantando*), and I must transpose them; 3 o'clock, A. M., 19th

October." He mentions (p. 91), too, the will of Petrarch bequeathing his lute to a friend. The will itself is quoted in many early editions of the *Canzoniere* such as that printed in 1568 in Venice by Bevilacqua. Tatham says that, knowing the melodies of the troubadours, he must have had some special cadence in mind in testing his poems by his lute.

56 These were inaccurately printed—one with the eleventh line divided between the tenth and the twelfth and the other with the false rhyme "despite" for "despair," to rhyme with "fair." These errors misled Sir Sidney Lee and O. F. Emerson ("Shakespeare's Sonneteering," *op. cit.*, p. 113n) into saying that this book contained no sonnets. The musical form is available in E. H. Fellowes, *The English Madrigal School*, Vol. XIV.

57 Byrd's *Songs of Sundrie Natures* (1589) contains six sonnets as two-part songs. Fellowes says that the practice of the musicians was to print the second part of a madrigal on a separate page and to number it as an independent composition. When the poem was a sonnet, the octave was treated as two quatrains and the sestet as an entirely separate poem. The treatment given the six sonnets from Byrd's 1589 edition is as follows (Fellowes, *op. cit.*, Vol. XV): The music for two sonnets ("When younglings" and "Upon a summer's day") is separately written and numbered for the two parts. Both are sung straight through and are for three voices. (Nos. x-xi, xii-xiii.) Two others ("Is Love a boy?" and "Wounded I am") repeat the quatrains as two stanzas, with separate music for Part II. (Nos. xv-xvi, xvii-xviii.) Both are for four voices. The one beginning "Weeping full sore" also repeats the second quatrain as the second stanza, but the sestet has no separate numbering. The song is for five voices. (No. xxvi.) The last sonnet, "Of gold all burnished," for five voices, is divided as a two-part song (Nos. xxxvi-xxxvii.) For the text see Bullen, *Some Shorter Elizabethan Poems*, pp. 33, 34, 35, 39, 45.

58 Gibbon's "Silver Swan," for instance, is built around six lines. Weelkes's "Welcome, Sweet Pleasure" and Morley's "Sing We and Chant It" are in dimeter measures. Sometimes the musicians shortened the sonnets. Farmer, in his 1599 *Madrigals,* used a sestet of a sonnet of Constable's *Diana* (Dec. V, No. 4) and of two of Bartholomew Griffin's *Fidessa* (Nos. XIII and XLVI). Ward used another method in his *Madrigals* (No. 26) in a sonnet (No. IX) from Davidson's *Poetical Rhapsody:* he omitted six lines, but not consecutive ones, from the poem. In 1630 many complete sonnets and lyrics from Greville's *Caelica* were put to music by Peerson in his "Motets of Grave Chamber Music." (Greville's sonnets themselves, however, were not published until 1633.) The sonnets to be found from Byrd to Peerson are usually sung straight through, although separate numberings are sometimes used for the sestet. Willa M. Evans, to whom I am indebted for several suggestions in this work, has recently discovered a hitherto-unknown musical setting by Henry Lawes for Shakespeare's Sonnet No. CXVI. See PMLA, LI (1936), 120–23.

[59] See Carlton's *Madrigals* of 1601 and Gibbon's *Madrigals* of 1612, both available in Fellowes, *English Madrigal Verse.*

[60] Translated in 1583, published in 1598, and dedicated, he says, to Lady Rich because of her knowledge of Spanish.

[61] See Jordan's *Robert Greene,* chap. v, for a discussion of Greene's sonnets. The doubtful one printed by Dyce and Collins is "Ah, were she pitiful as she is fair." Greene has only two genuine sonnets, one in *A Groats-Worth of Wit*—"What meant the Poets to invective verse," and one in *Francescos Fortune*—"Reason that long in prison of my will." Dyce prints as fourteen-line poems two seven-line poems from *Philomela (Dramatic and Poetical Works of Robert Greene and George Peele,* London, 1861, p. 315).

[62] Lodge added "sonnets"—but only one genuine one, and that translated from Desportes—to the end of *Scillaes Metamorphosis.* His novels have "sonets," "sonnettos," and "sonnets" which are almost never sonnets except in *The Life and Death of William Longbeard* and *A Margarite of America.* See *The Complete Works of Thomas Lodge,* "Hunterian Club Publications," Vols. IV–VIII.

[63] Miss Scott (*op. cit.,* pp. 15–17) says that these sonnets imitate foreign sonnets with less independence than do those of *Astrophel and Stella,* although even here Sidney is never servile—one can merely note from time to time the poem which gave him his inspiration.

[64] The total number is present only in the original version, now available in Feuillerat's edition (Cambridge, 1926). The sonnets are: Bk. I, pp. 25, 27; Bk. II, pp. 89, 91, 108, 118, 119; Bk. III, pp. 169, 170, 171, 179, 187, 189, 196, 202, 206, 216, 219, 236; Bk. IV, p. 256; Bk. V, p. 347.

[65] This edition was made by adding to the revised section (Bks. I, II, and 164 pages of Bk. III) the unrevised Bks. III, IV, V. Page 164 of the revised Bk. III was continued by beginning at about p. 5 of the unrevised Bk. III.

[66] Stated in the form of a summary by Sir Sidney Lee in his *Elizabethan Sonnets,* I, xxxix.

[67] See Scott, *op. cit.,* pp. 7–9.

[68] George Steevens suggested that Soowthern was a Frenchman with an Anglicized name and that the scarcity of the extant volumes of *Pandora* may have resulted from the suppression of the work by Elizabeth or by the Countess of Oxford because of the publication of their sonnets in it. Cf. Thomas Corser, *Collectanea Anglo-Poetica* ("Publications of the Chetham Society," CVIII. Manchester, 1880), 251–53.

[69] Quoted from the facsimile text edition based upon the Huntington Library copy. There are comments on Soowthern in Sir Sidney Lee's *Elizabethan Sonnets,* I, l-li; in Janet Scott's *Les Sonnets élisabéthains,* pp. 10–13; in Corser, *op. cit.,* and in Ritson's *Biographia poetica (op. cit.,* p. 337). There

is also a passage with marginal notations, in Michael Drayton's *Odes,* 1619,
"To Himselfe and the Harpe," which refers to John Soowthern:
"Southerne, *an*
English *Lyrick*"

> "*Sowtherne,* I long thee spare,
> Yet wish thee well to fare,
>   Who me pleased'st greatly,
> As first, therefore more rare,
> Handling thy Harpe neatly.

> To those that with despight
> Shall terme these Numbers slight,
>   Tell them their Iudgement's blind,
> Much erring from the right,
> It is a Noble kind. . . ."

[70] Lee suggests that they were made by Daniel (*Elizabethan Sonnets,* I, xlii.)

[71] See Brady's *Samuel Daniel; a Critical Study.* For a study of the names of the heroines of the sequences see Janet G. Scott's "The Names of the Heroines of the Elizabethan-Sequences," *The Review of English Studies,* II (1926), 159–62. *Delia* is from Scève's *Délie,* anagram for *L'Idée.*

[72] The facts in regard to the copies known of the early editions of Constable's work appear to be as follows: The first nineteenth century reference to the 1592 edition seems to be that of Payne Collier in his notes to a catalogue of the Heber Collection (London, 1834) as Item No. 513. Collier later refers to this volume in his comments on the *Catalogue of the Earl of Bridgewater's Collection* (London, 1837, p. 284), in *Notes and Queries,* 3 Ser., No. I, pp. 321–22, 1862, and at greater length in his *Bibliographical and Critical Account of the Rarest Books in the English Language* (London, 1866, I, 187–89).

Collier's 1592 copy passed to the Heber Collection (Hazlitt, *Handbook to the Popular, Poetical, and Dramatic Literature of Great Britain,* London, 1867, p. 119). It later went to the Britwell Library, thence to Dr. Rosenbach, who paid £2700 for it in 1924 (*Book Auction Records,* London, 1924, 379). From his ownership it went to the Huntington Library, and is probably unique.

Three copies of the 1594 edition are known. They are in the Bodleian, the British Museum, and the Huntington libraries, respectively. The copy in the Bodleian was once the property of Edmund Malone and seems to have been that known to Park and other early nineteenth-century readers. W. C. Hazlitt says of it: "The Malone copy is in a volume which was sold at Dr. Bernard's auction in 1698, and was about 70 years later bought off a stall in Salisbury by Joseph Warton for a trifle. It was presented by his brother Thomas to Malone." (*Bibliographical Collections and Notes on Early English Literature,* 1474–1700, Ser. 4, 1903, p. 83.)

The copy now in the British Museum was also owned by Malone, who passed it on to Bindley in 1796. It was later the property of Archibald Constable of Edinburgh in 1822 and of Corser in 1868 (Corser, *Collectanea Anglo-Poetica, op. cit.,* Pt. 4, p. 437). Some of Corser's comments indicate that he confuses this 1594 edition with that of 1592.

The Huntington Library copy has facsimile leaves which Dr. L. B. Wright informs me agree with the genuine leaves of the British Museum copy, but vary considerably from those of the Bodleian. This leads him to believe that there were two editions of 1594 and to the conjecture that when Bindley's copy was sold in 1818 Payne Collier "got hold of it and made a facsimile reprint supplementing the missing leaves by facsimiling those of the Malone copy, then in the hands of Boswell, Malone's posthumous editor. The dating of the book, 1584 [i. e., 1594] seems to have originated with Collier."

Collier refers, in his *Bibliographical and Critical Account of the Rarest Books in the English Language* (I, 187), and in *Notes and Queries,* 3 Ser., No. 1, pp. 321–22, to editions of 1597 and 1604. It appears, however, that there were no such editions. Hazlitt disposed of the "1604" edition as erroneous: the copy of the edition described in a catalogue of Bindley (1818) proved to be in reality a copy of the 1594 edition with the date cut off. That description had led to the belief in a 1604 edition (*Notes and Queries,* 4 Ser., II, p. 292; and *Bibliographical Collections and Notes on Early English Literature,* Ser. 2, p. 139).

Nothing is known of an edition in 1598, although Arber's *Transcript,* III, 44, November 6, contains the entry "Diana Sonnettes [by H. Constable] in 16°," for William Wood.

Modern readers, however, knew Constable's work from neither the 1592 nor the 1594 edition, but a third and a very different volume of his poems published in 1812 by Thomas Park from a sixteenth-century manuscript then owned by Todd, the editor of Milton ("The Harleian Miscellany," IX, 489–519). Todd nowhere states that the manuscript is in Constable's hand. He says that through the kindness of a Canterbury bookseller ("Mr. Alderman Bristow"), he possessed "a very curious little volume, in manuscript, of several Sonnets, Satires, Epigrams, etc., written by different poets in the reign of Elizabeth, among which are Constable's Sonets, commencing with a poetical address *To His Mistresse.*" He then describes the manuscript which Park published in "The Harleian Miscellany" (H. J. Todd, *The Poetical Works of Milton,* London, 1801, V, 443). Park, editing the manuscript, says that Bristow had purchased it "along with the library of a family in Kent." The manuscript itself seems to be no longer in existence, but presumably the whole was a transcript with the order of arrangement coming originally from Constable's own hand.

The sixty-three sonnets of this manuscript include all but one of the 1592 sonnets of *Diana* and five from the 1594 edition. The introductory sonnet, "To his absent Diana," is omitted. The remaining thirty-six are occasional sonnets addressed to persons ranging from Queen Elizabeth to King James of Scotland and from Lady Rich and other noble ladies to Arabella Stuart. At the end are two sonnets by unknown hands. That to "H.C., upon occasion of leaving his countrye" undoubtedly refers to one of the political flights of Constable:

> "England's sweete nightingale! What frights thee so,
> As over sea to make thee take thy flight?
> And there to live with native countryes foe
> And there him with thy heavenly songs delight? . . .
> Come then, feare thou not the cage, but loyall be,
> And ten to one thy Soveraigne pardons thee."

The extent of Constable's own work in the sonnets read today as his—the 1594 edition—is therefore by no means certain. Both the 1594 edition and Todd's sixteenth-century manuscript have curious divisions or groupings of the sonnets—the one into "decades," the other into three groups, "each part with three several arguments and every argument seven sonnets." These divisions may, however, have been made by the printer and the copyist rather than by Constable himself.

Various editors have followed different practices regarding the arrangement. Hazlitt's 1859 edition, which includes only the twenty-seven indicated by Warton as Constable's, follows neither the order of the 1592 nor that of Todd's manuscript. The result is a lack of continuity. Arber, Lee, and Martha Foote Crow (who had consulted the Harleian edition and supplied the titles from it to the poems there), all follow the 1594 edition. Ruth Hughey observes that a different order is given in the Harington Manuscript ("The Harington Manuscript at Arundel Castle and Related Documents," *The Library*, XV [1935], 433). The order there, as compared with the 1592 edition, is 1-11, 2-12, and so forth, in jumps of ten. Cf. Lowndes, *Bibliographer's Manual*, I, 512, for other modern editions.

Perhaps it should be stated that the pastoral poems which Hazlitt printed as signed "H.C." are by Henry Chettle. See Rollins's edition of *England's Helicon* (Cambridge, 1935), II, 26-27.

73 Ruth Hughey, *op. cit.*

74 *Ibid.,* p. 433.

75 It is clear that Constable knew Sidney. The date, however, of his sonnets addressed to Sidney's soul is puzzling. Of the three poems appearing in Sidney's *Defense of Poesy* in 1595, one begs the pardon of Sidney's soul because he has not felt the loss sustained in Sidney's death. Since that event had occurred in 1586 and since Sidney was universally mourned

in England, it is strange that Constable did not know of it. Constable may, however, have been in Italy in 1586, for in 1585 he wrote to the Earl of Rutland of his determination to travel there. (*Historical Manuscripts Commission Reports,* "Rutland Papers," I, 173.) Puzzling, too, is the date of composition of Constable's sonnet "To the Countess of Essex on Her Late Husband's Death."

[76] Scott, *op. cit.,* chap. iv.

[77] Cf. Sidney Lee, *Elizabethan Sonnets,* I, 137n.

[78] *Ibid.,* The Preface and p. 165.

[79] See the work of Mark Eccles on Barnes in the volume edited by C. J. Sisson called *Thomas Lodge and Other Elizabethans.* The word play is in passages such as the last lines of Sonnet XLIV.

[80] Lee, *A Life of William Shakespeare,* pp. 135–38.

[81] Scott, *op. cit.,* chap. vi. See also Sisson, *op. cit.,* E. A. Tenney's *Thomas Lodge,* and N. B. Paradise's *Thomas Lodge.*

[82] Scott, *op. cit.,* chap. vii.

[83] Available in its original form in Cyril Brett's edition of Drayton's *Minor Poems.*

[84] See Bullen's *Elizabethans* for such evidence as is known.

[85] Elton, *Michael Drayton, a Critical Study,* Appendix.

[86] Listed by Lee, *Life of Shakespeare,* p. 114.

[87] Cf. Schelling's *Elizabethan Drama* and V. E. Albright, *Modern Philology,* XI (1913), 237–46.

[88] *Daphnaïda and Other Poems,* edited by Renwick, p. 193.

[89] A. S. W. Rosenbach quotes the sonnet, with its verbal differences, and gives a facsimile from the 1590 copy of the *Faerie Queene* owned by him. (*Books and Bidders,* Boston, 1927, pp. 148–50.)

[90] *Times Literary Supplement,* May 10 and 24, 1923; Renwick, *Daphnaïda,* p. 198.

[91] Long, "Spenser and Lady Carey," *The Modern Language Review,* III (1908), 257–67; and "Spenser's Sonnets 'as published,' " *ibid.,* VI (1911), 390–96.

[92] *Daphnaïda and Other Poems,* pp. 195–96. Renwick (pp. 195–96) makes, too, the most satisfactory comment available upon the autobiographical nature of the sonnets of Spenser.

[93] See the introductory note to the edition of *Diella* published by Grosart in Vol. IV of his *Occasional Issues.*

[94] Lee, *Elizabethan Sonnets, II,* 335–36; Grosart, *Occasional Issues,* Vol. XII, and, for another work of Tofte, G. M. Kahrl, "Harvard Studies and Notes in Philology and Literature," Vol. XVIII (1935).

[95] Miss Scott notices some of them in her *Les Sonnets élisabéthains.* See also note 101, for Drummond.

[96] Sidney Lee, in his *Elizabethan Sonnets,* I, cv-cvi, lists poems belonging

"practically to the same category" as the collections of sonnets. Although they are in six, eight, or ten-line stanzas, he says that they "closely resemble in temper" the sonnet sequences. There seems small reason, however, for including *Willobie's Avisa* among them because of the narrative form and presumably satiric intent of the work. Cf. Pauline K. Angell, "Light on the Dark Lady: A Study of Some Elizabethan Libels," PMLA, LII (1937), 652–74.

[97] See Purcell's "Sidney's *Astrophel and Stella* and Greville's *Caelica*," PMLA, L (1935), 413–23. For Greville, see Bullen, *Elizabethans,* and M. W. Croll, *The Works of Fulke Greville* (Philadelphia, 1903).

[98] Brooke, *Shakespeare's Sonnets.* One of the best comments previous to this work is Bates's "The Sincerity of Shakespeare's Sonnets," *Modern Philology,* VIII (1910), 87–106. Bates gives, too, one of the best of the available short summaries of the history of the sonnet.

[99] There are numerous discussions of the more general phases of the subject. Leigh Hunt's introductory essay in his *The Book of the Sonnet* (Boston, 1867) is useful, especially for the form of the sonnet. A scholarly account of the sonnet form is to be found in Smart's preface to his edition of Milton's sonnets (Glasgow, 1921). "The Sonnet in England," by J. A. Noble (London, 1896), is a very general and very brief survey of the English sonnet. T. W. H. Crosland's *The English Sonnet* (London, 1917) is an inaccurate personal interpretation of certain sonnets and sonneteers. Of Charles Tomlinson's *The Sonnet, Its Origin, Structure, and Place in Poetry* (London, 1874) Bullock says that to it "may be traced most of the erroneous ideas as to the Italian sonnet still current with English and American writers." (PMLA, XXXVIII, 738.)

[109] Petrarch's rhymes are summarized by E. D. Hanscom in "The Sonnet Forms of Wyatt and Surrey," *Modern Language Notes,* XVI (1901), 274–80. The forms of the verse of Wyatt and Surrey are discussed in the articles mentioned earlier in this chapter. R. G. Whigam and O. F. Emerson present a study of Sidney's verse form in *Studies in Philology,* XVIII (1921), 347–53. Miss Scott, *op. cit.,* gives excellent brief comments on each poet discussed.

[101] Kastner has a series of articles in *The Modern Language Review* (II, III, IV, V, VII) on the relations of the French, English, and Scottish sonneteers, especially Drummond of Hawthornden. See, too, Koeppel, "Studien zur Geschichte des englischen Petrarchismus im sechzehnten Jahrhundert," *Romanische Forschungen,* V (1890), 65–98; Lee, *Elizabethan Sonnets,* Preface; and *The French Renaissance in England;* and Scott, *op. cit.*

[102] White, *Plagiarism and Imitation during the English Renaissance.*

[103] "The Elizabethan Sonnet," *The Cambridge History of English Literature,* III, 305–8.

[104] Discussed by Ruth S. Phelps in "The Forms of Address in Petrarch's *Canzoniere*," pp. 71–77. The sonnets termed "friendship-poems" are listed on p. 71.

[105] Reproduced by photograph in *L'originale del canzoniere di Francesco Petrarca Codice Vaticano Latino 3195* (Milano, 1905) and reprinted in facsimile in *Il canzoniere di Francesco Petrarca* (Roma, 1905).

[106] Phelps, *The Earlier and Later Forms of Petrarch's Canzoniere*, p. 201, says of these manuscripts: "As is well-known, the manuscript V.L. 3195 was written in part by Petrarch's scribe and in part by Petrarch himself. The scribe transcribed the first and larger moiety of Part I—190 poems—and the first and larger moiety of Part II—55 poems—while Petrarch finished the transcribing of both parts." Excellent studies of both manuscripts will be found in Wilkins, "On the Transcription by Petrarch in V.L. 3195, I and II," *Modern Philolgy*, XXIV (1926), 261–68, 389–401; and "The Dates of Transcription of Petrarch's Manuscript V.L. 3195," *Modern Philology*, XXVI (1928), 283–94.

[107] Tatham, *Francesco Petrarca*, I, 273.

[108] *Ibid.*, p. 277.

[109] *Ibid.*

[110] Phelps, *The Earlier and Later Forms of the Canzoniere*, p. 73.

[111] Ferrazzi, *Enciclopedia Dantesca* (Bassano, 1877), V, 760.

[112] The first copy listed in the British Museum Catalogue is 1784. This may not, however, be the earliest printing in England.

[113] The first complete translation seems to have been by R. G. MacGregor in 1851.

[114] Fletcher summarizes the points of similarity between the sonnets of Petrarch and Dante in the following comment upon Petrarch: "His *Canzoniere*, or sonnet sequence—as we say, though other forms than the sonnet are represented,—repeats the dramatic crises of the *Vita Nuova*: The sudden and almost mystical meeting and enamourment; the repulse by his lady; her death; her forgiveness and intercession in heaven; his imagined meeting with her there. Even the temporary turning for consolation to another is there. As Dante pays Beatrice the greater tribute of the *Commedia*, so Petrarch pays Laura that of the *Trionfi*. Both are 'visions' and in *terza rima*. Both emphasize the redeeming of the poet by the grace of his lady. And there are, moreover, innumerable coincidences in diction, phrase, metrics." (*Literature of the Italian Renaissance*, pp. 61–62.)

[115] Bates, "The Sincerity of Shakespeare's Sonnets," p. 92, says: "The Petrarchistic love situation was essentially static, not dynamic. By the terms of the hypothesis it could have no outcome. The lover does not act; he simply feels, and his variety of feeling is all conditioned by the larger unity of the unchanging situation. Eternal fidelity to an unresponsive mistress is the theme of nine-tenths of the Renaissance sonnets, and this theme does not permit development in time. The term 'sonnet sequence'

as applied to these collections is an entire misnomer. With the exceptions of Sidney, Spenser, and Shakespeare, the narrative element is rarely found in the Elizabethan or other Renaissance sonnets."

[116] Instances of independent Italian sonnets on similar themes may be read in Rossetti's translation in "The Italian Poets Chiefly before Dante" and in "Dante and His Circle," *The Poems and Translations of Rossetti* (London, 1926).

[117] "Dante and His Circle," *op. cit.*

[118] Within the cycles discussed there are only the following examples: Constable addresses a sonnet in *Diana* (Dec. I, No. 10) to Lady Rich; Fletcher one in *Licia* to the daughters of Lady Molineux (No. XL); Barnes one to Sidney's Stella (No. XCV). There are also instances in the later editions of Drayton's sonnets.

[119] Constable's *Diana*, however, has a sonnet appended to it on the death of an infant daughter of Lady Rich.

[120] *The Divine Comedy* (translated by Fletcher, New York, 1932), "Purgatory," XXVI, ll. 97–99.

[121] Moseley, *The "Lady" in Comparisons from the "Dolce Stil Nuovo";* mentioned more fully in Pt. II of this study.

[122] Merrill, "Platonism in Petrarch's *Canzoniere*," *Modern Philology*, XXVII (1929), 161–74.

[123] The material of this paragraph is condensed from Langley's "The Extant Repertory of the Early Sicilian Poets," PMLA, XXVIII (1913), 454–520, and Wilkins, "The Invention of the Sonnet," *Modern Philology*, XIII (1915), 463–94. The following paragraphs are based upon the work of Wilkins.

[124] Wilkins, *op. cit.*, pp. 493–94.

[125] Francis Hueffer, *The Troubadours* (London, 1878), p. 106, says that the only sonnet existing in the language of Provence was written, not by a Provençal, but by the Italian Dante da Maiano, a contemporary of Dante.

[126] *The Poetry of Giacomo da Lentino*, Sonnet XXIII and p. 123n. This sonnet, however, differs from some of the others of Giacomo in that the second quatrain does not begin with a capital letter.

[127] Wilkins, *op. cit.*, p. 493.

[128] *The Poetry of Giacomo da Lentino*, p. xxii.

[129] H. A. R. Gibb, the chapter called "Literature," in *The Legacy of Islam*, edited by Sir Thomas Arnold and Alfred Guillaume (Oxford, 1931); and A. R. Nykl, *A Book Containing the Risāla Known as the Dove's Neck-Ring* (Paris, 1931).

[130] Amy Kelly, "Eleanor of Aquitaine and Her Courts of Love," *Speculum*, XII (1937), 3–19.

[131] See Fletcher, *Literature of the Italian Renaissance*, chap. xiv; Vianey, *Le Pétrarquisme en France au XVIe siècle*, pp. 1–81,

[132] *Enciclopedia Italiana*, XVI, 385.

[133] *Ibid.*, XXXIII, 372.

[134] Vianey (*op. cit.*, pp. 19–20) says of Chariteo: "Chariteo a d'autres titres à l'attention que d'avoir, avec Tebaldeo, inauguré la préciosité. C'est chez lui, pour la première fois, que la poésie pétrarquiste rompt vraiment avec ses traditions. Vocabulaire, tours de phrases, façons de dire, images, composition du sonnet, métrique des sextines et des chansons, toute la rhétorique de l'*Endimion* est encore celle du *Canzoniere*. Et, à première vue, il ne semble pas que Pétrarque ait un imitateur plus docile que Chariteo; mais l'inspiration n'est plus pétrarquiste: la forme vient de Pétrarque; le fond vient de Catulle, de Tibulle, de Properce, d'Ovide, de Virgile . . . quelquefois il dérive directement des chansons populaires, quand il ne sort pas tout vivant du cœur même du poète."

[135] Fletcher, *Literature of the Italian Renaissance*, p. 222.

[136] Villey, *op. cit.*, pp. 54–57, "Me souvenant de tes grâces divines," to the Duchess of Ferrara (mentioned above, note 4, in connection with the date of Wyatt's earliest sonnet). Marot, has, however, in his *Cimetière*, two early fourteen-line poems, rhyming in couplets, which perhaps should be considered experiments in the sonnet form, although they were not published until 1544. One (to De Longueil) is dated 1522 by Jannet; the other is on the death of Queen Claude, who died in 1524.

[137] Olmsted, *op. cit.*, using the edition of Jannet (Paris, 1873) lists only ten. Two other sonnets, however, are to be found in the edition of Plattard (Paris, 1931), V, 324, 342.

[138] Jannet, *op. cit.*, I, 116; III, 59, 62, 76. The Petrarchan translations are on pp. 148–51 of Vol. III.

[139] Olmsted, *op. cit.*, p. 52; Molinier, *op. cit.*, pp. 389–99; 596–97. In Blanchemain's edition (Paris, 1873), the sonnets are as follows: I, 78, 280–301; II, 254, 262, 293, 300; III, 112. Saint-Gelais has, however, a number of poems in fourteen lines which do not follow the laws of the sonnet, for example, those in I, 207; II, 147; III, 64.

[140] Vianey, *op. cit.*, p. 61. The influence of Scève upon the Pléiade writers Du Bellay, Ronsard, and De Baïf is recorded by Eugene Parturier in the preface of his edition of *Délie* (Paris, 1916). Parturier, in two pages of tables, shows the similarity of themes in the work of the three poets.

[141] For Louise Labé, see Dorothy O'Connor, *Louise Labé* (Paris, 1936); Jean Larna, *Louise Labé* (Paris, 1934); E. M. Cox's preface to his translation of *The Debate between Folly and Cupid* (London, 1925); and Arthur Tilley's *The Literature of the French Renaissance* (Cambridge, 1904), II, 19–21.

[142] The following tabulations derived from Olmsted (not checked with recent editions of the poets) will show how copious is the verse of the Pléiade poets:

Pontus de Thyard: 176 sonnets—139 in *Les Erreurs amoureuses;* 21 in *Son-*

nets d'amour; the 12 of *Douze fables de fleuues ou fontaines;* and 4 scattered.

Pierre de Ronsard: 705 sonnets—229 in the *Amours de Cassandre;* 80 in the *Amours de Marie;* 16 in *Sonnets pour Astree;* 141 in *Sonnets pour Heléne;* 24 in *Les Amours diverses;* 215 others, many of them to different persons.

Joachim du Bellay: 480 sonnets—114 in *L'Olive;* 29 in *Les Amours de J. du Bellay;* 183 in *Les Regrets;* 32 in *Antiquitez de Rome;* 15 called *Songe;* 14 *Sonnets a la Royne de Navarre;* 13 in *Sonnets de l'Honneste Amour;* 16 in *Recueil de Sonnets;* and 64 miscellaneous.

Remy Belleau: 127 sonnets—45 in the first "Journée" of *La Bergerie;* 46 in the second "Journée" of *La Bergerie;* and 36 miscellaneous.

Étienne Jodelle: 183 sonnets—12 called *Hyménée;* 36 called *Contre les ministres de la nouvelle opinion;* 10 called *Tombeaux;* 47 called *Amours;* 71 miscellaneous; 7 called *Contr' amours.*

Jean Antoine de Baïf: 498 sonnets—42 in *Amours de Méline;* 247 in *Amour de Francine;* 85 in *Diverses amours;* and 124 miscellaneous ones.

Jean Dorat: 15 sonnets, mostly miscellaneous.

[143] Lee, *Elizabethan Sonnets,* I, xxv–xxvi.

The Classical Heritage

[1] In Roscher's *Ausführliches Lexikon der griechischen und römischen Mythologie,* p. 1340.

[2] *Ibid.,* p. 1344.

[3] *Ibid.,* p. 1348.

[4] Spencer, "The Literary Lineage of Cupid in Greek Literature," *The Classical Weekly,* XXV (1932), 123. I wish to acknowledge my great indebtedness to Professor Spencer's illuminating article.

[5] The first edition of the *Greek Anthology* appeared in Florence in 1494; the first Latin translation in 1529. Theocritus was published in 1495. See Laumonier's *Ronsard,* pp. 120–24, 592–94, for a detailed discussion.

[6] So many of the concepts which were used in later verse are drawn from the *Amores* that parts of Book I may be recalled briefly: The poet complains to Love because the god compels him to write of love instead of war: "Quis tibi, saeve puer, dedit hoc in carmina iuris?" (1. i. 5) Was not Love's kingdom, the poet asks, already great enough without his seeking new powers? The god, however, merely shoots another arrow at the poet and tells him that that will give him matter for his song. The arrow causes the poet great suffering:

"Me miserum! certas habuit puer ille sagittas.
uror, et in vacuo pectore regnat Amor."

(I. i. 15–26)

The poet, aware that Love is more cruel to those who resist than to those who yield, says he will submit to Cupid's laws and that the god, therefore, need not make war against him. He foresees the triumph of Love riding in the car of Mars with captives in his train and with the people crying his triumph. The god will be adorned:

"tu pinnas gemma, gemma variante capillos
ibis in auratis aureus ipse rotis."

(I. ii, 41–42)

Cupid's soldiers, Error, Madness, and Caresses, will help him vanquish gods and man; his arrows will wound many, his flame bring heat as his car approaches. (*Heroides and the Amores,* "The Loeb Classical Library," pp. 318–24.)
Ovid writes repeatedly (as, for example, in the ninth chapter of Book I of the *Amores*) of love as warfare. Others of his works add several details to this conception. All the later allusions, for instance, to the gold and lead arrows of Cupid come apparently from the *Metamorphoses* (i, ll. 468–75). These arrows came to symbolize happy and unhappy love.
[7] Its effect upon Chrétien de Troyes has been pointed out by Guyer in *The Influence of Ovid on Crestien de Troyes.* So many of the concepts of the verse of the Middle Ages are derived from the Ovidian conception of the nature, symptoms, and effect of love that it is worth while to quote at length Guyer's convenient summary of them: (*Op. cit.,* pp. 119–20).
"In the works of Ovid love is frequently personified as a god of irresistible power, as a tyrant who tortures his victims cruelly or punishes them with great severity. This harshness is sometimes treated as vengeance that Love takes on those who resist his will. He is provided with arrows which wound the hearts of lovers. Within his victims' breasts he enkindles the fire of love. On the other hand, love inspires men with great courage and increases their strength to a remarkable degree.
"Ovid also considers love as a science or art that must be learned. In the *Ars amatoria* Ovid poses as the teacher of love. At other times love is a sort of warfare. Love is the leader and the lover is a soldier. In Ovid's work love is also treated as a disease and Ovid becomes the doctor of love in the *Remedia amoris.*
"The love-sickness is distinguished from all other diseases by the peculiarity of being both pleasant and painful at the same time. The effects or symptoms of love are paleness, trembling, fear, loss of appetite, sighing, sleeplessness, weeping, crying out, fainting, mental absorption often leading to insane action and causing loss of the senses, insanity, and even

death. The disease can be cured by the lover; that is, by a return of affection."

⁸ For the nature of Provençal verse see Patterson's *Three Centuries of French Poetic Theory*, especially the bibliography, I, 39–40; Mott, *The System of Courtly Love Studied as an Introduction to the 'Vita nuova' of Dante* and *The Provençal Lyric;* Neilson, *The Origins and Sources of the Court of Love*, and Jeanroy, *Les Origines de la poésie lyrique en France* and *Le Poésie lyrique des troubadours.*

⁹ Mott, *System of Courtly Love*, p. 7; Neilson, *op. cit.*, p. 26.

¹⁰ For the influence of Ovid upon Chrétien de Troyes see Guyer, *op. cit.;* and Cross, T. P., and Nitze, W. A., *Lancelot and Guenevere; a Study on the Origins of Courtly Love* (Chicago, 1930). For the Provençal influence upon Chrétien see Mott, *op. cit.*, pp. 24–60. The possibility that Moorish culture in Spain was responsible for the knowledge of Ovid among the Provençal poets has already been mentioned in referring to Nykl's translation of the *Dove's Neck Ring.*

¹¹ Mott, *System of Courtly Love*, p. 57.

¹² Neilson, *op. cit.*, p. 26.

¹³ Neilson (*op. cit.*, p. 30. The Cheltenham *Court of Love* MS) notes one poem in which Love calls all his barons together at his dwelling on the top of Parnassus, thanks them for their services, and assigns them new tasks. Another poem, however, shows Love as a "very handsome and magnificently equipped cavalier conducting a very beautiful lady," accompanied by a squire who carries his bow and shoots it for him (*Ibid.*, pp. 26–27).

¹⁴ *The Romance of the Rose*, translated by F. S. Ellis (London, 1900), Bk., I, vi, ll. 911–32.

¹⁵ Dodd, *Courtly Love in Chaucer and Gower*, pp. 18–20. Dodd says that, in the ecclesiastical conception, terms of the medieval Christian worship are transferred to secular literature.

¹⁶ Gaspary, Adolf, *Die sicilianische Dichterschule des dreizehnten Jahrhunderts* (Berlin, 1878), pp. 62–73.

¹⁷ *The Poetry of Giacomo da Lentino*, pp. xxii–xxiii.

¹⁸ Rand, Edward K., *Ovid and His Influence* (Boston, 1928), p. 144.

¹⁹ Mott, *The System of Courtly Love*, p. 142. In the *Vita nuova*, Love, who sometimes speaks in Latin instead of the Italian of the remainder of the work, appears to the poet, as Rossetti phrases it, once in a mist of the color of fire, once in very white raiment, again as a pilgrim lightly clad, and so on. Professor Fletcher's *Dante* explains the allegory of these conceptions.

²⁰ The representations of Cupid in the work of Petrarch, especially in the *Trionfi*, as portrayed in a large number of paintings, miniatures, tapestries, and early editions of the poet's work, may be observed in the illustrations of *Pétrarque, ses études d'art, son influence sur les artistes*, by

Prince d'Esseling and Eugene Müntz (Paris, 1902). In the *Trionfi* Love is usually a very small child, but sometimes, as in the paintings of Botticelli and his school, a tall youth.

[21] Petrarca, *Le Rime*. Edition of Carrer, 1837, I, 484.

[22] Dodd, *Courtly Love in Chaucer and Gower*, p. 110.

[23] *Ibid.*, pp. 189–90; 211.

[24] One version of the Prologue (Text F of Robinson's edition) shows Love as having "gilte heer" crowned with a sun instead of with gold. The other version (Text G of Robinson) shows him as wearing on his head a garland of rose leaves and lilies.

[25] See Neilson, *op. cit.*, pp. 116, 142. Neilson also notes (p. 145) that the Prologue to the *Legend of Good Women* strongly approaches the medieval religious worship of the god.

[26] Dodd, *op. cit.*, p. 46.

[27] See note 6.

[28] Neilson, *op. cit.*, p. 3.

[29] Sidney, No. L; Greville, No. XXI; Smith, No. XI; and Percy, No. III.

[30] The importance of Ovid in this era is shown in the translations of the day. They are listed, among other sources, in the following:

Cambridge History of English Literature, IV, 503.

Bush, Douglas, "Classic Myths in English Verse (1557–89)," *Modern Philology*, XXV (1927), 37–47.

Lathrop, *Translations from the Classics into English from Caxton to Chapman*.

Palmer, *List of English Editions and Translations of Greek and Latin Classics Printed before 1641*, pp. 75–84.

Witz, Edmund, *Die englischen Ovidübersetzungen des 16. Jahrhunderts* (Leipzig, 1915).

Contemporary opinions with regard to Ovid are listed in Cooper's *Some Elizabethan Opinions of the Poetry and Character of Ovid*. The most valuable work on the period as a whole is in Bush's *Mythology and the Renaissance Tradition in English Poetry*. Two general studies of Ovid's influence are E. K. Rand's *Ovid and His Influence* and R. H. Coon's "The Vogue of Ovid since the Renaissance," *The Classical Journal*, XXV (1930), 277–91. Of particular interest to the general reader is the first chapter of Rudolf Schevill's *Ovid and the Renascence in Spain*. Feuillerat has pointed out the influence of Ovid on John Lyly in his *John Lyly*, pp. 582–98.

[31] Tottel's *Miscellany*, Nos. 50, 37, 51.

[32] The rondeau was published as a sonnet (No. 69) in Tottel. See Miss Foxwell's comment in her edition of Wyatt. The canzone based upon Petrarch is No. 64 of Tottel's edition.

[33] Rollins, in Tottel's *Miscellany*, II, 80.

[34] The Protestant divine Thomas Brice sums up the matter in a line in a ballad: "Tell me is Christ or Cupide Lord? Doth God or Venus reigne?"

(*Ballads and Broadsides Chiefly of the Elizabethan Period*, "Roxburghe Club Publications," CLX, Ballad 13.) Brice is said to have written the "Court of Venus Moralized" (1566–67), and "Songs and Sonnets" (1567–68).

Warnings against the sensual nature of love are expressed in "W.A.'s" "A Speciall Remedie against the Furious Force of Lawlesse Love." (*English Poetry of 1578–79*, "Roxburghe Club Publications," LXII.) Other poems by "W.A.," his "Remedy against Love," his "Discription of Love" and "Discription of a Lover," are greatly indebted to Ovid.

Spenser's *Teares of the Muses* (ll. 412–14) complains that the learned's meed is now "lent to the fool" who makes "loving layes" and is praised for them. Fletcher's preface to *Licia* states that the only persons really qualified to write of love are "some Gentlemen" of the Court and both universities whose learning and upbringing suit them for the task. He regrets that those of "mean reach, whose debased minds prey upon every bad dish" are the ones commonly "by learnless heads reputed for Love's Kingdom." Sidney admits the justice of the attacks against love, yet defends it in itself (*Defense of Poesy*, edited by A. S. Cook, Boston, 1890, p. 37).

[35] *Eglogs, Epytaphes, and Sonettes*, edited by Arber (London, 1871).

[36] *English Poetry of 1578–79*, "Roxburghe Club Publications," LXII. The poem, like *Cupido Conquered*, has a Chaucerian framework of a dream vision. *Cupido Conquered* shows the poet as borne aloft by Mercury, in the manner of the *Hous of Fame*, to gain new themes for his writing. In "Of Cupid His Campe" the guide is Morpheus. Every aspect of the god of love is satirized and his army described with surprising vividness. Audacity is captain. His leaders are Rage, Tyranny, Idleness, Drunkenness, etc. Morpheus takes the poet to Apollo's tent to observe the gods feasting there. Vulcan roasts the meats; the servitors, curiously enough, are laureate poets, ready "at becke to bow, when as the Muses call"—Homer, Hesiod, Virgil, Naso, "Chauser," "Goure," Skelton, Edwards. But nothing more is heard of these laureates, for Venus soon enters to tell of Diana's invasion. She weeps so that she falls "flatling" before the gods, whereupon the gods begin to weep, and everyone is moved. They agree, of course, to aid her against Diana; war is proclaimed, the gods depart, and Morpheus takes the poet to Diana's camp. Diana's forces are dismayed. Morpheus next takes the poet to see Cupid and his soldiers "banketing" at the palace, then disappears. "Sopor" also departs, and the poet awakes.

[37] See Fletcher's translations of Cavalcanti and Benivieni in his *Literature of the Italian Renaissance*, pp. 333–41.

[38] Any list of poems in England on this theme might well begin with Watson's "Quid Amor" (*Hec.*, No. XCVIII). Baskervill, in his article in the *Manly Anniversary Studies* (Chicago, 1923) on "Bassanio as an Ideal Lover," lists several illustrations. Among them are Watson's "When werte thou borne sweet love?" (*Hec.*, XXII, from Serafino); Greene's "What thing is Love?" (*Menaphon*) and "Ah, what is Love?" (*Mourning Gar-*

ment); Peele's "What thing is love" (fragment from *The Hunting of Cupid*); Lodge's "I'll teach thee, lovely Phillis, what love is" (*Phillis*, No. XXVI). *A Gorgeous Gallery of Gallant Inventions* has a poem "Aske what love is?" (p. 58) and *The Phoenix Nest* one called "Now what is love" (p. 90). The question of the nature of love is the theme, too, in the section of *England's Parnassus* on the subject of love (pp. 130–45).

A few other examples may be added. Howell's "And if love be Lorde" (in *Devises*, p. 36, translated from Petrarch); Raleigh's "Now what is love"; Griffin's (*Fidessa*, No. XLIII) "Tell me of love, sweet Love"; Florio's *First Fruits*, chaps. xiv, xxxi, xxxiv; and Davies's *Orchestra*, stanzas 104–19. Also, *Twelfth Night*, Act II, scene 1, second stanza of the lyric "O Mistress Mine"; Fletcher's *The Captain*, "Tell me, dearest, what is love"; and innumerable lyrics in the madrigal books. See, also, Ault's *Seventeenth Century Lyrics*, p. 522, under *Love Described*.

T. F. Crane's *Italian Social Customs of the Sixteenth Century* (New Haven, 1920) tells of games played in Italy which required "a knowledge of poetry, among them the game of the Figure of Love, where it must be explained why Love is represented blind, young, naked and armed with a bow" (pp. 278–79).

[39] *The Life and Works of Robert Greene* (edited by Grosart, 1881 ff.), Vol. IV. A modern translation of the poem of Louise Labé has been made by E. M. Cox (London, 1925).

[40] A contest between Love and Folly grows out of a dispute over the power of each: when Jupiter gives a banquet to the gods, the two arrive at the gates at the same time. Folly, however, pushes in ahead of Cupid, who is outraged at this affront to his rank. Folly maintains that she is greater than Love. In the ensuing argument Cupid attempts to wound Folly with his arrow, but she escapes injury because of her power to make herself invisible. Her revenge is to tear out Cupid's eyes and tie up his head with a scarf which he cannot remove. When Venus complains to Jupiter of this outrage to her son, Apollo and Mercury are appointed to plead the two cases before the gods. Jupiter, aware that the gods will be hard to placate by any decision, at length commands that Love and Folly should dwell together.

[41] See Koeppel, "Die englischen Tasso-übersetzungen des sechzehnten Jahrhunderts," *Anglia*, XIII (1890), 42–72. Child, writing in the *Cambridge History of English Literature* (III, 211), mentions Turbervile's "The Lover to Cupid for Mercie" as an expanded version of Wyatt's "Complaint upon Love to Reason," but does not mention the source of Wyatt's work as Petrarch's second canzone.

Poems of the Ovidian type long continued to be written, as in Barnfield's *Affectionate Shepherd*, 1594. Perhaps there is no larger (or more tiresome) medley of Ovidian themes in the era than the six-line poems of "J.C." called *Alcilia* (1595). Cf. Grosart's *Occasional Issues*, Vol. VIII,

Ballads, too, on the theme of Cupid continued to be written. Cf. *Roxburghe Ballads* (Hertford, 1893, VII, 97–124), "Cupid Ballads of the Last Years of the Stuart Period."

[42] See also the list of allusions to Cupid in C. H. Whitman's *Subject-Index to the Poems of Edmund Spenser* (New Haven, 1918, pp. 62–65).

[43] Fowler, *Spenser and the Courts of Love*, p. 63.

[44] Sawtelle, *The Sources of Spenser's Classical Mythology*, p. 42. *An Hymne in Honour of Love*, l. 43 ff.; and *Colin Clout*, l. 835 ff., show the cosmogonic Eros. It may be noted in passing that the same conception appears in Sir John Davies's *Orchestra*.

[45] See Sawtelle and Whitman for lists of allusions.

[46] *Muiopotomos*, l. 102; *An Hymne in Honour of Love*, l. 142; *Faerie Queene*, Bk. IV, canto 1, stanza 2; Bk. X, cantos 3, 4 and 54, *et passim*.

[47] Fowler, *op. cit.*, pp. 103–6.

[48] *Ibid.*, pp. 50–55. The anonymous *Court of Love*, it may be remembered, seems to present Cupid in effigy.

[49] *Ibid.*, pp. 63–65.

[50] Withington, *English Pageantry*, Vols. I–II. See especially I, 43–46, and notes.

[51] *Ibid.*, I, 212–13n.

[52] Nichols, John, *Progresses of Queen Elizabeth* (London, 1823), II, 188 ff. The masque is found on pp. 190–98.

[53] Other allusions are: *Romeo and Juliet*, Act I, scene 4, ll. 4–5; *The Merry Wives of Windsor*, Act II, scene 2, ll. 141, and Act V, scene 5, l. 31; *Troilus and Cressida*, Act III, scene 1, ll. 120; *King Lear*, Act IV, scene 6, l. 141; *Othello*, Act I, scene 3, ll. 270–71; *Antony and Cleopatra*, Act II, scene 2, ll. 207–10; *Cymbeline*, Act II, scene 4, ll. 88–90, and Act III, scene 2, l. 39; *Pericles*, Act I, scene 1, l. 38.

[54] A play of Edward Sharpham, *Cupid's Whirligig*, acted by the children of the King's Revels, has a foreword and epilogue spoken by Cupid. His mother has commanded him to stop shooting his arrows, telling him "on a whirligig goe play." The complications of the plot purport to be the result of his power. ("The Berkshire Series," edited by Allardyce Nicoll, 1926.)

[55] Ogle, "The Origin and Tradition of Literary Conceits," *The American Journal of Philosophy*, XXXIV (1913), 127. Scott, *op. cit.*, often stresses the fact that the continental poems are analogues instead of sources. In this chapter the studies of Ogle and of Hutton have been accepted for the sources of the classical conceits.

[56] Hutton, *op. cit.*, pp. 46–47.

[57] A summary of even a few of the sonnets is revealing: He repents ever having scorned Love, for now he lives in a servile manner under his yoke. Love, transforming himself into air, enters into the poet's breast and holds possession there. The poet protests vainly of Love's hurtful effect and

usual tyranny. Cupid shoots an arrow from a lady's eye which cleaves the poet's heart. Those who suffer from haughty Love endure more than those who know not Love. Watson lists (from Petrarch) all the contrary passions of a lover. He becomes the vassal of Love and calls upon him for aid; Love is the lord and ruler of his will. Watson also describes the gold and lead arrows of Cupid; an arrow is left sticking in his heart. His heart, he says, fleeing from the warfare of Cupid, is captured and locked up in the Tower (i. e., "endless toil"). One who lives under the command of the god of love is a double thrall. The poet finally, however, escapes from the rule of love and rejoices that he has forsworn the god who delights to wound and does not care who is injured by his dart. (Nos. I, XIV, XVIII, XXIV, XXVII, L, LVI, LX, LXIII, LXVIII, LXX, LXXIII, LXXV, LXXXI and XCII.)

[58] Ogle, "The Origin and Tradition of Literary Conceits," pp. 130–39.

[59] *Ibid.*, p. 139.

[60] *Ibid.*, p. 138.

[61] Ogle (pp. 142–43) mentions instances, for example, from Theocritus, Musaeus, Alciphron, Catullus, and the *Anacreontea.*

[62] Hutton, "The First Idyll of Moschus," *The American Journal of Philology,* XLIX, 110.

[63] *The Greek Anthology,* V, 389, "The Loeb Classical Library." The version in the *Anacreontea* is very similar. See *Elegy and Iambus,* II, No. 6, "The Loeb Classical Library."

[64] Hanford, "The Debate of Heart and Eye," *Modern Language Notes,* XXVI (1911), 161; Mott, *op. cit.,* p. 31; and Ogle, *op. cit.,* pp. 136–37.

[65] Spenser, No. LX; Constable, Dec. IV, No. 1; Linche, No. IV.

[66] Smith, Kirby Flower, "Pupula duplex," *Studies in Honor of Basil Gildersleeve* (Baltimore, 1902), pp. 295–96. Cf. Sidney, No. XI, and Drayton's poem in *England's Helicon* called "Rowland's Madrigal":

> "See where little *Cupid* lyes
> Looking babies in her eyes
> Cupid helpe me now . . .
>   To wound her that wounded me."
>   (Edition by Rollins, Cambridge, 1935, p. 114.)

[67] See also No. 29 of the 1599 edition.

[68] Cf. Lodge, No. XXXIX; *Zepheria,* No. IV; and Drayton, Nos. IV and XXXIX of the 1599 edition.

[69] Watson, No. VI; Fletcher, No. II; Greville, No. XXV.

[70] *The Greek Anthology,* I, 213, "The Loeb Classical Library."

[71] "The Anacreontea," in *Elegy and Iambus,* II, 55, "The Loeb Classical Library."

[72] As in Sidney, Nos. XVII and XX, to be mentioned later.

[73] Fletcher, *The Religion of Beauty in Women,* p. 150.

[74] Nos. X, LVII, XII, and so forth. Sonnet XVI is on the theme of Petrarchan warfare, but adds a reference to the little loves instead of merely to Cupid. Sonnet XXIV says that when the lady's eyes shoot death from their shining beams he thinks a new Pandora is sent to be his scourge.

[75] It may be noted that Sonnet VIII, in the "English" form, not Spenser's usual interlocking rhyme scheme, opens with lines nearly identical with those of Greville's third sonnet:

> SPENSER: "More than most fair, full of the living fire,
> Kindled above unto the Maker near.
> GREVILLE: "More than most fair, full of that heavenly fire,
> Kindled above to show the Maker's glory."

Miss Scott suggests (*op. cit.,* p. 61) that there is here an exercise of the Areopagus group.

[76] No. LXVII. Other references in Barnes are more commonplace. Love's golden arrows take aim from her bright eyes, her eyes are the quiver whence the darts are drawn that fix his bondage to her, her eyes are love's quiver, and so forth. (Nos. XXVI, LXXXVII, and XCIV.)

[77] Percy, No. II. See also his first, third, fourteenth, and eighteenth sonnets.

[78] Constable, Dec. IV, No. 8; Dec. VI, Nos. 5, 8, 9. Also, see Lodge, No. XIX; Daniel, No. XIV; Linche, Nos. I, XXXVI; and Tofte, Pt. II, No. 4.

[79] Scott, *op. cit.,* p. 305.

[80] "Datemi pace." Edition of Carrer, II, 47.

[81] Another instance of the poet's proclaiming his slavery is in Barnes, No. LIV. Barnes, stealing love's bow to shoot at boys and girls, as well as redbreasts, goldfinches, and sparrows, was caught and punished. He is then a slave to Parthenophe and to love.

[82] Lee, *Elizabethan Sonnets,* I, 109, "Since shunning pain."

[83] Fletcher, Nos. V, VII, IX, XIV. The last two are the Anacreontic manner.

[84] Griffin, Nos. XXXII, XLIII, LXII. See similar allusions in *Zepheria,* No. XIII; Drayton, No. 26 of 1594 and No. IV of 1619; Linche, No. XXXIV; and Tofte, Pt. III, Nos. 27 and 29.

[85] Barnes

No. XXVIII: His heart burns within him.

No. LXXVII: Fire rages within his heart with "heat's extremes."

No. LXXX–VII: His heart is consumed with rage of fire. He lives by the fire of his love, which is incense to his soul.

No. XCII: Her beauty makes an "endless burning fire of Fancy's fuel."

No. C: He pleads for pity because of his hidden flames and secret smarts.

Constable

Dec. I, No. 2: Her eye is a fire that draws up his love as "earthly vapours drawn up by the sun": his love is a fire, and so ascends above.

Dec. I, No. 3: Love is warned not to fly too close to Diana, the poet's sun, lest his wings be burned.

Dec. I, No. 5: He wishes that the fires kindled by her eyes would dry the flowing streams of his eyes.

Dec. I, No. 6: His heart is "damned in love's sweet fire."

Dec. II, No. 5: Since his heart is found to be murdered by fire, love decrees that his eyes, guilty of looking upon Diana, shall be drowned in tears.

Dec. V, No. 1: Love maintains a continual furnace which "burns inward, yields a smouldering flame."

Dec. V, No. 6: The fire of her eye's disdain causes his pain.

Dec. V, No. 10: As Prometheus was punished for stealing fire, so the poet is punished for stealing living beauty's fire to put it into his verse.

Dec. VI, No. 3: Her beauty causes the flame of his love.

Dec. VI, No. 5: A flame of fire from her eyelids burns his heart.

Dec. VI, No. 6: Her beauty is the brightest living flame.

Dec. VI, No. 7: His heart says that his eyes let in the fire which burns him with an everlasting light.

Dec. VI, No. 8: Love's flame burns eternally.

Dec. VIII, No. 5: His love burns like the fires of hell because he must henceforth keep it concealed.

[86] Constable (Dec. V, No. 10) and Smith (No. XXIII) also write of frying in flames.

[87] Sidney

No. XVI: Not finding in himself the restless flames which others endured, he underestimated the power of love.

No. XXV: Stella causes him to burn in love.

No. XXVIII: His writing breathes out the flames which burn in his heart.

No. XXXV: What Nestor's counsel can his flames allay? Patience is asked to help him bear his fire with patience.

No. LIX: In comparing his love with that of Stella's dog, he says that, although the dog may love her, he himself burns in love.

No. LXVIII: Stella is asked why she tries to quench in him the noble fire fed by her worth.

No. LXXII: The fire of his heart is blown by Desire.

No. LXXX: Her lip is "Cupid's cold fire."

No. LXXXI: His heart burns and he cannot be silent.

No. LXXXIX: Even in blackest winter night he feels the flames of hottest summer day.

[88] Nos. VII, XV, XXIX. Also, Nos. XIX, XXVII, XXXIII, XLI, XLIV, and so forth. See Miss Scott, *op. cit.*, p. 313, for sources.

[89] Nos. II, XXV, XXXV, XXXVII, XXXVIII. See Miss Scott, *op. cit.*, p. 312, for sources.

[90] Griffin

No. I: Fidessa, he says, can surely not be so cruel as to make his heart the fuel for her fancy.

No. VIII: His heart is set on fire by his thoughts.

No. XI: The wind blows upon his face to cool the fire which hot Desire has made in his breast.

No. XXIII: Love is asked to kindle the coals of love about her heart.

No. LIX: Fidessa is the fire, he the fuel that feeds it.

Linche

No. I: When he boldly gazes upon Diella's heavenly face, she darts huge flames of fire upon him.

No. III: Her eyes, though crystal fountains, dart fire more glorious to behold than the midday sun.

No. XIV: He will cease to burn in hot flames only when a number of impossible things in Nature are achieved.

Nos. XXXIV–XXXV: The lady should not rejoice, as she does, to see him consumed in fire.

Smith

No. V: The flames of Etna are not half so hot as is the fire which her disdain causes. (The same figure is also used in No. XIII.)

No. XVII: If Chloris will show pity and quench the flames boiling in his breast, he will attempt more for her than Leander did for Hero.

No. XXIII: He has endured fire as great as that which the phoenix has endured.

[91] Pt. II, Nos. 12, 17. See also Pt. I, Nos. 8, 15, 19, 22, 27, 34; Pt. II, No. 29; Pt. III, Nos. 3, 8, *et passim.*

[92] Ogle (*op. cit.,* p. 129) mentions Meleager, Plautus, Lucretius, Ovid, and other authors.

[93] For love as a yoke see Watson, *Hecatompathia,* No. I; *The Tears of Fancie,* No. XVII; Barnes, No. LXV; Sidney, unnumbered sonnet "Since shunning pain."

[94] For love as a labyrinth see Watson, *Hecatompathia,* Nos. XVIII and XCV; *The Tears of Fancie,* No. LIII; Barnes, No. XII. For love as a maze see Barnes, No. XXVII, and also Fletcher's poem, "A Lover's Maze," published with *Licia.* Gascoigne's sonnet "To the brown beauty" has the phrase "of craftie Cupid's maze."

[95] Vianey, *Le pétrarquisme en France au XVIe siècle,* pp. 19–20, says of Chariteo: "Et, à première vue, il ne semble pas que Pétrarque ait un imitateur plus docile que Chariteo; mais l'inspiration n'est plus pétrarquiste; la forme vient de Pétrarque; le fond vient de Catulle, de Tioulle, de Properce, d'Ovide, de Virgile, quelquefois de Lucrèce, et de Sénèque le tragique, et quelquefois il dérive directement des chansons populaires, quand il ne sort pas tout vivant du coeur même du poète."

Hutton states that coincidences in theme between the Italian poets of the late fifteenth century and the *Greek Anthology* indicate that the Italians drew, in most cases, from the "common stock of amatory ideas gathered by the medieval vernacular poets." He says that some of these doubtless go "back to the older reservoir of Graeco-Roman literary themes to which Greek epigrams themselves belong. The verses of Serafino and Tebaldeo are often a tissue of these commonplaces." A reader today might think of Meleager in reading a certain *rispetto* from Politian, but "Politian was almost certainly thinking of Petrarch." *The Greek Anthology in Italy to the Year 1800*, pp. 46–47.

[96] Laumonier, *Ronsard*, pp. 592–93. Laumonier discusses other aspects of the Anacreontic background on pp. 120–24.

[97] See Hughes, "Spenser and the Greek Pastoral Triad," *Studies in Philology*, XXIII (1923), 203.

[98] A painting by Veronese, "Wisdom and Strength," in the Frick Art Gallery, in New York, gives Cupid peacock-spotted wings.

[99] See Jones, *A Spenser Handbook*, pp. 54–56, for a comparison of Spenser and Bion. See also Renwick, *The Shepherd's Calender and Other Poems*, pp. 187–88. Renwick p. 187 considers Spenser's effort to "adapt the artificial Cupid-idyll style to English detail" not entirely successful. The poem, he says, was available to Spenser in Latin, "as usual printed with the Greek text," and in the French of Baïf (189n.).

[100] Fletcher has an interesting sonnet (No. XIV) here based on Angerianus (Scott, *op. cit.*, p. 313). Licia cuts Cupid's wings and uses them as a fan until the poet's heart is given in exchange for them. Greville (No. XV) gives a characteristic allegorical turn to the image when he speaks of clipping self-love's wings in order to lend wings to love.

[101] Spencer, in "The Literary Lineage of Cupid," lists several instances in Greek literature. The many little loves, or *putti*, are still frequently seen in paintings, marginal decorations of books, architectural details, etc.

[102] Jones, *Spenser Handbook*, pp. 348–50; Lee, *Elizabethan Sonnets*, I, xciin.; and Renwick, *Daphnaïda and Other Poems of Spenser*, pp. 194; 203–4. Renwick suggests that Spenser inserted these poems as the equivalent of Petrarch's sestines and canzoni.

[103] Kendall, Timothy, *Flowers of Epigrammes*, in the section called "Trifles," XV, 287–88. "Publications of the Spenser Society" (Manchester, 1874).

[104] Hutton, "The First Idyl of Moschus," 104–36; Fucilla, "Materials for the History of a Popular Classical Theme," *Classical Philology*, XXVI (1931), 135–52. See also, Koeppel, "Die englischen Tasso-übersetzungen des 16. Jahrhunderts," *Anglia*, XIII (1890), 42–72.

Fucilla (*op. cit.*) says that the popularity of Meleager's epigram in Italy owes much to the numerous echoes which this same conceit had in Petrarchistic poetry: "Petrarch, to go no farther, uses this figure, which had previously been a commonplace of the poetry of the *Dolce stil nuovo*, at least a half-dozen times. On the other hand, Sannazaro went straight to the Petrarchistic tradition for his notion of Love's dwelling within the lover's heart and troubling it, rather than to the Anacreontic verses of Julianus . . ." (p. 138). The story first appeared in England in 1567 in Turbervile's *Of Lady Venus*. It next appeared in a charming version (not noted by Hutton or by Fucilla) in Lyly's *Gallathea*. Cf. Jeffrey *John Lyly and the English Renaissance*, pp. 80–82.

Neither Hutton nor Fucilla mentions, either, the tale from John Dickinson (1594) called "Arisbas, Euphues amidst his slumbers: Or Cupids Iourney to Hell." Cupid runs away to hell to visit his "Uncle Pluto." He is welcomed with pomp by the "blodlesse ghoasts" and dines so well that he falls asleep. Proserpine then takes his arms, since they had been so misused by the boy; and bestows them upon Plutus, "God of Coyne." Cupid, awakening, does not know what course to follow—he is afraid to hide in hell, where so many accuse him of their woes, and equally afraid to return to Venus without them. (In Grosart's *Occasional Issues*, Vol. VI.)

Another poem derived from the same source is Drayton's *Ode* of 1619 called *The Cryer,* in which he makes a proclamation for his lost heart.

[105] Lee, *A Life of William Shakespeare,* p. 448, expresses the belief that Barnes had worked from French adaptations. Hutton, however, says in "The First Idyl of Moschus," p. 127, that none of the French versions he examined lent color to this belief, and that the lines appear to come directly from the Greek.

[106] Apparently the only sonneteer to repeat this reason for Cupid's flight was Griffin in his twenty-second sonnet.

[107] The conceit concerning the burning of Cupid's wings seldom recurs in the cycles. Watson's *The Tears of Fancie,* however, mentions Cupid's burning his "parti-colored wings" while gazing at the lady's eyes and his being thrown into the poet's breast, where he builds his bower and remains (No. VI).

[108] Scott, *op. cit.,* pp. 32–33. For the poem of Paulus Silentiarius see the *Greek Anthology,* I, No. 267, "The Loeb Classical Library." For Propertius see the translation by H. E. Butler, p. 95.

The poem of Paulus says that no one else need fear the coming of the love-god, for since Cupid has set his cruel foot on him and trampled his heart, he remains there because he has shed the feathers of his wings. Propertius, using the same theme, mourns that Love must have lost his wings, since he never flies away from his heart.

[109] Scott, *op. cit.,* p. 32: "Nous ne pouvons donner des précisions (mais combien vagues encore!) que pour quelques sonnets, le VIII, le XVII, et le LXV."

[110] *Anacreontea, op. cit.,* No. 33, pp. 61–62. It may be noted in passing that Lord Byron included a translation of this poem in his *Hours of Idleness.* He adds descriptive details such as glossy curls and azure wings.

[111] This play alludes in Act IV, scene II, ll. 20–28, to the story:

Samais: "Is he still in love?"

Epiton: "In love? Why, he doth nothing but make sonnets."

Samais: "Canst thou remember any one of his poems?"

Epiton: "Ay, this is one:

> 'The beggar Love that knows not where to lodge,
> At last within my heart, when I slept,
>
> > He crept.
>
> I waked, and so my fancies began to fodge.' "

[112] Miss Scott (*op. cit.,* p. 34) points out that the figure, in the last lines of the sonnet, of the arrow head left with the poet is derived from the Sidney coat-of-arms.

[113] Dec. II, Nos. 6 and 7.

[114] *The New English Dictionary* lists, among the definitions for wanton, the following: "Undisciplined, ungoverned. Of children: naughty, unruly. A child spoiled by over-indulgence; a child of playful, roguish, or sportive conduct." Cf. Greene's *Menaphon,* "Weep not, my wanton." Watson, in the *Hecatompathia* (No. LXXXIX) calls Cupid a wanton child. Sidney, No. LXXIII, attributes the "wanton" nature of Cupid to the fact that he is schooled only by his mother's tender eyes, and that so soft a rod encourages him to miss his lessons. Greville, No. XII, Watson, No. VI, Fletcher, No. II, and Lodge, No. XXXVI, all call Cupid a wanton boy. "Wag" is used by Sidney, No. XLVI, Greville, Nos. XIII, XXVIII, and so forth. Greville describes Cupid as little lad Cupid, silly boy, faithless boy, base boy, and the like. Fletcher uses phrasings such as "sweet boy" and "sweet Love" (Nos. IV, V, IX, X, XXI.) Griffin probably follows Sidney in his phrasings in Nos. XIV, XXII, XLII. Watson (*Tears of Fancie,* No. I) calls Cupid a boy "not past the rod"; Greville, No. XXXVII, stanza 11, refers to Cupid as a lad who fears the rod.

[115] Nos. XXVI, XXXVII, LXII, LXVIII, LXX.

[116] Scott, *op. cit.,* p. 34. See also p. 304.

[117] Mentioned by G. C. Moore Smith in a review of Bullen's *Elizabethans* (*The Modern Language Review,* XX, 90). Moore Smith quotes a letter from Bullen, written only a few days before his death, which suggests that Greville's "meadow-god" may be derived from the following lines:

> "Rura fecundat voluptas: rura Venerem sentiunt:
> Ipse Amor puer Dionæ rure natus creditur:
> Hunc ager cum parturiret ipsa suscepit sinu,
> Ipsa florum delicatis educavit osculis."

[118] See Alden, *The Sonnets of Shakespeare,* pp. 369–73.

[119] Chiefly Nos. VIII, XI, XVII, XLVI, LXV, LXX, LXXIII, CI.

[120] Nos. LIII, LXVII, LXXXIII.

[121] Chiefly Sonnets XXIV, LXXV, XCIII; Madrigals 3, 25, and Ode 15.

[122] Drayton, Nos. XXII, XXIII, XXXVI, XLVIII; Constable, Dec. II, Nos. 6, 7; Griffin, Nos. XVII, XXII, XLIII; Linche, No. XVIII; *Zepheria,* No. XXVIII; Tofte, Pt. III, No. 23.

[123] Scott, *op. cit.,* p. 113. The chief sonnets of this group are Nos. II, IV, V, IX, X, XIII, XIV, XXI, XXIX.

ANATOMY OF MELANCHOLY

[1] Guyer, *The Influence of Crestien de Troyes.* Guyer gives a convenient list of citations of the symptoms of love in Ovid. Among them are paleness, fear, loss of appetite, sighing, sleeplessness, weeping, and mental absorption.

[2] This code is discussed by Neilson, *op. cit.,* pp. 176–81; and by Mott, *op. cit.,* pp. 59–60.

[3] Neilson, *op. cit.,* p. 181. For these aspects of Provençal verse see also Mott's *The Provençal Lyric,* pp. 16–38.

[4] Neilson, *op. cit.,* p. 185. It is interesting to observe the effect that this convention had upon a later poet, the fourteenth-century Machaut. Lowes sums it up as follows: "His chief preoccupation (and that for us is the rub) was with fine-spun niceties and labored technicalities of the dominant system of courtly love and of his verse a canonical *ars amatoria* of the fourteenth-century could readily be compiled, not omitting the bead-rolls of the secret symptoms of heroic love—changes of colour between white, red, black and bluish-green (I am not improvising, but meticulously following Machaut); shuddering, shivering, starting, paling, flushing, swooning—'reeling and writhing and fainting in coils.' For in blissful ignorance of both Machaut and courtly love, the Mock Turtle parodied in one imperishable phrase the medieval symptoms of the malady." John L. Lowes, *Geoffrey Chaucer* (New York, 1934), pp. 84–85.

[5] Neilson, *op. cit.,* p. 186.

[6] *The Poetry of Giacomo da Lentino,* pp. 116–27. Garver, in "Sources of the Beast Similes in the Italian Lyric of the Thirteenth Century," *Romanische Forschungen,* XXI (1908), 276–320, traces of the Provençal origins of these similes in a very illuminating article .

[7] Mott, *op. cit.,* pp. 130–40, gives an excellent analysis of the poem. For Dante's references to his weeping see Sonnets II, XVII, XXI, Song LV and several of the prose commentaries.

[8] Lawrence, W. W., *Shakespeare's Problem Comedies* (New York, 1931), pp. 142–44.

[9] Campbell, Oscar James, *Jacques,* "Huntington Library Bulletin" No. 8.

[10] Lee, *Elizabethan Sonnets,* I, lviii-lix; Scott, *op. cit.,* p. 305, the note on the thirty-ninth sonnet of Sidney, and Fletcher, *Literature of the Italian Renaissance,* pp. 224–27.

[11] Lee, *op. cit.,* pp. lviii-lix, and *A Life of William Shakespeare,* p. 447. Lee notes the phrase in De Baïf and Pierre de Brach. Theodore Spencer, in *Death and Elizabethan Tragedy,* p. 90, quotes these passages from Homer and Hesiod and says that the association of night, sleep, and death is thus very ancient and that sleep and death are connected hundreds of times in classical authors. The analogy, although rarely found in the Middle Ages, was quite common in the sixteenth century.

[12] Sidney's references here suggest comparison with a passage in Chaucer's *Book of the Duchess* (ll. 240–60) of a reward offered to Morpheus of a feather bed made of the down of pure white doves, "ryght well cled in fyn blak satyn doutremer," which had "many a pilowe."

[13] Lee, *Elizabethan Sonnets,* I, lviii, says that the sonnet is for the most part a mere adaptation of Desportes (*Amours d'Hippolyte,* LXXVI). Kastner (*The Modern Language Review,* III, 272–73) believes the last lines of Daniel's sonnet point to Chariteo rather than to Desportes. Brady (*Samuel Daniel,* p. 15) suggests that the opening lines owe more to della Casa than to Desportes and says that it is unfair to call the poem a mere adaptation of Desportes.

[14] *The Minor Poems of Michael Drayton,* p. 24.

[15] The phrase "care-charmer sleep" alone was sometimes used, as in Smith's sonnet (No. XXXIV) of the nightingale:

> "Because care-charmer sleep should not disturb
> The tragic tale which to the night she tells."

[16] From his play *Valentinian.*

[17] Sidney, No. LXXXIX; Spenser, No. LXXXVI.

[18] Nos. XCVIII, XCVI, XCIX.

[19] Nos. XXXII, XXXVIII.

[20] Lodge, No. XVII; Linche, No. XIX. Daniel's apostrophe to sleep, already quoted, ends with the desire not to wake to reality.

[21] Watson, No. XL; Fletcher, No. XXXI; Constable, Dec. II, No. 3; Smith, No. XVI; Linche, Nos. II, XXXIII.

[22] Hanford, J. H., "The Debate of Heart and Eye," *Modern Language Notes,* XXVI (1911), 161–65.

[23] *Ibid.,* p. 161.

[24] *Ibid.,* p. 164.

[25] Especially No. LV, "Occhi, piangete," and No. XCIX, "Che fai, alma?"

[26] Neilson, *op. cit.,* p. 60.

[27] Sidney Lee seems unnecessarily severe against Shakespeare's use of this conceit (*Life of Shakespeare,* p. 116) in calling it the "unexhilarating notion" of the eyes and heart in perpetual dispute.

[28] The theme is fairly common in Elizabethan literature. See, for example, Donne's "The Message" and Drayton's lyrics (1619 edition) "The Heart," "The Cryer," and "To His Coy Love." The last-named one begins:

"I pray thee, leave, love, me no more,
Call home the heart you gave me."

The cleverest poem on the migration of the heart is Donne's "The Broken Heart."

[29] The sonnets are Nos. CCIV–CCV in the edition of translations by various hands in the "Bohn Library" (London, 1907). Carrer, Nos. CLXXXIV–CLXXXV.

[30] It is clear that this narrative must have been begun earlier than No. XVII—at some point in the eight missing poems of the only known first edition of the work—because the opening word "then" of Sonnet XVII, "Then from her fled my heart in sorrow wrapped," implies a continuity in the telling.

[31] The extent to which Barnes may be original in using legal phraseology seems difficult to determine. The medieval debates and trials of the heart certainly contain all the elements needed, and both Petrarch and Gascoigne had written accounts of a case pled before a bar. Closer parallels for the legal phrases than that of Petrarch may possibly exist among the French or Italian poets. Barnes's narrative is probably indebted somewhat to that of Watson—or perhaps both poets follow some as-yet-unnoted source.

[32] Some of the earlier sonnets of *Parthenophil and Parthenophe* appear to have been written to one Laya, but the poet soon gives his allegiance to Parthenophe. See, too, the madrigal appended to Percy's *Coelia*. Addressed to "Parthenophil," it twits the poet for his fickleness and prophesies that Parthenophe's charms will also be of brief interest to him.

[33] Hutton, *The Greek Anthology in Italy, op. cit.,* pp. 46–47.

[34] *The Greek Anthology,* I, 203, 271, "The Loeb Classical Library." The Petrarchan translations are from the edition of the "Bohn Library," Canzone 13, ll. 35–36, and Sonnet LXXV.

[35] Nos. IV, XXXII, XXXIX.

[36] Scott, pp. 313, 315.

[37] The image of Will appears before him, too, in his dreams, but not as an image carved in his heart. In these sonnets of the image appearing before him the figure is always that of a shadow—a fair imperfect shade (No. XLIII), a shadow to his sightless view (No. XXVII), and shadows that are like Will (No. LXI). No. CXIII, of the memory in the poet's mind of the features of Will seen wherever he looks and in every aspect of his life, is entirely free from allegory. Sidney (No. XXXVIII) writes of Stella's image driving away sleep. Drayton has a sonnet (No. XIII), "To the Shadow."

[38] Scott, p. 319, gives Spenser's sources in Desportes and Tasso.

[39] Lowes, *Geoffrey Chaucer,* the passage quoted in note 4 above.

[40] See also the mention in Part I of a few others of those available.

[41] So many of the conceits appear within the same sonnet or are so briefly presented that separate headings would give inevitable repetitions. They are therefore listed in the appendix under the one heading *despair*.

[42] Similar is the theme in Sonnet XLIV, well known as a "reduplicating" sonnet: His words set forth his mind, his mind bemoans his smart, his smart should conquer any heart, her heart is not that of a tiger—yet he finds no pity. The reason is that "sobs his annoy," when they come to Stella's lips, are "metamorphosed straight to tunes of joy."

[43] For example, see *Zepheria,* Nos. XIV, XV, XXXI, and Tofte, Pt. I, Nos. 14–15; Pt. II, Nos. 7, 18, 34; and Pt. III, No. 37.

[44] Constable: Dec. I, No. 1; Dec. II, No. 4; Dec. III, No. 9; Dec. IV, No. 6; Dec. V, Nos. 3, 6–10; Dec. VI, No. 9; Dec. VII, Nos. 7, 10; Dec. VIII, Nos. 2, 3.

Fletcher: Nos. VII, XVII, XVIII, XXXI, XXXII, XXXIII, XXXV, XXXVI, XXXIX, XLI, XLII, XLIV, XLVI, XLIX, L.

Griffin: Nos. VII, IX, XVI, XXIV, XXV, XXVIII, XXIX, XXX, XXXII, XXXVI, XLIV, XLVI, XLVIII, LX.

Smith: Nos. IV, VI, IX, XII, XIV, XV, XXIII, XXIX, XXX–XXXI, XXXVII, XLII.

[45] Lodge: Nos. II, V, VI, X, XIV, XVII, XIX, XXI, XXIII, XXIX, XXXII, XXXVII.

Watson: Nos. XVIII, XIX, XX, XXVII–XXXIX, XLIII, LVI, LX.

[46] See also Shakespeare, No. CXIV; Daniel, No. XXII; Griffin, No. XXX; Lodge, No. XXXVII; Drayton, No. VII; and Linche, No. XIX.

[47] Only a few by Barnes are noticed here: Nos. XV, XXX, LXI, LXXVII, LXXX, XCV. Other laments are in Nos. XIV, XXIV, XXV, XXVII, XXIX, LIII, LVI, and so forth.

[48] Nos. I, II, IV, XIV, XVIII, XXII, XXIV, XXXII, XXXV, XLII, XLIII.

[49] Nos. VII, XI, XXVI, XXXII, XLII, LIV.

[50] Nos. XXIV–XXV, XXXV. For No. XXXV see Scott, p. 312.

[51] Griffin echoes these lines in his eighteenth sonnet: "Thus absent, presence; present, absence maketh."

[52] *Zepheria,* No. XXX; Lodge, Nos. XXIV–XXV; Griffin, No. XVIII.

[53] Nos. XLV, LI, LVII, and so forth.

[54] The excellence of this sonnet is all the more apparent when it is compared with one in *Zepheria* (No. XXXV) in which the same questioning method is used for any joy that comes to the poet's spirit: He articles joy with felicity and deposes him on these interrogatories: first, does he come from Zepheria? Next, will he restore his light? If, in the end, he finds the joy has come only to "unbend his thoughts from her," he strangles it in its infancy.

[55] Nos. XCVII, CVI. These reflect the convention found in the *Vita nuova* and in Petrarch of the lover who turns to other ladies for comfort after the death of the lady.

[56] Lee, *Elizabethan Sonnets*, I, 122. This is one of the sonnets published in 1594 in Constable's *Diana*.

[57] *Ibid.*, p. 122. This passage is imitated by Drayton in the "Elegies" of 1627: The opening lines of his elegy "Upon the Noble Lady Aston's Departure for Spaine" are:

> "I many a time haue greatly marueil'd, why
> Men say, their friends depart when as they die,
> How well that word, a dying, doth expresse
> I did not know (I freely must confesse)
> Till her departure . . ."

Another imitation of Sidney is Griffin's phrase of "traitor absence" (No. XVIII). Griffin's sixth sonnet is also on the theme of absence. The stylistic device of variations upon "Unhappy sentence! Worst of worst of pains" seems to be his own contribution.

[58] Nos. LXXXVII–LXXXIX, XCI, CVI, CVII. In Sonnet CVII, on despair, he says that the only light that came to him in his darkness was from Stella, but that despair drove away even that. Fletcher's Sonnet XLIII, of the darkness of absence, is similar in tone.

[59] Garver, *op. cit.*, pp. 276–320.

[60] *Ibid.*, p. 287.

[61] Not published until the 1598 edition. In *Elizabethan Sonnets*, I, 117. Note the metaphor, also, in Sonnet CVIII, of his young soul fluttering to rest in his thoughts of Stella.

[62] 1590 edition, edited by Feuillerat (Cambridge, 1912), p. 96. Linche's comparison of his watching for a glimpse of Diella's face (No. VIII) is that of a falcon watching its prey, while a falcon is mentioned in *Zepheria* (No. XXVII) and the expression "falcon-like" used by Lodge (No. XXVII).

[63] Scott, *op. cit.*, pp. 163–64.

[64] *Ibid.*, p. 320.

[65] This is a favorite method of Spenser. The lady, not the lover, is compared to a lion and lioness (No. XX), a spider's web (No. XXIII), a cockatrice (No. XLIX), a leech (No. L), a panther (No. LIII), and a tiger (No. LVI).

[66] Renwick, *Daphnaïda and Other Poems*, p. 202.

[67] Other brief comparisons, usually in the customary sense, occur in various cycles, as Lodge's reference to the swan's song (No. X), and Barnes's (No. LVII) and Smith's to the nightingale (No. XXXIV). Watson, for example, compares himself to a hawk (No. VII), to a bird lacking the sun (No. LII), and to a wounded bird and a wounded deer (No.

LVIII). Narratives, not comparisons, are found in Sidney's imitation of Catullus (No. LXXXIII) and Spenser's sonnet of the cuckoo as harbinger of spring (No. XIX).

[68] Daniel's sonnets of 1591 include a sonnet on the phoenix. (Not reprinted in 1594. In *Elizabethan Sonnets*, I, 90.)

[69] No. XXXV in the 1594 edition, not reprinted in the 1619 collection.

[70] Griffin (No. XIII), "the weeping wounded hart"; Linche (No. XXIII), "a deer late wounded very sore"; *Zepheria* (No. III), the frightened deer; Tofte (Pt. III, No. 15), "a gentle tame deer called a hart." Watson (No. XLIX), has word play upon "hart" and "heart."

[71] For the relation of this sonnet to Petrarch and Horace see Scott, *op. cit.*, p. 172; and Renwick, *Daphnaïda and Other Poems*, p. 203.

[72] For the quotation from LXVII and its relation to Tasso and Petrarch see Renwick, *ibid.*, p. 202, and Scott, *op. cit.*, pp. 166–67.

[73] Salamander and gnat, Barnes, No. XXIV. Salamander, Lodge, No. XXXVIII. (Watson's *Hecatompathia*, No. XLIII, has a sonnet on the salamander, translating, in part, a sonnet on that theme by Serafino.) Fly in a flame, Sidney ("Finding those beams"); Griffin, Nos. XIII, XXVI. The spider is twice used by Spenser, once in a comparison of the spider and the web (No. XXIII); again, of the spider and the bee (No. LXXI). The scorpion is used by Smith (No. XIX) in comparing himself to animals able to heal themselves—a sick hound, an old eagle, a snake shedding its skin. He, however, is wounded by a scorpion and is unable to heal himself. Griffin compares himself to a boar struck with a butcher's knife (No. XIII). Barnes says his fears are like lambs beset with lions (No. LXXX).

[74] Lee, *Elizabethan Sonnets*, Vol. I, "Finding those beams." From the 1598 edition of Sidney's works.

[75] For the subject as a whole see Bush, *Mythology and the Renaissance Tradition in English Poetry*.

[76] Acteon, Watson, No. XLIX. Ixion, Drayton, No. XL; Linche, No. XXV; Tofte, Pt. II, No. 40. Charon, Fletcher, No. XLI. Narcissus, Spenser, No. XXXV; Lodge, No. XXXIV; Tofte, Pt. III, No. 11. Medusa, Watson, No. XXI. Atlas, Lodge, No. III; Sidney, No. LI. Medea, Drayton, No. XLIV.

[77] Nos. XLI–XLII. See Scott, *op. cit.*, p. 313.

[78] Spenser, No. LVI; Linche, No. XX. The mention in Lodge (No. XIV) and Smith (No. VI) of pine trees is, on the other hand, the pastoral one of the trees heeding their woe when the hard-hearted lady will not.

[79] Drayton, No. I; Constable, Dec. IV, No. 3; Spenser, No. LXIII; Smith, No. XXXV; Linche, No. XVIII.

[80] Spenser (No. LIX) also compares the lady to a ship that keeps a steady course in a tempest.

[81] 1591 edition only. See Lee, *Elizabethan Sonnets*, I, 94, No. XII.

[82] George Wyndham gives a discussion of this point in the introduction to his edition of Shakespeare's poems, London, 1898, pp. cxxii–cxlvii.

[83] "Il mio avversario," and "L' oro, e le perle," Nos. XXX–XXXI.

[84] See Lee, *Elizabethan Sonnets*, I, lvi, for the facts of Daniel's translation of this sonnet from Desportes.

[85] Barnes, No. CIV; Percy, No. IV.

[86] Spenser, No. VII; Constable, Dec. I, No. 5.

[87] Watson tells his "idle lines, unpolished, rude, and base" that if they can succeed in making the lady repent the grief that she has caused him, or even laugh at him, and "laughing, so mislike thee," then they are to tell her to look into his heart to see her ruthlessness. Percy bids his verse that, if it falls into Coelia's cruel hands, to say only—"Alas, he was too Passionate!" The tone of the first sonnet of the *Amoretti* is likewise an expression of the joy that will come to the poet if the lady looks upon his leaves, lines, and rhymes. There is, however, the possibility that this dedication was written, not for the *Amoretti,* but for the *Faerie Queene* (cf. Rosenback, *op. cit.,* pp. 148–50). The second sonnet of the *Amoretti,* presumably always of the cycle, reads in part:

> "But if in presence of that fairest proud
> Thou chance to come, fall lowly at her feet;
> And, with meek humbleness and afflicted mood,
> Pardon for thee, and grace for me, entreat."

[88] Also in *Zepheria,* No. XVIII: The copying scribe deserves no credit if his verse is good.

[89] Drayton, Nos. VIII, XXI, XLV; Griffin, No. LX; Linche, No. VI; Percy, No. III; Sidney, Nos. XIX, LV; Smith, Nos. V, XIV, XV.

[90] Constable, Dec. I, No. 1; Daniel, Nos. VI–VII, LII; Fletcher, No. XLVII; Percy, No. VIII; Sidney, No. LXX; Smith, Nos. III, XLI, XLIV, XLVI; *Zepheria,* Nos. XVIII, XXX.

[91] Barnes, No. XVII; Drayton, Nos. XXXV, XXXIX; Shakespeare, Nos. XXXVIII, LXXVI, LXXVIII–LXXXIX, CIII; Sidney, Nos. XV, LV, LXXIV; Smith, No. I; Spenser, Nos. III, XVII.

[92] Constable, Dec. II, No. 1; Dec. III, No. 9; Dec. IV, No. 1; Dec. V, No. 5; Dec. VI, Nos. 3, 6; Dec. VII, No. 5; Daniel, dedicatory sonnet to the Countess of Pembroke, Nos. II, XVII, LI; Fletcher, dedicatory sonnet to Licia; Lodge, No. XX.

[93] Smith, Nos. I, II, XLI; Tofte, Pt. I, No. 36; Watson, introductory sonnet to *The Tears of Fancie,* and also, No. LIV; *Zepheria,* No. II.

[94] *Elizabethan Sonnets,* I, lv; *A Life of William Shakespeare* (pp. 114 ff.); and "Ovid and Shakespeare's Sonnets," in *Elizabethan and Other Essays* (edited by F. S. Boas, Oxford, 1929). Lee quotes, in the *Life of Shakespeare,* the prose references in Sidney and Nash to this subject (pp. 118–19). Shakespeare uses the theme in many sonnets, among them Nos. I–XIX, XXI, XXXII, LV, LX, LXIII, LXV, LXXXI, C–CI, CVII.

[95] Nos. XXXIII, XXXVII, XXXVIII, XXXIX, XL, L, LIII. The sources are listed by Lee and Miss Scott.

[96] Daniel, Nos. XXXIX, LI, and Constable, Dec. V, No. 5.

[97] Daniel, No. III; Smith, No. XLVIII.

THE SONNET LADY

[1] The Rossetti translation.

[2] Gaspary, *Die sicilianische Dichterschule des dreizehnten Jahrhunderts,* pp. 46–48.

[3] Moseley, *The 'Lady' in Comparisons from the Dolce Stil nuovo.*

[4] *Ibid.,* p. 56.

[5] Ogle, M. B., "The 'White Hand' as a Literary Conceit," *The Sewanee Review,* XX (1912), 459–69. Ogle's article was written to supplement one by M. P. Tilley, "The 'White Hand' of Shakespeare's Heroines" (*The Sewanee Review,* XIX (1911), 207–12. Ogle does not agree with Tilley that Shakespeare's heroines are described as they are in order to conform to the standards of the day, but thinks the descriptions are the results of long literary tradition.

[6] Ogle, "The 'White Hand' as a Literary Conceit," p. 466.

[7] See also Fletcher's *Literature of the Italian Renaissance,* pp. 223–24.

[8] D. E. Owen's *The Relations of the Elizabethan Sonnet Sequences to Earlier English Verse* (Philadelphia, 1903), places, it seems, too much stress upon the direct influence of Chaucer upon the Elizabethans and nowhere appears to consider the fact that Chaucer had drawn these images from the common storehouse of French and Italian themes. Much of the work of Owen has been supplanted by present-day knowledge of the sources of Chaucer and of the sources and analogues of the English sonnets.

[9] Quoted by Rollins in his edition of *The Phoenix Nest,* pp. 147–48. This passage by Rich may be compared with another denunciation from him quoted in L. B. Wright's *Middle Class Culture in Elizabethan England* (Chapel Hill, 1935), pp. 483–84, from Rich's *My Ladies Looking Glass,* 1616. Rich rebukes the courtier poet, the writer of amorous verse, who will "hatch out Rimes, and learne to indite amorous verses in the praise of his mistress (that is many times scarce worth the speaking of) and will borrow colours from lillies and red roses to beautify her cheekes; her eyes will be saphires, her lippes coroll, her teeth, pearle, her breathe balme, a Pallas for her wit but he never streines so farre as to her honesty."

[10] *Reliquiae Wottonianae,* "A Parallel of Robert Devereux and George Villiers," (London, 1672), p. 165.

[11] *Literature of the Italian Renaissance,* p. 218. See Professor Fletcher's entire chapter on Petrarchism, pp. 217–27.

¹² Drayton dedicated his *Ideas Mirrour,* of 1594, to his "ever-kind Maecenas," Anthony Cooke. Griffin's *Fidessa* is to William Essex, Smith's *Chloris* is to Spenser, and *Zepheria* is to the "modern laureates."

¹³ The list could be extended indefinitely. The work of Alexander Craig is published by the Hunterian Club, Vol. I. The works of Davies are ed· ited by Grosart in the Chertsey Worthies' Library.

¹⁴ Grey eyes are mentioned in the description of Julia in the *Two Gentlemen of Verona,* Act IV, scene 4, ll. 197; *Twelfth Night,* Act I, scene 5. ll. 266. Crystal eyes are mentioned in *Love's Labour's Lost,* Act IV, scene 3, ll. 142; *Cymbeline,* Act V, scene 4, ll. 81; and *Midsummer's Night's Dream,* Act III, scene 2, ll. 139. Golden hair is mentioned in *Merchant of Venice,* Act I, scene 1, l. 170; Act III, scene 2, l. 122; scene 1, l. 179. Ruby lips are mentioned in *Cymbeline,* Act II, scene 2, l. 17; coral lips, in *Taming of the Shrew* Act I, scene 1, l. 179. White hands, rosy cheeks, and the like, are also mentioned; e. g., *As You Like It,* Act III, scene 2, l. 413; *Merchant of Venice,* Act II, scene 4, l. 12.

¹⁵ Cf. Alden's Variorium edition of the sonnets: "reek" = emits vapour, steams; but "here probably used for the sake of rhyme." Cf. *Love's Labour's Lost,* Act IV, scene III, l. 140, "saw sighs reek from you."

¹⁶ Sidney, Nos. IX, XIII, XXXII, XCI, and Song V; Barnes, Nos. XIX, XXVI, XLVIII, LVIII, LXVIII, LXXI, LXXXIV, LXXXIX, XCVI; Daniel, Nos. XIV, XIX, XXXIII, XXXVI–XXXVII; Lodge, Nos. IX, XXII; Percy, No. XII; Griffin, No. XXXIX; Tofte, Pt. I, Nos. 29, 31; Pt. II, Nos. 21, 38; Pt. III, Nos. 6, 14, 16, 25, 35; Linche, Nos. III, XVI, XXVII; Spenser, Nos. XV, XXXVII, LXXIII, LXXXI; Greville, No. LVIII; Fletcher, No. XXX; Constable, Dec. I, Nos. 6, 9, 10; Drayton, No. IV of 1594; *Zepheria,* No. XVII; Smith, No. IX.

¹⁷ Sidney, No. XII; Constable, Des. II, No. 8, and Dec. IV, No. 2; Spenser, No. XXXVII; Daniel, No. XIV. Variants are in Spenser, No. LXXIII; Fletcher, No. LII ("trammels of hair"); and Tofte, Pt. III, Nos. 6, 16. Ogle ("Origin and Tradition of Literary Conceits") says that he has not found this conceit in exactly this form in ancient literature, but that it is evidently developed from the theme of love as a hunter ensnaring lovers in a net. The next step was to make the eyes of the lady the net. Ogle says: "Who was responsible for this shift from eyes to hair it is impossible to say. Petrarch seems to have been the first to make the change, inspired, perhaps, by some such passage as in Chrétien, *Cligés,* 1194 sq. where Fenice's hair is woven into the web of a garment and is indistinguishable from the gold thread" (p. 130).

¹⁸ Sidney, No. CIII, of Stella on the Thames; Spenser, No. LXXXI; Fletcher, No. XXX; Tofte, I, 31.

¹⁹ Also, Smith, No. XXVI.

²⁰ Lodge, No. IX; Smith, No. IX. Smith probably copies Lodge outright.

[21] Lodge, No. XXII, "and gold more pure than gold doth gild thy hair."

Fletcher, No. XXX,

> "When as her hair, more worth, more pale than gold
> Like silver thread lies wafting in the air."

Tofte (Pt. I, No. 16), wishing to exchange the hair for gold, assures Laura that the one is not worth more than the other; Pt. III, No. 35, her hair is finer gold than a golden brooch.

[22] Owen, *op. cit.*, and Davis, Horace, *The Critic*, XIX (1893), 419. Spenser uses the phrase in the *Faerie Queene*, Bk. II, canto 3, stanza 30; *An Hymne in Honour of Beautie*, l. 97, and the *Epithalamion*, l. 154. The last is:

> "Her long loose yellow locks lyke golden wyre."

[23] *The Modern Language Review*, XX (1925), 398.

[24] Instances of the figure are in Barnes, Nos. XIII and XLVIII; Linche, No. III; Percy, No. XII; Daniel, No. XXXIII; Lodge, No. IX; *Zepheria*, No. XVII; Smith, No. IX.

[25] See Ogle's "The 'White Hand' as a Literary Conceit."

[26] See F. N. Robinson's edition of Chaucer (Cambridge, 1933), p. 885, for a list of medieval usages of this type of description. From this usage Chaucer may have drawn suggestions for his detailed description of the Duchess in *The Book of the Duchess* (ll. 816–1040).

[27] Sidney, Nos. IX, XII, XIII, XXIX, XXXII, XLIII, LII, LXXVII, CII, and the unnumbered sonnet "Woe, woe, to me."

[28] Sidney, No. XIII; Constable, Dec. I; No. 10; Barnes, No. XC.

[29] Barnes, Nos. LXIV, LXXI, LXXVIII, LXXXV, LXXXIX, XC, XCII, XCVI, XCVIII; Constable, Dec. VI, No. 4; Dec. VII, No. 1; Daniel, No. VI; Drayton, Nos. VIII, XXIX; Fletcher, Nos. V, XXX, LII; Griffin, No. XXXIX; Linche, Nos. III, IV, XXII, XXXI–XXXII; Lodge, Nos. VIII, XXII; Percy, Nos. XII, XV; Smith, No. XVIII; Spenser, Nos. XVII, LV, LXXVI–LXXVII; Tofte, Pt. I, No. 29; Watson, No. XXXI; *Zepheria*, Nos. XVII, XXIV, XXXIII, XXXIV.

[30] Ogle, "The Origin and Tradition of Literary Conceits," p. 146, says that perhaps the earliest appearance of the word is in Phrynichus. Simonides used the same figure, and it is also found in Bion. It is mentioned only once he says, in the *Greek Anthology*, in the work of Rufinus.

[31] *Ibid.* Roses and lilies are terms in Ovid's *Amores*, II. v, 34; Virgil's *Aeneid*, and elsewhere. The combination of snow and roses in describing the blonde type of beauty is likewise a classical conception found frequently in the Latin poets and in Petrarch, but it does not occur in the English sonnets. Another classical comparison which Ogle traces is "apple-cheeked." This does not occur in the sonnets, although it is found in the *Arcadia* and in Spenser's *Epithalamion*.

[32] For sources see Lee's *Elizabethan Sonnets*, I, lxii, lxiii, notes.

[33] Barnes, Madrigals 4, 11, 24; Sonnets No. XXVI, XLVI, LXXI, XCVI;

several odes (as Nos. 2 and 16) and sestines (as No. I). See, also, Griffin, No. XXXVII, and *Zepheria,* No. XXXIII.

[34] Lee notes that these ideas are particularly common in French poetry, especially in Ronsard and in Du Bellay (*Elizabethan Sonnets,* I, lxii–lxiii).

[35] Barnes, No. XCVI; Constable, Dec. I, No. 9 (see Miss Scott for scources); Lodge, No. XXXVII. See also *Zepheria,* No. XVII; the rose and hyacinth borrow her colors; No. XXXIII, Zepheria is fairer than any of the flowers, the nymphs of Phoebe; Tofte, Pt. II, No. 8, Laura gives him a flower and then he breathes only the scent of flowers.

[36] Renwick, *Daphnaïda and Other Poems* (p. 202), notes that this sonnet is "outside the range of correct Petrarchan sentiment, but has precedent in Ronsard and a few others."

[37] See Lee, *Elizabethan Sonnets,* I, lxii–lxiii; Barnes, No. LVIII and LIX; Fletcher, No. XXVIII; Constable, Dec. IV, No. 10; Daniel, Nos. XXXIII–XXXVII, XLV–XLVI; Drayton, No. VIII; Spenser, Nos. LXX, LXXIX; Smith, No. XXXI. Shakespeare (No. VI) writes "Then let not winter's ragged hand deface / In thee thy summer."

[38] Sidney, Nos. CI–CII; Barnes, Madrigal 20; Lodge, No. VII; Fletcher, No. XX.

[39] With this group may be noted the sonnets of Sidney and Spenser which imitate Petrarch's identification of Laura with the laurel. Sidney (No. XC) speaks of his verse as a laurel tree; Spenser evolves sonnets (Nos. XXVIII–XXIX) from the laurel leaf worn by the lady.

[40] The question is debatable. Certain passages indicate dark eyes: Canzone III, ll. 22–24, "Nero e nel bianco"; Canzone IX, l. 50, "bel nero e'l bianco"; Sonnet CLI, "bianco e nero." Canzone XXV, however, calls the eyes "fenestre di zaffiro." Cf. Tatham, *op. cit.,* I, 250–51n. Sidney, in No. VII, describes Stella's black eyes as being mourning for those who died for her. See, too, Nos. XX, XLVII, XCI, and No. IX, which has a reference to "touch," evidently touchstone, a black marble, drawn from the "mind of beauty"—a pun upon "mine."

[41] Constable, *Diana: Sonnets and Other Poems,* edited by Hazlitt; "To Mr. Hilliard: Upon Occasion of a Picture he made of my Ladie Rich," p. 44.

[42] H. E. Rollins, *The Phoenix Nest,* p. 153, notes other instances of sapphire eyes in his comment on a line from Lodge in *The Phoenix Nest* (p. 58, l. 31): There is an example in Tottel (p. 204) of the eyes as "polisht Diamondes, or Saphires at the least," and one in Turbervile's dedication to Lady Anne, Countess of Warwick, of his *Epitaphes, Epigrams, Songs and Sonets.* Lady Anne had an eye "that saphire-like doth shine."

[43] Diamond, Barnes, Nos. XLVIII, XCII, Madrigal 10; crystal, Daniel, No. XIV; "crystal-painted," Griffin, No. II; crystal fountains, Linche, No. III; crystal beam, Smith No. II; transparent crystal casements, *Zepheria,* No. XVII; clearest crystalline, Barnes, No. CIII; sparkling chrysolites,

Barnes, No. XCIV; fair eyes, Daniel, No. L, Lodge, Nos. XXVII, XXXII, Spenser, Nos. VII, XVII, XXIV.

[44] Ogle, "The Origins and Traditions of Literary Conceits," pp. 130–32.

[45] Professor Fletcher translates a madrigal of Michelangelo to Vittoria Colonna which illustrates the belief that within her eyes he saw the trace of the high stars. (*Literature of the Italian Renaissance,* pp. 211–12.)

[46] Frances A. Yates, in *A Study of Love's Labour's Lost,* advances the belief that there is a relationship between this phase of Sidney's cycle and *Love's Labour's Lost* in that the reference of the play to eyes are in defense of Lady Penelope Rich. Cf. pp. 88–136.

[47] Nos. VIII, IX, X.

[48] Nos. LXXXVII, LX.

[49] Barnes seems to imitate this poem in Sonnet No. XXII. See note 58.

[50] Nos. XCI, XCVI–XCVII, CVIII.

[51] Lee, *Elizabethan Sonnets,* I, 122.

[52] "Passa la nave," No. CXXXVII, edition of Carrer.

[53] Watson, No. XXXI; Fletcher, Nos. XLIII, XXXVIII. Such lines recall, of course, Chaucer's description of the friar:

> "His eyen twinkled in his head aright
> As doon the sterres in the frosty night."

[54] So published in the 1619 edition, but included with no heading in the 1602 edition.

[55] Instances are:

Barnes: No. XXIII, "Bright orbs of day"; No. LXXIX, her sunbright smile is bestowed upon his rival.

Daniel: No. VI, Her sunny eyes; No. XLVIII, she is fairer than the sun.

Fletcher: No. XV, Licia shines fairer than Phoebus; No. XXXVIII, he will praise his heaven for such a sun if she will grant a sun-bright smile.

Griffin: No. II, her sight both gives and takes away light; No. X, "there is no sun but thee."

Linche: No. VIII, the sight of her eyes is more pleasing to him than the warmth of the sun is to naked savages; No. IX, her sun-like rays; No. XIII, her sun-bright eye; No. XXXI, "fair suns that shine when Phoebus' eyes are gone."

Lodge: No. XIX, Her assaulting eyes are the lamps which light his desire.

Tofte: Pt. I, No. 3, Laura's sweet face is "like to the sun most fair"; Pt. II, No. 4, "Shoot forth no more those darts from lightning eyes."

Zepheria: No. XVII, her eyes are suns, the "crystal transparent casements" of her face; No. XIX, she is asked to shine forth her "comfort's sun"; No. XXVII, Zepheria is his sun; No. XXXIX, her sunny shine.

[56] Sidney, No. LXVIII; Barnes, Nos. XXIII, LXXVIII; Fletcher, No. XXV; Percy, No. VI; Spenser, No. LX.

[57] Dec. I, Nos. 2 and 7; Dec. II, Nos. 3 and 10; Dec. VI, No. 1; Dec.

VII, Nos. 1 and 3. Among the minor sonneteers, Smith and Tofte are notable for the fact that entire sonnets are given to these themes. *Chloris:* No. XXXVIII, when he cannot see her he is debarred from heaven's light; No. XLIII, she is the glorious sun from whence his lesser light borrows its shine. Tofte: Pt. I, No. 5, the strife between his fair sun and the sun on high; No. 20, when she frowns the clouds are dark; when she smiles, the sun springs forth; No. 24, compares Laura to the sun. Pt. II, No. 15; a tortured figure expressing his wish that he, like a cloud covering the sun, could kiss Laura; No. 24, her absence removes his sun; Pt. III, No. 38; he wishes he were Argus-eyed so that he might properly behold his sun.

[58] Barnes no doubt took his idea from one of Sidney's sonnets already mentioned, No. LXXVI: In his absence from Stella, he is numb with cold, when she comes before him, it is like the coming of Aurora. By noon, the heat grows greater; finally, he says:

"My heart cries, 'Ah, it burns!' Mine eyes now dazzled be.
No wind, no shade can cool. What help then in my case?
But with short breath, long looks, stayed feet, and walking head;
Pray that my sun go down with meeker beams to bed."

[59] See Miss Scott's chapter on Barnes, pp. 77–79.

[60] See also the last lines of Sonnet XLIV:

"That saints divine are known saints by their mercy!
And saint-like beauty should not rage with pierce-eye!"

See Mark Eccles, in Sisson's *Thomas Lodge and Other Elizabethans,* pp. 171–72.

[61] The extent of the Platonic influence of the beauty of the lady upon the poet is discussed in J. S. Harrison's *Platonism in English Poetry of the Sixteenth and Seventeenth Centuries.* For Spenser's Platonism see also Renwick's *Edmund Spenser,* pp. 155–57, 163–68. For the Platonism in *Astrophel and Stella* the best discussion is Fletcher's "Did 'Astrophel' Love 'Stella'?" in his *The Religion of Beauty in Women,* pp. 147–66. For the period as a whole, we may accept the comment of Harrison (p. 127): "Sidney, Spenser, and Shakespeare are the three chief sonnet writers of the last decade of the sixteenth century in whose work this phase of Platonism [i. e., the elevating influence of beauty] is to be found, but its presence, though faint, can be felt in others." Harrison says that, since the writing of love lyrics in the Petrarchan manner was "never anything more than a courtly way of making love through exaggerated conceit and fine writing," the love of the idea of beauty in its absolute nature is nowhere present in the mass of love lyrics written between 1590 and 1600 (pp. 137–38).

[62] Renwick, W. L., *Daphnaïda and Other Poems,* p. 202.

[63] Griffin (No. XXXIX) uses some of these details in an enumeration sonnet with several other figures.

[64] Pt. I, Nos. 7, 25, 29, 30; Pt. II, Nos. 20, 32; Pt. III, Nos. 12, 14, 35.

[65] See Act IV, scene III, ll. 75–78. Berowne, overhearing Longaville's sonnet containing a reference to a goddess, says:

> "This is the liver-vein, which makes flesh a deity;
> A green goose a goddess; pure, pure idolatry.
> God amend us, God amend!"

[66] Barnes, No. LXXXV: (on the four directions) Her rosy color comes from the east, where Aurora arises. See, also, Barnes, No. XXVI and Madrigal 18.

Daniel, No. XIX: "Restore thy blush unto Aurora bright."

Griffin, No. XXXIX: Fidessa's blush is like Aurora or the morning sky.

Sidney, No. LXXVI: Stella brings warmth and light like that of Aurora.

Tofte, Pt. I, No. 37: Her beauty is like that of Aurora.

[67] The lady's beauty the gift of the gods: Lodge, No. XXXIII; Fletcher, No. LI, Smith, No. XLV.

The lady's beauty as stolen from the gods or goddesses: Barnes, No. LXIV; Drayton, No. XIV; Daniel, No. XIX; Tofte, Pt. I, No. 28.

The lady's beauty as equaling that of the goddesses: Sidney, No. XCVII (describes a lady seen in Stella's absence as Diana's peer); No. CII (on Stella's illness); Barnes, No. XIX, Parthenophe matches the qualities of Jove, Mercury, Minerva, Phoebus, Bacchus, and Venus; No. LXVIII, her eye is as powerful as that of Medusa; *Zepheria,* No. XXIII, Zepheria equals Minerva. Constable, Dec. I, Nos. 3, 4; Dec. II, No. 10; Dec. VI, No. 10.

The lady's beauty as surpassing that of the goddesses: Sidney, No. XLII, the eyes of Stella are schools where Venus learns chastity. Watson, No. LV, "More bright than Cynthia." Barnes, No. XXVI, Aurora's blush is yellow in comparison with that of Parthenophe (No. XCV says that Sidney's Stella, not Parthenophe, surpasses Aurora); No. XCVI, Venus sends the beauty of Parthenophe to aid the beauty of sick Flora. Lodge, No. XXII, Phoebe spices her nectar with the breath of Phillis. Linche, No. V, Cupid thinks that Diella is more beautiful than Psyche; Venus fears to let Mars see her. *Zepheria,* No. VII, Zepheria is fairer than Phoebe; No. XIII, she surpasses Venus; No. XXIII, several details. Tofte, Pt. I, No. 13, the anger of Laura is greater than that of Juno. Drayton, No. IV, graces and goddesses dwell in the lady's face; No. XXXIX, Idea surpasses Minerva and Astrea. Griffin, No. LVII, in a contest between Diana, Cupid, and Fidessa, Fidessa wins. Percy, No. XI, Coelia is fairer than Polyxena; No. XIII, Coelia is as fair as Venus but as dangerous as a gorgon.

[68] Angry or jealous goddesses:

Sidney, No. LXXVII: Venus weeps because she lacks Stella's grace.

Barnes, No. LXXI: Diana's arrows wound him less than does Parthenophe's kiss.

Lodge, No. IX: Aurora wept with jealousy over the beautiful golden locks of Phillis.

Smith, No. IX: Diana weeps with jealous rage at the beauty of the hair of Chloris.

[69] See pp. 62–63.

[70] Garrod, H. W., *The Times Literary Supplement*, May 10 and 24, 1923. The passages suggested by Garrod as containing these puns are in Nos. XI, XIV, XXII, XXXVI, XLIV, LVII, LXV, LXXXIII, LXXXV. Direct references in Spenser to "warrior" are No. XI, cruel warrior, and No. LVII, sweet warrior. As was said on page 22, however, Renwick (*Daphnaïda*, p. 198) doubts this identification because evidence for the marriage is lacking. See also Long, "Spenser and Lady Carey," *The Modern Language Review*, III (1908), 257 ff.; and "Spenser's Sonnets 'as published,' " *The Modern Language Review*, VI (1911), 390 ff.

[71] Queen of love, Barnes, No. XLV; Lodge, No. IV; *Zepheria*, No. XIII; Smith, No. XII; Linche, No. VI. Queen of beauty, Constable, Dec. V, No. 10; Griffin, No. LV. Queen of summer, *Zepheria*, Nos. XI, XXXII. Queen of worldly pleasures, Daniel, No. X. Merely as queen, Lodge, XX; Fletcher, Nos. III and XLIX.

[72] Some of the sonnets, already mentioned, which describe Licia as a goddess also call her queen: Nos. III, X, XI.

[73] Queen of the poet's heart or soul, Barnes, Madrigal 5; Linche, No. XXXVI; Fletcher, No. XXXVI; Daniel, Nos. VIII, XVI, XIII, all in the 1592 edition. No. XIII was reprinted as No. XLIII in 1594, with the verbal differences of "soul's queen" changed to "her deity."

[74] No. XXVIII and No. CVII. The latter sonnet has an interesting allusion in which the poet asks Stella to give her lieutenancy to his thoughts "for his great cause which needs both use and art" and that she dismiss him "from her wit" as one sent by the queen on some mission.

[75] Spenser, Nos. III, LXXII; Drayton, No. L.

[76] Barnes (No. XLIV) enumerates examples of the hard fates of poets that should teach Parthenophe that saints divine are known by their mercy and that saint-like beauty should not rage with pierce-eye, i. e., *Percy*.

[77] Barnes (No. LXXXIX) says:

"What saints are like her? Speak, if you be!
                                    (Echo) Few be!"

Percy, apparently in direct imitation of Barnes, writes (No. XV):

"What is her face, so angel-like?   *Angel-like.*
Then unto saints in mind, she's not unlike? *Unlike.*"

Smith's contribution is the following line (No. XXII): "Attentive be unto the groans, sweet saint!   sweet saint!"

[78] Lodge (No. X) professes that all his joyful hymns are written to exhort others to die for such a saint as Phillis; Daniel's Delia, sacred on earth, is "designed a saint above" (No. VI). Idea is Drayton's soul-shrined saint living on the Ankor's silver-sanded shore (No. LIII). Linche, in an "enumeration" or cataloguing list, sets forth his image—he who can count

the candles of the sky, the hours since the world began, and so on, would have sufficient skill to express not only his grief but also his praises of Diella as a saint above (No. XXX). Griffin worships his saint among the gods and saints (No. XXXVI). A curious set of images is to be found in *Zepheria* (No. XXXIII): Zepheria is more beautiful than the nymphs of Phoebe (anemone, daffodilly, hyacinth, rose, amaranthus, and lily) who come annually to Nature's fair, where men gaze upon them with "mazed-admire," thinking that for some transgression "heaven's angels were un-paradised." "Heaven's paradise" contains but few saints such as these nymphs.

[79] Spenser, No. XXII, quoted on page 102; Constable, Dec. VI, No. 1, "One saint I serve, one shrine with vows I dight," and so forth. Spenser twice refers to the lady's celestial hue, Nos. III, XLV; twice to her lovely hue, Nos. VII, XXXI; once each to the goodly semblance of her hue (No. LIII), her glorious hue (No. LXXIX), and her heavenly hue (No. LXXX).

[80] Sidney, in his eighth song, calls Stella an angel. Barnes (No. XXVI) says Parthenophe has an angel's grace. Linche writes of Diella's angel face (No. XXII) and of her celestial look (No. XII). Drayton, as did Shakespeare, writes of his good angel (No. XVIII, "in my soul, divine") and of the evil spirit of her beauty which haunts him—"this good-wicked spirit, sweet angel-devil" (No. XX).

[81] Flint: Watson, No. XXXVIII; Barnes, Nos. XXV, LXXXVII; Daniel, Nos. XIII, XVIII; Griffin, Nos. LII, LV; Linche, Nos. IX, XIII (b); Spenser, No. XVIII; Tofte, Pt. I, No. 39; Fletcher, Nos. VIII, XXXV; Smith, No. XXXIX.

Marble: Fletcher, No. VIII; Spenser, No. LI.

Steel: Fletcher, No. VIII; Spenser, No. XVIII; Smith, No. XXXIX.

Stone: Spenser, No. LIV, and Griffin, No. LV (both say "senseless stone"); Smith, No. XL; Daniel, No. XIII. Tofte, Pt. II, No. 31, compares his worship of Laura to that of a painted wooden idol, and, in Pt. I, No. 31, to the turning of Fortune's wheel. Sidney, No. LXVI, refers to Fortune's wheel, but merely as turning slowly for him.

[82] Fletcher, No. VIII; Linche, Nos. XVI, XXI; Spenser, Nos. XX, LVI; Griffin, No. LIX. All these, it will be noticed, are comparisons of the lady —not, like those in Part II, comparisons of the poet himself to various things in natural history.

[83] Spenser, Nos. XX, XLIX, L, LIII.

[84] Smith, No. XIX; Tofte Pt. I, No. 32. These references and those in footnote 83 are apart from the comparisons listed in the second chapter, in which the poet compared himself, not the lady, to various things in natural history.

[85] The dove is also mentioned by Linche, Nos. VI, XXXIV.

Conclusion

[1] Nos. XL, LI, LVI, LXIX, LXXI, LXXXII, LXXXIII, CLVIII, Sestine in Pt. II, No. II.

[2] Phelps, "The Forms of Address in Petrarch's *Canzoniere*."

[3] As, for example, Nos. III, LXXVII, CLVII, CXLII and Canzones XIV–XV.

[4] No. IX, "Se la mia vita," and, apparently, all the implied references to the green leaves of the laurel, as in Sestine II.

[5] Neilson, W. A., and Thorndike, A. H., *The Facts about Shakespeare,* (New York, 1923), p. 88.

Notes on Appendix

[1] Wilson *Sir Philip Sidney,* p. 203.

[2] *The Elizabethan Sonnets,* pp. xliii-liv. Lee expresses over views, however, in earlier articles, as in that on Lady Rich in the *Dictionary of National Biography.* Lee's attitude toward Renaissance imitation is aptly characterized in a protest by R. M. Alden in regard to a comment of Lee about Shakespeare's Sonnet 29. Lee's remark, Alden says, is "the sort of comparative criticism of the sonnets which has repeatedly vexed the souls of those who cherish great admiration for the writer's learning . . . the implication that that which has been abundantly uttered by others is not likely to be uttered anew in personal sincerity . . ." (*The Sonnets of Shakespeare,* p. 83).

[3] Koeppel, "Studien zur Geschichte des englischen Petrarchismus im sechszehnten Jahrhundert," *Romanische Forschungen,* V, 1890, 97.

[4] Scott, *op. cit.,* pp. 52–53.

[5] Osborne, *Sir Philip Sidney en France,* p. 52.

[6] Henry Osborn Taylor, *Thought and Expression in the Sixteenth Century* (New York, 1920), II, 225.

[7] Conyers Read, Mr *Secretary Walsingham and the Policy of Queen Elizabeth* (Oxford, 1925), III, 425.

[8] Lee, *Elizabethan Sonnets,* I, xliii note, says that "Astrophel" "deprives of serious autobiographical significance" Sidney's "description in the sonnets of his pursuit of Stella's affection." Fletcher, *The Religion of Beauty in Women,* in the chapter, "Did Astrophel Love Stella," advances this poem as a reason for accepting Sidney's sonnets purely as platonic love. Wallace's *The Life of Sir Philip Sidney,* p. 256, thinks that Spenser's absence in Ireland prohibited his knowledge of the true identity of Stella.

H. R. Fox Bourne, *Sir Philip Sidney*, p. 244, says that Sidney's friends evidently took the sonnets as works of fancy, "with no greater basis of fact than served for the building thereon of an imaginative superstructure." A. H. Bill's *Astrophel*, the most recent life of Sidney, accepts the identity of Stella as Lady Rich.

[9] *Op. cit.*, p. 699.

[10] H. H. Hudson, "Penelope Devereux as Sidney's Stella," p. 119n. The date of Spenser's own contribution is not known. Dodge notes that it cannot have come before 1591 when, in the Preface to the "Ruines of Time," the poet says that his friends had reproached him for not having shown any thankful remembrance to the house of Dudley. Royden's, Raleigh's, and the poem attributed to Greville had appeared in the *Phoenix Nest* in 1593. Nash, however, had referred in 1589 in his Preface to Greene's *Menaphon* to Royden's "immortal Epitaph of his beloved Astrophel." This, it may be observed, is one of the earliest references known to Sidney as Astrophel. Bryskett's "The Mourning Muse of Thestylis" was entered in the Stationers Register in August, 1587, but if printed then, no copy is known to have survived. (Cf. Arber's *Transcript*, II, 220b.)

[11] Robert Shafer, "Spenser's Astrophel," *Modern Language Notes*, XXVIII (1913), 225.

[12] W. P. Mustard, "Lodowick Bryskett and Bernardo Tasso," *The American Journal of Philology*, XXXV (1914), 194.

[13] Renwick, *Daphnaïda and Other Poems*, pp. 236–37; Long, "Spenseriana: *The Lay of Clorinda*," *Modern Language Notes*, XXXI (1916); C. G. Osgood, "The Doleful Lay of Clorinda," *Modern Language Notes*, XXXV (1920).

[14] Renwick, *Daphnaïda*, p. 191, suggests, as one explanation, that Spenser tacitly puts Lady Sidney into the place of Stella. Wallace's explanation (*Life of Sidney*, p. 256) of the dedication of "Astrophel" as resulting from the fact that Spenser may not have known in 1595 the real identity of Stella is not tenable. Wallace overlooks the fact that Spenser had already mentioned in *Colin Clouts Come Home Againe* (ll. 532–35) the presence of Stella at court:

> "No lesse praiseworthie Stella do I read,
> Though nought my praises of her needed arre,
> Whom verse of noblest shepheard lately dead
> Hath prais'd and rais'd above each other starre!"

The date of *Colin Clout* is uncertain. The poem was based upon Spenser's visit to court in 1589, was dated 1591, and published in 1595. An early date is implied in the words "of noblest shepheard lately dead." Spenser, however, even before the publication of *Astrophel and Stella*, could have seen a manuscript copy of Sidney's sonnets, for Newman the printer speaks of them as having been spread abroad in written copies, presumably after Sidney's death. Spenser's own interest in writing sonnets and his interest in Sidney make it seem improbable that he would not have ferreted out the identity of Stella.

[15] Thomas Watson, "Meliboeus." In *Poems* "Arber Reprints," Vol. XXI.

[16] The last two lines of a song in William Byrd's *Songs of Sundrie Natures* of 1588 allude, I believe, to Lady Rich—though not, of course, to her as Stella. "Diana" is surely Queen Elizabeth. The sonnet is as follows:

> "Weeping full sore, with face as fair as silver,
> Not wanting rose nor lily white to paint it,
> I saw a lady walk fast by a river
> Upon whose banks Diana's nymphs all danced.
> Her beauty great had divers gods enchanted
> Among the which Love was the first transformed,
> Who unto her his bow and shafts had granted,
> And by her sight to adamant was turned.
>
> 'Alas,' quoth I, 'what meaneth this demeanour,
> So fair a dame to be so full of sorrow?'
> 'No wonder,' quoth a nymph; 'she wanteth pleasure;
> Her tears and sighs ne cease from eve to morrow.
> This Lady Rich is of the gifts of beauty,
> But unto her are gifts of fortune dainty.' "

[17] *The Diary of Lady Hoby* (New York, 1930), p. 161.

[18] Symonds, *The Life of Sir Philip Sidney* (New York, 1906), p. 116.

[19] For the sonnets evolved from this type of personification, see Scott, *op. cit.*, pp. 35–37.

[20] Frances A. Yates expresses the opinion in *A Study of Love's Labour's Lost*, p. 112, that Sidney's doubts arise from his attitude toward philosophy, not from the struggles of a Puritan conscience. His recognition of the futility of sonneteering, Miss Yates says, grows out of the effect upon him of the opinions of Giordano Bruno, who came to England in 1583 and dedicated to him in 1588 his *De gli eroici furori*. This work was prefaced by a violent attack against Petrarchistic worship of women (see Yates, p. 105). It is quite possible that Sidney's attitude grew in part out of his study of Plato and others, but I do not believe that the sonnets came late enough to have been affected by Bruno, even if that influence began as early as 1583.

[21] Similar lines occur in Sonnets X, XIX, XXXIII, XLVII, LXII, LXIV, LXXII.

[22] Since the order of arrangement in the 1591 edition was not changed by the Countess of Pembroke in 1598, it may be accepted as sufficiently authentic. She set the lyrics within the sequence and added material presumably not known before that time. Sonnet XXXVII is the chief invective against Lord Rich. All of Song XI was new, No. VIII had eight new stanzas, and No. X added four stanzas.

[23] Hughey, *op. cit.*

[24] See Hoyt H. Hudson's "Penelope Devereux as Sidney's Stella" for a complete refutation of J. M. Purcell's *Sidney's Stella*. Hudson quotes this passage from Harington.

[25] Philip Gawdy, "Roxburghe Club Publications." CXLVIII (London, 1906).

[26] *Historical Manuscripts Commission Report XII*, Appendix, Coke MSS, I, 63.

[27] Mentioned by Gerald Massey in *Shakespeare's Sonnets* (London, 1866), p. 410, and referred to vaguely by Maude S. Rawson in *Penelope Rich and Her Circle* (London, 1911).

[28] Edition by Pollard, Introduction. Wallace, *op. cit.*, p. 249, says: "The first 32 sonnets, with the single exception of Number 24—the punning invective against Lord Rich—were obviously written before Penelope's marriage, and they bear out the theory that up to this time both Sidney and Penelope were heart-whole." Mona Wilson, *op. cit.*, p. 312, says that the more mature of the early sonnets date from the summer and autumn of 1580 and that "the workmanship of this early group is so uneven as to suggest that, in composing the cycle, Sidney made a selection from occasional verse going back to 1579, or even 1578." A. H. Bill, *op. cit.*, p. 221, implies that some of the sonnets came early but says that Sidney's infatuation for Lady Rich must have begun after the end of 1581.

[29] *The Dictionary of National Biography*, articles on Sidney and Lady Rich. In the article on Sidney, Lee says that the sonnets were probably begun in 1575 and ceased soon after Sidney's marriage. The article on Lady Rich implies the same dates. In his Preface to the *Elizabethan Sonnets*, I, xlii, he refers to the series of sonnets which occupied Sidney's leisure through the "last six years of his life" [1580–86]. His article in the *Cambridge History of English Literature* (III, 289), on the "Elizabethan Sonnet" says that "although the date cannot be stated with certainty, it is probable that Sir Philip Sidney's ample collection of sonnets . . . was written between the years 1580 and 1584."

[30] Symonds, *op. cit.*, p. 116, says that the poems were "composed, if not wholly, yet in by far the greater part, after Lady Rich's marriage. . . . In the first place, then, the poems would have no meaning if they were written for a maiden." W. J. Courthope, *History of English Poetry* (London, 1920), II, 230–31, says: ". . . it is hardly doubtful that the whole series was designed after the marriage had been accomplished, or at least after it was arranged." H. R. Fox Bourne, (*op. cit.*, pp. 224–25), says that No. XXX refers to events "in the autumn of 1580 or soon after."

[31] *Modern Language Notes*, XLV (1930), 310. This comment, however, was not known to me until it appeared in 1934 in Purcell's *Sidney's Stella*, at the same time that my note, "The Date of the Marriage of Penelope Devereux," appeared in PMLA, XLIX (1934) 961–62.

[32] *Historical Manuscripts Commission*, 12th Report. Appendix, Pt. IV

(London, 1888), "Manuscripts of the Earl of Rutland," I, 127–28. The single line, "My Lady and mistress will be married about Allhallow's tide to Lord Rich," is quoted in Cokayne's *Complete Peerage*, VIII (1898), 65, as determining the date of the marriage of Lord Rich, later Earl of Warwick. No source, however, is stated in Cokayne for the reference.

[33] Lodge's *Illustrations*, III, 14–15. There are several references to Brakenbury in the *Calendar of State Papers, Domestic Series*, and the volumes of the Reports of the *Historical Manuscripts Commission*.

[34] It may as well be said here as elsewhere that this marriage, whatever its date, broke up no romance between Sidney and Lady Penelope. The probable attachment of Lady Penelope to Sir Charles Blunt, later Earl of Devonshire, may, however, have caused some trepidation if we may trust accounts such as that of Peter Heylin in his life of Archbishop Lawd. There is, it seems, no contemporary evidence that Sidney was in love with Lady Penelope before her marriage, and the sonnets imply that the contrary was the case. Heylin, commenting upon Lady Rich and Devonshire, says in part: ". . . a Lady in whom lodged all attractive Graces of Beauty, wit, and sweetness of Behavior, which might render her the absolute Mistress of all Eyes and Hearts. And she so far reciprocated with him in the like affection (being a compleat and gallant man) that some assurances past between them of a future Marriage. But her friends looking on him as a younger Brother, considerable only in his depending at the court, chose rather to dispose her in Marriage to Robert Lord Rich, a man of an independent Fortune, and a known Estate, but otherwise of an uncourtly disposition, unsociable, austere, and of no very agreeable conversation to her. Against this Blunt had nothing to plead in Bar, the promises which passed between them being made in private, no Witnesses to attest unto it, and therefore not amounting to a pre-Contract in due form of Law." The "friends" of Lady Rich are presumably her guardians, Huntington, Walsingham, and Burghley.

The anger of James I at the remarriage of Lady Rich, whose divorce decree, it turned out, had not permitted remarriage, is known from many sources, including the letter of Devonshire himself to the king in regard to the matter. Other facts of Devonshire's life are to be found in the letters of Chamberlain in Winwood's *Memorials of Affairs of State* (London, 1725). An account of his death is given in II, 206. Also, see Fynes Moryson's *Itinerary*.

[35] The Catalogue of the Manuscripts in the British Museum (1854–75, Vol. II) lists a manuscript of miscellaneous poetry, satire, and "other pieces in verse by members of the Caryll family and others," containing a copy, dated 1584, of Sidney's "Ring out Your Bells" (Add. MSS. 28, 253). I have not seen this MS. Presumably the poem itself was written much earlier than the transcript in the 1584 copy.

[36] Purcell, *op. cit.*, p. 24.

[37] *Fugger News-Letters,* second series (Queen Elizabeth), London, 1926, p. 71, No. 135, May 19, 1582, says: "Letters from London of May 12 report that with the consent of the King of Barbary the Turks have taken Laraish, so that the Straits of Gibraltar have become exceedingly unsafe. They also say in London that Frenchmen have landed on the coast of Portugal and done much damage."

[38] The *Calendar of State Papers, Venetian,* 1581–91, p. 33, No. 79, 1582, has a letter from the Venetian ambassador in Spain which says: "The news that the Turkish fleet is about to take the sea, is believed in Lisbon. But the number of the vessels will exceed by very little the number of last year. For while the Persian War lasts the Turks will not care to break the truce with the king of Spain; they merely desire to keep him in anxiety, in order to impede his designs and to favour those of his opponents." On June 21, 1582, an English representative, writing Walsingham from Paris that the Turkish fleet had departed at last from Genoa, gave the number of galleys and said that "this and the other fleet from here are keeping the mind and plans of the King of Spain in suspense, and gave and will give us much convenience. God grant that we may recognize it." (*Calendar of State Papers, Foreign,* 1582, p. 99, No. 102.) Earlier in the same year (March 7) the Venetian Ambassador wrote from Vienna of news from Constantinople that the French urged the Sultan to attack Spain, "pointing out how weak his Majesty is in Flanders, that England is an open foe, Portugal disturbed, the Azores sure to hold for Don Antonio. The Pasha is said to have promised to make the Turkish fleet take the sea in force this year" (*Calendar of State Papers, Venetian,* 1581–91, p. 31).

[39] *The Correspondence of Sir Philip Sidney and Hubert Languet* (Ed. by Pears, London, 1845), pp. 141–42.

[40] *Encyclopedia Britannica,* XXV, 887, under "Stephen, Bathory." It may be noticed that on April 22, 1582, Fremyn wrote Walsingham from Antwerp that the Poles had made peace with the Muscovites (*Calendar of State Papers,* 1581–82, p. 644) as if he had only then heard the news. In October, 1582, Cobham, the English Ambassador to France, had written Walsingham at length of the affairs of the Pope, the Muscovites, and the Polish king (*Calendar of State Papers,* 1582, p. 380), and so forth.

[41] Orvis, J. S., *A Brief History of Poland* (New York, 1916), p. 108. Walsingham's foreign ambassadors often refer in 1582 and 1583 to the affairs of Poland and Muscovy. See the *Calendar of State Papers, Foreign,* 1581–82, 1582, 1583.

[42] Motley, *The Dutch Republic,* III, 498.

[43] *The New English Dictionary,* Vol. X, Pt. 2. The line is either misquoted there, as it omits the word "no," or it follows the wording of the quarto editions of the sonnets (rather than the authorized one of 1598), where the line is "If in the Scottish Court be weltering yet." Pollard's

Astrophel and Stella, 1888, collates the editions. Pollard's note is found on page 192.

⁴⁴ Blok, *History of the Netherlands* (translated by Ruth Putnam, New York, 1890), III, 159; Motley's *Rise of the Dutch Republic,* III, Pt. VI ("Alexander of Parma"), p. 505 ff., 549 ff.

⁴⁵ Blok, *op. cit.,* pp. 163–64.

⁴⁶ Motley, *op. cit.,* III, 555.

⁴⁷ Blok, *op. cit.,* pp. 163–64.

⁴⁸ *Ibid.,* pp. 168–69.

⁴⁹ *Fugger News-Letters,* second series (Queen Elizabeth), No. 124, December 5, 1582.

⁵⁰ See articles in the *Dictionary of National Biography* for her and her son by the Earl of Clanrickard. Since her poem on the death of Sidney is little known, it may be quoted. It is on p. 11 of the *Academiae Cantabrigiensis lacrymae.*

> Vita mea, o coniux, mea mors, te pendet ab uno.
> Nanq̃; tui nobis fixus inhaeret Amor.
> Scilicet orba meo iam Coniuge viuere possum?
> Ne viuam, cupiam viuere si sine te.
> Et iuuet ergò mori, quoniam sic viuere frustrà
> Non iuuat? ipse Deus si iubet ante mori.
> Ergò vita mea ô Coniux, te pendet ab uno?
> Chare magis vita, dum tua vita, mea.
> Ergò mori & cupiam, sine te quia viuere nolim?
> Viuo, sed moriar, si licuisse datur.
> Induperatoris sic stat sententia summi,
> Quando licet moriar. Non licet ante mori.
>
> Viuo, non moriar. Quod facio ergò, licet.

BIBLIOGRAPHY

Chief Articles Consulted

Alden, Raymond M., "The Lyrical Conceit of the Elizabethans." *Studies in Philology*, XIV (1917), 129–53.

Bates, Ernest S., "The Sincerity of Shakespeare's Sonnets." *Modern Philology*, VIII (1910), 87–106.

Berdan, John M., "A Definition of *Petrarchismo*." PMLA, XXIV (1909), 699–710.

———— "The Migrations of a Sonnet." *Modern Language Notes*, XXIII (1908), 33–36.

———— "Professor Kastner's Hypothesis." *Modern Language Notes*, XXV (1910), 1–4.

———— "Wyatt and the French Sonneteers." *The Modern Language Review*, IV (1909), 240–49.

Bullock, Walter L., "The Genesis of the English Sonnet Form." PMLA, XXXVIII (1923), 729–45.

Bush, Douglas, "Classic Myths in English Verse (1557–89)." *Modern Philology*, XXV (1927), 37–47.

Campbell, Oscar James, *Jacques*. Huntington Library Bulletin, No. 8, 1935.

Carpenter, Frederich I., "Thomas Watson's *Italian Madrigals* Englished." *Journal of Germanic Philology*, II (1898), 323–58.

Coon, R. H., "The Vogue of Ovid since the Renaissance." *The Classical Journal*, XXV (1930), 277–91.

Emerson, Oliver F., "Shakespeare's Sonneteering." *Studies in Philology*. XX (1923), 111–36.

Fucilla, Joseph G., "Materials for the History of a Popular Classical Theme." *Classical Philology*, XXVI, (1931), 135–52.

Garrod, H. W., Letters in *Times Literary Supplement*, May 10 and 24, 1923.

Garver, Milton S., "Sources of the Beast Similes in the Italian Lyric of the Thirteenth Century." *Romanische Forschungen*, XXI (1908), 276–320.

Hanford, J. H., "The Debate of Heart and Eye." *Modern Language Notes*, XXVI (1911), 161–65.

Hanscom, Elizabeth D., "The Sonnet Forms of Wyatt and Surrey." *Modern Language Notes*, XVI (1901), 274–80.

Hartung, P. N. U., "The 'Sonnettes' of Barnabe Googe." *English Studies*, XI (1929), 100–102.

Hudson, Hoyt H., "Sonnets by Barnabe Googe." PMLA, XLVIII (1933), 293–94.

———— "Penelope Devereux as Sidney's Stella." *The Huntington Library Bulletin*, No. 7, 1935.

Hughes, Merritt Y., "Spenser and the Greek Pastoral Triad." *Studies in Philology*, XXIII (1923), 184–216.

Hughey, Ruth, "The Harington Manuscript at Arundel Castle and Related Documents." *The Library*, XV (1935), 388–444.

Hutton, James, "The First Idyl of Moschus in Imitations to the Year 1800." *The American Journal of Philology*, XLIX (1928), 105–36.

Kastner, L. E., "Wyatt and the French Sonneteers." *The Modern Language Review*, IV (1909), 249–53.

—— "The Elizabethan Sonneteers and the French Poets." *The Modern Language Review*, III (1907–8), 268–77.

Koeppel, Emil, "Die englischen Tasso-Übersetzungen des 16. jahrhunderts." *Anglia*, XIII (1890), 42–72.

—— "Studien zur Geschichte des englischen Petrarchismus im sechzehnten Jahrhundert." *Romanische Forschungen*, V (1890), 65–98.

Langley, Ernest, "The Extant Repertory of the Early Sicilian Poets." PMLA, XXVIII (1913), 454–520.

Lea, Kathleen M., "Conceits." *The Modern Language Review*, XX (1925), 389–407.

Long, Percy W., "Spenser and Lady Carey." *The Modern Language Review*, III (1908), 257–67.

—— "Spenseriana: the Lay of Clorinda." *Modern Language Notes*, XXXI (1916), 79–82.

—— "Spenser's Sonnets 'as published.'" *The Modern Language Review*, VI (1911), 390–96.

Merrill, R. V., "Platonism in Petrarch's *Canzoniere*." *Modern Philology*, XXVII (1929), 161–74.

Padelford, Frederick M., "The Scansion of Wyatt's Early Sonnets." *Studies in Philology*, XX (1923), 137–53.

Purcell, James M., "Sidney's *Astrophel and Stella* and Greville's *Caelica*." PMLA, L (1935), 413–23.

Ogle, M. B., "The Classical Origin and Tradition of Literary Conceits." *The American Journal of Philosophy*, XXXIV (1913), 125–53.

—— "The 'White Hand' as a Literary Conceit." *The Sewanee Review*, XX (1912), 459–69.

Osgood, Charles G., "The *Doleful Lay of Clorinda*." *Modern Language Notes*, XXXV (1920), 90–96.

Scott, Janet G., "The Names of the Heroines of the Elizabethan Sonnet-Sequences." *The Review of English Studies*, II (1926), 159–62.

Shafer, Robert, "Spenser's *Astrophel*." *Modern Language Notes*, XXVIII (1913), 224–26.

Spencer, Floyd A., "The Literary Lineage of Cupid in Greek Literature." *The Classical Weekly*, XXV (1932), 121–27, 129–34, 139–44.

Villey, Pierre, "Marot et le premier sonnet français." *Revue d'histoire littéraire de la France*, XXVII (1920), 538–47.

Wilkins, Ernest H., "On the Transcription by Petrarch in V. L. 3195, I and II." *Modern Philology*, XXIV (1926), 261–68, 389–401.

Wilkins, Ernest H., "The Dates of Transcription of Petrarch's Manuscript V. L. 3195," *Modern Philology,* XXVI (1928), 283–94.
———— "The Invention of the Sonnet." *Modern Philology,* XIII (1915), 463–94.

Chief Works Consulted

Anacreontea, The, In Elegy and Iambus, Vol. II. "The Loeb Classical Library." Translated by J. M. Edmonds. London, 1931.
Berdan, John M., Early Tudor Poetry. New York, 1931.
Bill, A. H., Astrophel. New York, 1937.
Bourne, H. R. Fox, Sir Philip Sidney. New York, 1891.
Bowers, Fredson Thayer, Notes on Gascoigne's A Hundreth Sundrie Flowers and the Poesies. "Harvard Studies and Notes in Philology and Literature," Vol. XVI (1934).
Brady, George K., Samuel Daniel; a Critical Study. Urbana, 1923.
Bullen, Arthur H., Elizabethans. London, 1925.
Bush, Douglas, Mythology and the Renaissance Tradition in English Poetry. Minneapolis, 1932.
Byrd, William, "Psalms, Sonnets, and Songs of Sadness and Piety," and "Songs of Sundrie Natures." Bullen, Shorter Elizabethan Poems. Westminster, 1903.
Cambridge History of English Literature, The, Vols. III–IV. New York, 1910.
Chambers, Sir Edmund K., Sir Thomas Wyatt and Some Collected Studies. London, 1933.
Constable, Henry, Diana. . . Sonnets and Other Poems. Edited by W. C. Hazlitt. London, 1859.
———— The Sonnets of. . . "The Harleian Miscellany," Vol. IX. London, 1813.
Cooper, Clyde Barnes, Some Elizabethan Opinions of the Poetry and Character of Ovid. Menasha, Wis., 1914.
Dante Alighieri, Vita nuova. Translated by Dante Gabriel Rossetti, in Poems and Translations. London, 1926.
Dodd, William George, Courtly Love in Chaucer and Gower. Boston, 1913.
Drayton, Samuel, Minor Poems. Edited by Cyril Brett. Oxford, 1907.
Elizabethan Sonnets, Vols. I–II. Edited by Sir Sidney Lee. Westminster, 1903.
Elton, Oliver, Michael Drayton. London, 1905.
English Poetry of 1578–79. "Roxburghe Club Publications," Vol. LXII. London.
Fellowes, Edmund H., English Madrigal Verse. Oxford, 1920.

Fellowes, Edmund H., The English Madrigal School, Vols. XIV–XV. London, 1920.

Fletcher, Jefferson Butler, Dante. New York, 1916.

―――― Literature of the Italian Renaissance. New York, 1934.

―――― The Religion of Beauty in Women. New York, 1911.

Foscolo, Ugo, Essays on Petrarch. London, 1823.

Fowler, Earle Broadus, Spenser and the Courts of Love. Menasha, Wis., 1921.

Furtwängler, A., Eros. Roscher, Ausführliches Lexikon der griechischen und römischen Mythologie. Leipzig, 1884.

Gascoigne, George, The Complete Works of . . . Cambridge, 1907 and 1910. Vols. I–II.

Gaspary, Adolf, Die sicilianische Dichterschule des dreizehnten Jahrhunderts. Berlin, 1878.

Gawdy, Philip, Letters of . . . "Roxburghe Club Publications." Vol. CXLVIII. London, 1906.

Giacomo da Lentino, The Poetry of . . . Edited by Ernest F. Langley. Cambridge, 1915.

Gorgeous Gallery of Gallant Inventions, A, Edited by Hyder E. Rollins. Cambridge, 1926.

Greek Anthology, The, Vols. I, V. "The Loeb Classical Library." Translated by W. R. Paton. London, 1916–19.

Greene, Robert, The Life and Complete Works of . . . Edited by Alexander Grosart, Vols. IV, IX, XII.

Greville, Fulke, Lord Brooke, Caelica. Edited by Martha F. Crow. London, 1898.

Guyer, Foster E., The Influence of Ovid on Crestien de Troyes. New York, 1921.

Harrison, John Smith, Platonism in English Poetry of the Sixteenth and Seventeenth Centuries. New York, 1903.

Howard, Henry, Earl of Surrey, The Poems of . . . Edited by F. M. Padelford. Seattle, 1928.

Howell, Thomas, Devises. Edited by Sir Walter Raleigh. Oxford, 1906.

Hutton, James, The Greek Anthology in Italy to the Year 1800. Ithaca, 1935.

James I, King of England, New Poems. New York, 1911.

Jeanroy, Alfred, Le Poésie lyrique des Troubadours. Paris, 1934.

―――― Les Origines de la poésie lyrique en France. Paris, 1889.

Jeffery, Violet M., John Lyly and the Italian Renaissance. Paris, 1928.

Johnston, Robert, Historia rerum Britannicarum, 1572–1628. Amsterdam, 1655.

Jones, H. S. V., A Spenser Handbook. New York, 1930.

Jordan, John Clark, Robert Greene. New York, 1915.

Lathrop, Henry B., Translations from the Classics into English from Caxton to Chapman, 1477–1620. Madison, 1933.

Laumonier, Paul, Ronsard, poète lyrique. Paris, 1909.

Lee, Sir Sidney, A Life of William Shakespeare. New York, 1909.

Molinier, H. J., Mellin de Saint-Gelays (1490?–1558). Rodez, 1910.

Moseley, Thomas Addis Emmet, The "Lady" in Comparisons from the Poetry of the "Dolce Stil Nuovo." Menasha, Wis., 1916.

Mott, Lewis Freeman, The Provençal Lyric. New York, 1901.

——— The System of Courtly Love Studied as an Introduction to the Vita nuova of Dante. Boston, 1896.

Myrick, Kenneth Orne, Sir Philip Sidney as a Literary Craftsman. Cambridge, 1935.

Neilson, William Allan, The Origins and Sources of the Court of Love. Boston, 1899.

Olmsted, E. W., The Sonnet in French Literature. Ithaca, 1897.

Osborn, Albert W., Sir Philip Sidney en France. Paris, 1932.

Ovid, The Heroides and Amores. Translated by Showerman. "The Loeb Classical Library." New York, 1931.

Owen, Daniel E., The Relations of the Elizabethan Sonnet Sequences to Earlier English Verse. Philadelphia, 1903.

Palmer, Henrietta, List of English Editions and Translations of Greek and Latin Classics Printed before 1641. London, 1911.

Paradise of Dainty Devices, The, Edited by Hyder E. Rollins. Cambridge, 1927.

Patterson, Warren F., Three Centuries of French Poetic Theory, Vols. I and II. Ann Arbor, 1935.

Phelps, Ruth S., The Earlier and Later Forms of Petrarch's Canzoniere. Chicago, 1925.

——— "The Forms of Address in Petrarch's Canzoniere." "The Todd Memorial Volumes." New York, 1930, Vol. II.

Phoenix Nest, The, Edited by Hyder E. Rollins. Cambridge, 1931.

Poetry of the English Renaissance. Edited by J. W. Hebel and H. H. Hudson. New York, 1929.

Propertius, The Works of . . . Translated by H. E. Butler. London, 1912.

Renwick, William L., Edmund Spenser. London, 1925.

Rossetti, Dante Gabriel, Poems and Translations. Oxford, 1926.

Sawtelle, Alice E., The Sources of Spenser's Classical Mythology. New York, 1896.

Schevill, Rudolf, Ovid and the Renascence in Spain. Berkeley, 1913.

Schrötter, Wilibald, Ovid und die Troubadours. Marburg, 1908.

Scott, Janet G., Les Sonnets élisabéthains. Paris, 1929.

Shakespeare, William, Shakespeare's Sonnets. Edited by Tucker Brooke. New York, 1936.

——— Shakespeare's Sonnets. Edited by Israel Gollancz. London, 1919.

——— The Sonnets of Shakespeare. Edited by R. M. Alden. Boston, 1916.

Sidney, Sir Philip, Sir Philip Sidney's Astrophel and Stella. Edited by A. W. Pollard. London, 1888.

——— Defense of Poesy. Edited by A. S. Cook. Boston, 1890.

——— Complete Works of . . . Edited by A. Feuillerat. Cambridge, 1912–26.

Sisson, Charles Jasper, Thomas Lodge and Other Elizabethans. Cambridge, 1933.

Spencer, Theodore, Death and Elizabethan Tragedy. Cambridge, 1936.

Spenser, Edmund, The Complete Works of. Edited by R. E. N. Dodge. Boston, 1908.

——— Daphnaïda and Other Poems. Edited by W. L. Renwick. London, 1929.

——— The Shepherd's Calendar. Edited by W. L. Renwick. London, 1930.

Symonds, John Addington, Sir Philip Sidney. New York, 1887.

Tatham, Edward Henry Ralph, Francesco Petrarca. London, 1925–26.

Tottel's Miscellany, Vols. I–II. Edited by Hyder E. Rollins. Cambridge, 1928–29.

Vianey, Joseph, Le Pétrarquisme en France au XVe siècle. Montpellier, 1909.

Wallace, Malcolm William, The Life of Sir Philip Sidney. Cambridge, 1915.

Watson, Thomas, The Poems of . . . Edited by Arber. London, 1870.

White, Harold O., Plagiarism and Imitation during the English Renaissance. Cambridge, 1935.

Wilson, Mona, Sir Philip Sidney. New York, 1932.

Withington, Robert, English Pageantry, Vols. I–II. Cambridge, 1918.

Wyatt, Sir Thomas, The Poems of . . . Edited by A. K. Foxwell. London, 1913.

Yates, Frances A., A Study of Love's Labour's Lost. Cambridge, 1936.

INDEX

INDEX